THE VILLANS

ABOUT THE AUTHOR

Born in London, Graham Betts attended his first game in 1965 and has seldom been absent since, family commitments notwithstanding. Aside from a number of football books he has also written extensively on music, an industry he has worked in for the last 20 or so years. He lives in Aston Clinton in Buckinghamshire with his wife and two children.

THE VILLANS

DAY-TO-DAY LIFE AT VILLA PARK

GRAHAM BETTS

MAINSTREAM
PUBLISHING

EDINBURGH AND LONDON

First published in Great Britain in 1998 by
MAINSTREAM PUBLISHING COMPANY (EDINBURGH) LTD
7 Albany Street
Edinburgh EH1 3UG

ISBN 1 84018 033 1

The photographs for this book have been supplied by Wellard Huxley Promotions and
John Allen, proprietor of *The Football Card Collector* magazine

A catalogue record for this book is available from the British Library

Typeset in Times
Printed and bound in Great Britain by Butler and Tanner Ltd

INTRODUCTION

Like many of today's truly big clubs, Aston Villa were established after a humble collection of youths formed a football club in order to enjoy some form of recreation during the winter months, for they already had cricket to occupy them in the summer. It was under a gas lamp in Heathfield Road in 1874 that the idea of the club was first mooted, and whilst Heathfield Road has long since disappeared, Aston Villa Football Club continues to go from strength to strength.

Even before the century was out, Aston Villa were one of the most illustrious of names in the world of football. League champions four times (and on their way to their fifth title come the summer of 1900) and FA Cup winners three times (although they managed to have it stolen from them in 1895!), their tally of honours also included a coveted double of League championship and FA Cup in 1896–97. It was another 64 years before the feat was achieved again.

If their domination of the game at this stage was confined to England, with European competition not a part of the football calendar until the 1950s, their influence had already extended far beyond these shores; a Berlin club assumed the name Aston Villa in their honour! For all of Villa's accomplishments on the field, their place in the development of the game is assured because of a committee member's activities off it. In March 1888 William McGregor wrote to the secretaries of some of the leading clubs of the day, including his own, and suggested that the clubs meet in home and away fixtures. It was a suggestion that was heartily taken up, and the Football League came into being. It could only have been Aston Villa who could found the League and lose the Cup!

Whilst countless Villa books before have tended to start with the club's humble beginnings and work their way through to the present day, this book tells the story day by day and enables the reader to follow the historic double, the run that led to the European Cup in 1982 and the ending of the championship barren spell in 1981. There is the joy of winning countless trophies and honours, tempered with the theft of the FA Cup and the murder of Tommy Ball.

A book of this kind could not have been written without the invaluable help and assistance of numerous others, and I am therefore indebted to the following people for the part they have played in getting this project off the ground: Nigel Walmsley, Rob and Denise Fallon, who've known the best of times and worst of times following Villa over the years, and John Betambeau and John Roberts for their material help. Thanks also to Phil Robinson, Richard Lerman and Brian Watts for their encouragement, and to Bill Campbell at Mainstream. I would also like to thank my family, Caroline, Jo and Steven, who have lived with this project almost as long as I have!

JANUARY 1ST

1881 Aston Villa entertained Heart of Midlothian, one of the top sides in Scotland, in a prestigious friendly and won 4–1 thanks to goals from Richards, Hunter, Davis and Brown.

1886 Harold Halse born in Stratford in East London. After a remarkable two seasons with Southend United, during which he scored 200 goals, Harold was snapped up by Manchester United for £350 in March 1908. Although he didn't score with the same regularity at Old Trafford, he was one of the most dangerous forwards of his age and would go on to score six goals in the FA Charity Shield match against Swindon. He won a League championship and FA Cup winners' medal whilst at United and was sold to Aston Villa for £1,200 in 1912, adding a second FA Cup winners' medal at the end of his first season at Villa Park. His third appearance in the final came in 1915 when he was playing for Chelsea, although this time he had to settle for a runners-up medal. At the end of the First World War he returned to Chelsea, subsequently moving on to Charlton in 1921, retiring in 1923 and then scouting for the club for a further two years.

1938 A 1–1 draw at Upton Park was enough to take Villa to the top of the Second Division for the first time in the current campaign and one that was to end in triumph: Second Division champions and a return to the First Division after a two-year absence.

1987 A second-half goal spree turned a 1–0 lead over Hull City into a comprehensive 5–0 win, and with it Villa took over at the top of the Second Division table for the first time in the season.

JANUARY 2ND

1912 Frank Shell born in Hackney. In his early career at Villa Park Frank seemed to be set for a prosperous future, but the Second World War cut across his career and he was sold to Birmingham City at the end of hostilities and later wound down his career with Hereford United, returning to the League with Mansfield Town, scoring once in 22 games.

1932 Aston Villa won 8–3 at Filbert Street, the home of Leicester City, with five of Villa's goals being scored by George Brown, thus equalling the individual record for the most number of goals in a game jointly held by Harry Hampton, Harold Halse and Len Capewell. However, George Brown was the first player to have scored as many as five goals on an opponent's ground. This was also the second time Villa had scored as many as eight goals away from home, the previous occasion being a cup replay against Clapton Orient in 1929. Brown was known as 'Bomber Brown' during his career, which had begun with Huddersfield Town, George successfully coming through a trial and being able to give up his occupation of miner. Whilst at Leeds Road he won eight caps for England and joined Villa in 1929, remaining with the club until 1933 when he joined Burnley. He later played for Leeds United and was then player-manager with Darlington.

JANUARY 3RD

1885   The local clash between Villa and West Bromwich Albion drew a crowd of 22,088 to Perry Barr for the FA Cup third-round replay. Despite being roared on by their biggest-ever crowd, Villa went down 3–0.

1920   Harry Hampton made his 373rd and final appearance for the club in the 2–2 home draw with Burnley, leaving the following month to sign for local rivals Birmingham City. He had begun his Villa career back in 1904 and would surely have made considerably more appearances and scored more goals (he left with 242 to his credit) had the First World War not interrupted his career. Even so, he survived being gassed during the war and recovered to resume his playing career, a remarkable achievement. He topped the League's list of goalscorers in 1911–12 with 25 goals to his credit.

1976   Villa were drawn away at Second Division Southampton in the third round of the FA Cup and seemed to have the measure of their opponents, taking the lead through Andy Gray in the second half. With time running out their presence in the next round seemed assured until Hugh Fisher grabbed an equaliser in the very last minute to set up a replay at Villa Park.

1998   Villa survived a scare in the FA Cup third-round clash at Fratton Park against Portsmouth, only equalising in the very last minute through Simon Grayson to grab a replay after a 2–2 draw.

JANUARY 4TH

1890   Villa went down 7–0 in the League at Everton, although midway through the game centre-forward Archie Hunter collapsed suffering from a heart attack. He was taken to hospital but never fully recovered, dying four years later. Hunter had come to join Villa almost by accident, for he was in the Midlands on a business engagement in 1879 and trying to find the Calthorpe club when fate lent a hand and brought him to Aston Villa. Even then in his early days he had to play under an assumed name as he faced almost certain dismissal from his company had it been known he was playing football! He later became club captain, guiding them to the FA Cup final in 1887, the very first Villa player to get his hands on the coveted trophy.

1920   Harry Parkes born in Birmingham. Signed by Villa just before the Second World War, he guested for Villa, Northampton and West Bromwich Albion during the hostilities and returned to Villa at the end of the war. He made his debut in 1946–47 and went on to make 345 appearances for the first team, appearing in every outfield position at some point during his career. He retired at the end of 1954–55 season.

1930 Eric Houghton made his debut for Villa in the 4–3 home defeat by Leeds United, although it was not a dream start; he missed a penalty. He went on to become one of the deadliest penalty-takers in the history of the game, scoring 17 times for Villa from the penalty spot.

1958 Villa's defence of the FA Cup began with a 1–1 draw at the Victoria Ground in Stoke, but after a replay at Villa Park (drawn 3–3) Stoke finally knocked them out at Molineux 2–0. What made the game memorable was the appearance of Stan Crowther in the Villa side; later in the competition he played for Manchester United, the club having been given permission to sign otherwise ineligible players after the Munich air disaster. Stan Crowther along with United made it all the way to Wembley, this time being beaten by Bolton in the final.

1964 Villa had struggled during the opening half of the League campaign, seldom able to string a decent run of results together and had slipped down the table. The FA Cup offered a welcome respite, especially when they were drawn at home to lowly Aldershot, but at Villa Park Aldershot rode their luck, produced a battling performance and one or two saves from the goalkeeper that on any other day would have gone in and held Villa to a goalless draw. When Villa were tumbled out of the competition a few days later, it spelt the end of the road for manager Joe Mercer, the strain of trying to restore Villa to their former glories too much for him. Assistant Dick Taylor took over for the rest of the season with much the same brief Mercer had been given when he first took over; keep Villa in the First Division. It was a feat he achieved.

JANUARY 5TH

1924 Teddy Bowen made his debut for Villa in the 2–0 win at Ninian Park against Cardiff City. Born in Hednesford, he had signed professional forms shortly before making his debut and went on to make 199 appearances for the club. He lost his place in 1934 and was allowed to join Norwich City in October of that year, turning out 130 times for the Canaries.

1957 After the trauma of the previous season, Villa gave their fans something to cheer about with a run towards Wembley. The start could hardly have been more scary, surviving a 2–2 draw at Kenilworth Road against Luton that earned a replay at Villa Park.

1982 On paper Villa were given a potentially difficult trip to Notts County for the FA Cup third round, but fortunately football is played on grass and Villa were quite superb on the day, 4–0 ahead by half-time and cruising to a 6–0 victory. David Geddis grabbed a hat-trick, Gary Shaw and

Gordon Cowans scored one apiece and Jackson of County turned through his own net to complete the scoring.

JANUARY 6TH

1934 Spurs visited Villa Park and slipped away 90 minutes later with both points after administering a 5–1 defeat, Villa's worst of the season in front of their own supporters.

1951 Shortly before the start of the season Villa had parted company with manager Alex Massie and then taken three months to appoint his successor, George Martin. By the time he arrived at Villa Park the club was in something approaching turmoil, too far down the League in order to mount a campaign for the title and needing some medicine quickly. Martin duly administered the right doses and Villa were on their way to recovering in the League, which left the FA Cup as one way of salvaging something from the season. A fine 2–0 home win over Burnley saw them safely through the first hurdle and set up a local clash with Wolves. That's where the story ended; they were beaten 3–1 at Molineux.

1996 Villa were paired with non-League opposition in the FA Cup for the first time in 76 years when they were drawn against Gravesend and Northfleet. Although the Beazer League home side were drawn at home they agreed to switch the tie to Villa Park and thus took their share of receipts generated by a crowd of 26,021. Any chance of a shock result evaporated as early as the second minute when Mark Draper gave Villa the lead, and second-half goals for Savo Milosevic and Tommy Johnson wrapped up a 3–0 win.

JANUARY 7TH

1888 Such was the interest generated by the pairing of Villa, the cup holders, with Preston North End in the FA Cup fifth round that the ground at Perry Barr was packed to overflowing with 26,849 spectators. Twice the crowd spilled out on to the pitch and eventually the police had to call for assistance from the mounted branch and a couple of Hussars stationed nearby so that they could maintain order. Although the visitors were winning 3–1 the conditions were such that a conference took place on the field and both teams agreed that the game would be considered a friendly and the cup-tie played at a later date. However, the FA insisted that the result should stand and Villa were therefore eliminated from the cup they had won the previous year.

1928 Aston Villa scouts were at Prenton Park to check on the progress of Tranmere Rovers centre-forward Tom 'Pongo' Waring, a player who had been earning rave reviews less than two years since breaking into the side. Villa were not to be disappointed; Waring scored six of Tranmere's goals in the 11–1 win over Durham City and immediately opened negotiations with the Merseyside club to bring him to Villa Park, finally landing him the following month. His signature cost them £4,500; he repaid that sum many times over during his near-on-eight-year stay with the club.

1957 Two days after being held at Kenilworth Road, Villa brought Luton back to Villa Park and saw off the challenge with a 2–0 win in front of a crowd of almost 28,000 thanks to two goals from Johnny Dixon.

1976 Villa Park was packed with 44,623 fans for the FA Cup third-round replay with Southampton, with Villa favourites to progress. On the night, however, Southampton belied their Second Division status with a dogged display. Ray Graydon scored for Villa and Jim McCalliog for Southampton during an even first half, and with no further scoring in the second period extra time beckoned. There McCalliog was waiting to score his second of the night and send Southampton through, on their way to winning the cup at the end of the season.

JANUARY 8TH

1921 Villa's defence of the FA Cup won the previous season began with a home tie with Bristol City, with a record crowd of 49,734 present to see Villa win 2–0. Sadly, Villa were knocked out at the quarter-final stage by Spurs, who later won the cup.

1983 With Villa safely through to the next round of the European Cup, scheduled for March, thoughts could turn to making progress in the major domestic cup competition, the FA Cup. A trip to Northampton's County Ground, where the three sides held a 14,529 crowd (Northampton shared their ground with the county cricket club), was a potential banana skin waiting to trip Villa up, but a goal from Mark Walters in the first half eased the fears and enabled Villa to go through 1–0 victors.

1994 A trip down the M5 saw Villa at Exeter City's St James' Park for the FA Cup third-round clash. The pitch was atrocious, prompting many to believe the game should have been called off, but Villa made the best of a bad situation, with Dean Saunders converting a second-half penalty to win the game 1–0 on a day other big guns had been humbled and dumped out of the competition.

JANUARY 9TH

1897 The double season of 1896–97 saw Villa win 21 of their 30 matches during the season, with their away record even better than that of their home. Villa had been beaten at home the previous week by bottom-of-the-table Burnley at home; this week they went down 4–2 at second-bottom Sunderland! It was Villa's last defeat of the season however.

1954 Villa's interest in the FA Cup ended at the very first hurdle, thumped 5–1 at Highbury by an Arsenal side who on their day could be devastating, as they proved against Villa, or mediocre, as they proved in the next round losing 2–1 at home to Third Division Norwich City! It was just Villa's luck to have caught them the wrong way round!

1961 Villa had been given a scare in their first clash with Bristol Rovers in the FA Cup third round at Eastville, with Rovers doggedly holding on for a 1–1 draw. At Villa Park it was a different story with Villa rarely troubled in a 4–0 win to set up a meeting with Peterborough United at London Road in the fourth round.

1962 Ray Houghton born in Glasgow. He began his career with West Ham but made only one substitute appearance before being allowed to join Fulham on a free transfer in 1982. A £147,000 move took him to Oxford United in 1985 and he helped them win the Milk Cup in his first season. Liverpool signed him for £825,000 in October 1987 and he went on to add two League titles, two FA Cups and two FA Charity Shields to his honours collection before a £900,000 move to Villa Park in 1992. Although just over 30 years of age by this time he proved himself to be an industrious midfield player and helped the club win the League Cup in 1994. He was sold to Crystal Palace for £300,000 in March 1995, helping them gain promotion to the Premier League in 1997.

1991 An extra time goal from Alan Cork was enough to give Wimbledon a 1–0 win in the FA Cup third-round replay at Plough Lane, the two sides having drawn 1–1 at Villa Park.

JANUARY 10TH

1920 Billy Walker made his debut for the club in the FA Cup first-round tie with Queens Park Rangers, scoring both goals in the 2–1 win. Born in Wednesbury in October 1897 he played for Hednesford Town, Darlaston and Wednesbury Old Athletic before joining Villa. His goals in 1920 enabled the club to win the FA Cup at the end of the season, and he went on to make 531 appearances for the club, scoring 244 goals, his appearance record finally being overtaken by Charlie Aitken in 1973. He retired from playing in 1933 and went into management, taking over at Sheffield Wednesday, Chelmsford and then Nottingham Forest. After guiding Forest to the FA Cup in 1959 he retired the following year owing to illness. He won 18 caps for England whilst playing for Villa and died in November 1964.

1948 One of the most dramatic games Villa have played in the FA Cup saw them at home to Manchester United in the third round and take the lead after only 13 seconds through George Edwards, without United having even touched the ball. But United responded to the challenge and scored five times before half-time. It was Villa's turn to hardly get a kick! Whatever was said in the dressing-room at half-time obviously worked, for Edwards added a second when the United keeper failed to hold a corner, Smith reduced the deficit to two goals with 20 minutes to go and Dorsett made it 5–4 with just nine minutes left on the clock. Ford hit the bar as Villa pressed for an equaliser and with everyone committed to attack, it was almost inevitable that United would steal away and make it safe at 6–4. If there was disappointment that Villa had fallen at the first hurdle, it was tempered by the fact they had more than played their part in an absorbing game.

1996 Having beaten Peterborough United, Stockport County and QPR in the early rounds of the Coca-Cola Cup, Villa faced a potentially tricky home tie with Wolves in the fifth round. A crowd of 39,277 were at Villa Park for an intriguing contest, finally settled in Villa's favour by a goal from Tommy Johnson in the second half. With Birmingham City also through, there were hopes of a possible meeting in the final at Wembley, but whilst Villa made it (against Arsenal in the semi-final), Birmingham did not, beaten by Leeds over two legs.

JANUARY 11TH

1902 Billy Brawn made his debut for the club in the 4–0 defeat at Blackburn Rovers. Signed from Sheffield United the previous month after beginning his career at Northampton Town, he went on to earn international recognition whilst with Villa, collecting two England caps and helping Villa win the FA Cup in 1905. He left Villa in 1906 for Middlesbrough and later played for Chelsea and Brentford, serving the latter club as a director when his playing career came to an end.

1955 Ken McNaught born in Kirkcaldy. The son of a former professional footballer with Raith Rovers, Ken was signed by Everton as an apprentice after completing his school exams. He made his debut for the club during the 1974–75 season and made 84 appearances for the first team before a £200,000 move to Villa in August 1977. He remained at Villa Park for six seasons, helping them win the League and European Cup before moving on to West Bromwich Albion for £125,000, finishing his career through injury with Sheffield United.

1958 Stan Lynn scored a hat-trick for Villa as Sunderland were beaten 5–2 at Villa Park. In so doing he became the first full-back to have scored a hat-trick in the First Division.

1961 Adrian Heath born in Stoke. He began his career with his local side and spent three years at the Victoria Ground before a £700,000 move to Everton in 1982. Over the next seven years he helped Everton win the League title in 1985 and 1987, the FA Cup in 1984 and the FA Charity Shield for four consecutive seasons. He was sold to Aston Villa for £360,000 in 1989 but made only 12 appearances for the club before joining Manchester City and later played for Stoke, Burnley, Sheffield United and a second spell at Burnley, where he was later manager.

JANUARY 12TH

1889 The Perry Barr patrons had another six goals to cheer as Villa saw off Bolton 6–2 in the Football League, the first season of the competition. The previous October Villa had hit six past Blackburn in a 6–1 win and in September had scored nine against Notts County, winning 9–1.

1929 A crowd of over 51,000 were at Villa Park for the FA Cup third-round clash between Villa and Cardiff City. Villa turned in an impressive performance to emerge 5–1 winners and went into the next round to face Clapton Orient.

1970 Defeat by Charlton Athletic in the FA Cup third-round replay at the Valley spelt the end for Villa manager Tommy Docherty. With the club firmly rooted at the bottom of the Second Division and out of both cup competitions at the first hurdle, there was nothing left but a battle to maintain Second Division status, a battle that was ultimately lost. Docherty was replaced by his assistant Vic Crowe, but in fairness to Crowe there was too little time to try and rescue a club that had been in free fall for far too long.

1994 Victories over Birmingham, Sunderland and Arsenal had brought Villa to White Hart Lane for the Coca-Cola Cup fifth-round clash with Spurs, and goals from Ray Houghton and Earle Barrett booked a semi-final place thanks to a 2–1 win.

JANUARY 13TH

1906 Villa's defence of the FA Cup began with an easy 11–0 win over King's Lynn at Villa Park, their biggest win in the competition this century. Villa survived until the third round, where they went out 5–1 to Manchester United at Old Trafford.

1970 Mark Bosnich born in Sydney, Australia. He first came to England in 1989 with Manchester United but after only three appearances was released, as a work permit problem proved difficult to overcome. He returned in 1992 with Villa, initially as understudy to Nigel Spink, but he forced his way into the side in 1993 and became a regular player. He helped the club win the League Cup in both 1994 and 1996 and is also a full Australian international.

JANUARY 14TH

1882 Villa and Notts County had already met twice in the FA Cup fourth round, both matches finishing all-square at 2–2. Perry Barr was the venue for the decisive third meeting, drawing a crowd of 12,000, some 5,000 more than had witnessed the first meeting between the two on New Year's Eve. This time Villa proved too strong for County, running out 4–1 victors.

1893 League champions Sunderland were on their way to retaining their title, the first time it had been done since Preston won the first two League championships. Unfortunately for Villa, Sunderland were in no mood to drop more than two points at home all season, handing out a 6–0 beating, having already won at Perry Barr 6–1 earlier in the season.

1967 Lew Chatterley became the first Villa substitute to score, netting in the 3–2 home win over Blackpool.

1998 A goal from Savo Milosevic finally overcame Portsmouth in the FA Cup third-round replay at Villa Park, earning Villa a home clash with local rivals West Bromwich Albion in the fourth round.

JANUARY 15TH

1898 The visit of Sheffield United, on their way to taking the League championship mantle from Villa, attracted a then record crowd of 42,000 to Villa Park. United won 1–0 to strengthen their grip at the top of the table.

1932 Jimmy Dugdale born in Liverpool. He began his career with West Bromwich Albion, signing professional forms in June 1952, and switched to Villa Park in 1956 for £25,000. Whilst at Villa he helped the club win the FA Cup, League Cup (he was one of the first players to win winners' medals in both domestic cup competitions) and the Second Division title, and left the club in October 1962 for Queens Park Rangers. His career was brought to an end by injury seven months later.

1971 Tommy Johnson born in Newcastle-upon-Tyne. He began his League career with Notts County in 1989 and switched to Derby County for £1.3 million in 1992. Just under three years later he came to Villa Park as part of the deal that took Gary Charles to the Baseball Ground.

1975 Villa had reached the League Cup semi-final after seeing off Everton, Crewe Alexandra, Hartlepool and Colchester. With the exception of Everton it had hardly been the toughest of routes to a semi-final, but both Crewe and Hartlepool had forced replays. The draw for the semi-final also favoured Villa, pairing them with Chester when Manchester United or Norwich City could have come out of the hat. The first leg took them to Sealand Road where Chester gave Villa something of a fright, coming back from behind twice to earn a 2–2 draw in front of a sell-out crowd of 19,000.

JANUARY 16TH

1897 Villa were on their way to winning the double of League championship and FA Cup at the end of the season, but their 2–1 win over Sunderland at Perry Barr heralded an unbeaten run that would last until September 25th 1897 when they were defeated 4–3 at Ewood Park against Blackburn Rovers, a run of 16 League games without tasting defeat.

1932   Villa scored 64 goals at Villa Park during the course of the season, the second highest tally for the First Division (unbelievably, Everton scored 84), with six of them coming in the 6–1 win over Liverpool.

1947   John Woodward born in Stoke. He began his career with the local club and joined Villa in October 1966, going on to make 27 League appearances and scoring seven goals. He left for Walsall in 1969 and later played for Port Vale and Scunthorpe.

1951   Alex Cropley born in Aldershot. He was brought up in Scotland and began his career with Hibernian, winning two caps for Scotland whilst at Easter Road. Signed by Arsenal for £150,000 in December 1974, he made just 30 League appearances for them before moving to Villa Park for £125,000. At the end of his first season he helped the club win the League Cup and he went on to make 65 League appearances for the club before moving on to Newcastle United in 1981. He later played for Portsmouth before returning to Hibernian to finish his career.

JANUARY 17TH

1880   Villa had entered the FA Cup for the first time in the 1879–80 season and had had the good fortune to receive a bye in the first round. They were then paired with Stafford Road of Wolverhampton in the second round, although they lost the toss for choice of venue (until 1882, the venue for cup-ties was decided by a toss of a coin, thereafter the first club drawn was at home), but Villa performed admirably and came away with a 1–1 draw.

1891   The Casuals were the visitors for the FA Cup first-round match at Perry Barr, with Villa registering a 13–1 win. This remains one of only two occasions the club has scored as many as 13 goals in a first-class fixture, the 13–0 drubbing of Wednesbury Old Athletic in 1886 being their record score. The Casuals beaten in this match should not be confused with the Corinthian Casuals, one of the leading amateur sides of the day who would beat Villa 3–2 at Perry Barr in 1894 shortly before Villa won the title.

1920   Aston Villa signed Newcastle United's centre-half Tommy Ball. After a hesitant start to his Villa Park career he settled down well at the heart of the defence and was set to become an integral part of the side for possibly the next ten years or so, but sadly he was shot dead by his neighbour, a policeman, in 1923 at the age of only 24.

1970   A high scoring game at Villa Park against Plymouth Argyle as Villa went down 5–3. Evenly poised at half-time at 2–2, Villa slipped further into trouble despite goals from Bruce Rioch (two) and Willie Anderson. Villa conceded 21 goals at home during the course of the relegation season, with almost a quarter coming in this one match!

1990   Leeds United were the visitors for the Zenith Data Systems Cup Northern Area semi-final with a crowd of 17,543 at Villa Park, one of the better attendances for the much-maligned competition. Villa won 2–0 thanks to goals from Stuart Gray and a David Platt penalty.

JANUARY 18TH

1936   Gordon Hodgson made his debut for Villa in the 3–0 defeat at Deepdale against Preston. Born in Johannesburg he was invited to join Liverpool after impressing in a match against them whilst they were on tour in the Transvaal in 1925. He spent 11 years at Anfield, scoring 240 goals in 378 appearances for the first team before switching to Villa in January 1936. He was with Villa for 14 months before joining Leeds United in March 1937, later coaching the same club and then taking up the position of manager of Port Vale, a job he held until his death five years later at the age of 47.

1943   George Cummings was handed a *sine die* ban from football following incidents in the match against Leicester on Christmas Day. With the country at war the football authorities were in the habit of handing out similar bans to almost all and sundry but later rescinding them, just as they did with Cummings whose ban was lifted on August 20th.

1993   Villa's pursuit of Manchester United at the top of the Premier League gathered momentum with an impressive 5–1 demolition job on Middlesbrough. Goals from Garry Parker, Paul McGrath and Dwight Yorke gave Villa a 3–0 lead, and there were second-half strikes from Dean Saunders and Shaun Teale to round off a third consecutive win.

JANUARY 19TH

1888   A friendly match with local rivals West Bromwich Albion drew a crowd of 10,000, but it was already apparent that a fixture list that comprised of friendlies and cup-ties, with no guarantee that the former would actually take place, was hardly ideal, and at the end of the season the Football League was introduced.

1969   Steve Staunton born in Dundalk. Signed by Liverpool from Dundalk for £20,000 in 1986, he was a member of the side that won the FA Cup in 1989 and League title in 1990, but he was unable to command a regular place in the side and was surprisingly sold to Villa for £1.1 million in 1991. He went on to prove the bargain of the decade, helping Villa win the League Cup in 1994 and 1996 but returned to Liverpool on a free transfer in 1998. He has won over 70 caps for the Republic of Ireland.

1983   Having won the European Cup the previous season Villa were scheduled to play European Cup-Winners' Cup holders Barcelona over two legs for the European Super Cup. The first leg at the Nou Camp saw them go down 1–0.

JANUARY 20TH

1965 Villa had reached their third League Cup semi-final in five years and were drawn against Chelsea. Having disposed of Luton, Leeds, Reading and Bradford City Villa had proved that they could raise their game when it mattered (they had beaten Bradford 7–1, with Tony Hateley scoring four of the goals), but Chelsea were renowned cup fighters and enjoying a remarkable season (they were to reach the FA Cup semi-final and topped the League for lengthy spells in addition to their League Cup exploits). At Villa Park Chelsea's hunger for success and a side on top of their game showed itself against a Villa side using the cup as a diversion from their League shortcomings, and a 3–2 win for the visitors gave Villa an almost impossible task for the second leg at Stamford Bridge.

1993 Bristol Rovers had pulled off a shock 1–1 draw at Villa Park in the FA Cup third round and fancied their chances of seeing off Villa at the compact Twerton Park ground in Bath. With scouts from Wimbledon, awaiting the winners in three days' time, among the crowd of 8,880 Villa saw off the threat and emerged 3–0 winners thanks to goals from Dean Saunders (two) and Ray Houghton.

JANUARY 21ST

1933 Seven goals at Villa Park sent the crowd home happy, with Villa recording a 5–2 win over Liverpool and keeping the pressure on Arsenal at the top of the table. Although Villa were ultimately to finish the season in second place behind their rivals from London, Villa Park fans witnessed 89 goals during the campaign, 60 of them in the opponents' net.

1961 Gary Shaw born in Birmingham. Signed by Villa as an apprentice, he made his first-team debut in 1978 and quickly established himself as a first-class striker, helping the side win the League in 1981 and the European Cup the following year, linking especially well with Peter Withe. His Villa career was effectively ended by a succession of injuries, although he remained with the club until 1988, later playing in Denmark and Austria before returning to English shores and turning out for Walsall and Shrewsbury.

JANUARY 22ND

1949 The visit of Arsenal, challenging at the top of the table whilst Villa languished at the bottom, brought 64,190 to Villa Park. Billy Goffin scored the only goal of the game to kick-start Villa's recovery; the remaining 17 League games would yield 26 points and they would finish the season in mid-table respectability.

1971 Stan Collymore born in Cannock. After failing to make the grade with Wolves, Stan rebuilt his career with non-League Stafford Rangers and cost Crystal Palace a fee of £100,00 when he signed in 1991. Palace got their money back when they sold him to Southend and it was here that his career took off. A £2 million fee took him to Nottingham Forest in 1993 and he developed into a highly feared striker. Liverpool paid £8.5 million for him in 1995 but he failed to settle in Merseyside, refusing to move nearer the club's training facilities and frequently falling foul of disciplinary measures. At the end of the 1997–98 season he was sold again, this time to Villa for £7 million, although he has yet to reproduce the form that once made him such an in-demand player.

1975 Ron Saunders notched up a notable hat-trick, guiding a side to the League Cup final for the third successive season. This time it was Villa's turn to benefit, overcoming spirited opposition from Chester on their way to a 3–2 win on the night in front of a crowd of 47,632 at Villa Park. Two goals from Keith Leonard and one from Brian Little gave Ron Saunders his record, but all Villa fans now prayed he would be able to do better than in either of his previous visits to the final; both Norwich City and Manchester City had been beaten! Villa's opponents at Wembley were to be Saunders' former club Norwich, conquerors of Manchester United in the other semi-final.

JANUARY 23RD

1897 Villa took a break from the rigours of League and cup football to journey to London to play a friendly against Spurs. Whilst Villa would end the season double champions, Spurs were enjoying their first proper taste of League football, having entered the Southern League at the start of the season. In the event Spurs were mightily pleased to have forced a 2–2 draw against the reigning League champions.

1982 A single goal from Gary Shaw eased Villa into the FA Cup fifth-round draw thanks to a 1–0 win at Ashton Gate against Bristol City. It was a controlled performance from Villa, drawing on their European experiences to frustrate City when required and hit hard on the break. It earned them a tie at Spurs in the next round.

1988 Villa maintained their position at the top of the Second Division with a 2–0 win over Manchester City at Maine Road. With City beginning to lose sight of the sides at the top of the table a win was vital for them in front of their own supporters, but a strike from Tony Daley in the first half put Villa in control and Garry Thompson finished them off in the second in front of a crowd of 24,668.

JANUARY 24TH

1880 The visit of Stafford Road for an FA Cup second-round replay drew a then record crowd of 4,000 to Perry Barr, with Villa winning the tie 3–1. They were then drawn against Oxford University in the third round but subsequently withdrew before the tie was played. Whether this was because they were in awe of a side that had reached the final three times and won the cup once is not known, but Oxford went on to reach the final for a fourth time, being beaten 1–0 by Clapham Rovers.

1927 Jackie Sewell born in Whitehaven. He began his career in the Third Division (South) with Notts County and helped them to the title in 1949–50, forming a partnership with Tommy Lawton in the process. He was sold to Sheffield Wednesday in 1952 for £34,500 and averaged a goal every other game during his spell with the club, costing Villa £20,000 when he signed in December 1955. A member of the 1957 FA Cup winning side he moved on to Hull City in 1959 and later coached on the African continent.

1947 Willie Anderson born in Liverpool. He spent four seasons with Manchester United but found first-team opportunities severely restricted owing to the continued form of George Best and joined Villa in January 1967 for £20,000. A member of the League Cup runners-up in 1971 and Third Division championship side the following year, he made over 200 appearances for the team before joining Cardiff City and finished his career playing in America.

JANUARY 25TH

1930 A then record crowd of 74,626 were at Villa Park to see the FA Cup fourth-round clash between Villa and local rivals Walsall, with Villa winning the game 3–1 and earning another home tie, this time against Blackburn Rovers. Despite the defeat, Walsall's goalkeeper Fred Biddlestone had impressed the Villa management so much they signed him to the club following the game!

1975 Villa's twin assault on Wembley continued with a comprehensive 4–1 win over Sheffield United in the FA Cup fourth round at Villa Park. A tense first half saw Villa lead by a single goal from Keith Leonard, followed by second-half strikes from Chris Nicholl, Ray Graydon and a second goal for Leonard in front of a crowd of 35,881 settled the game.

1986 The lowest crowd at Villa Park for an FA Cup tie was the 12,205 present to see the 1–1 draw with Millwall, with Steve Hodge scoring for Villa. Millwall won the replay 1–0 to end Villa's interest in the competition for another 12 months.

JANUARY 26TH

1924 Although the Trinity Road stand had been open and in use since the previous August, the Duke of York (later King George VI) visited Villa Park to officially open the stand, with Villa recording a 1–0 win over Bolton Wanderers in honour of the event.

1957 The long trek to the North East was duly rewarded as Villa won 3–2 at

Middlesbrough in the fourth round of the FA Cup. Brian Clough and Bill Harris had scored for Middlesbrough in the first half, whilst Brown had scored for Villa. But in the second half Villa took control, equalising through Derek Pace and Johnny Dixon scoring the winner for a memorable result.

1983   Aston Villa won the European Super Cup, overcoming a 1–0 defeat in the first leg in Barcelona with a 3–0 home victory thanks to goals from Gary Shaw, Gordon Cowans and Ken McNaught for a 3–1 aggregate victory.

JANUARY 27TH

1951   Villa's season effectively came to a close with a cup exit at the hands of Wolves. Having begun the season in poor form the cup remained the last tangible hope for gaining any glory, and having seen off the challenge of Burnley in the last round hopes were high that this might be the year that Villa made it back to Wembley. Unfortunately, they came up against a Wolves side enjoying a welcome respite from League action and who played with much more confidence. A 3–1 win for Wolves was probably the fairest result on the day, but the cup defeat hurt for some time given the proximity of the opposition.

1990   David Platt and Paul Birch gave Villa a comfortable 2–0 lead at half-time in the FA Cup fourth-round tie with Port Vale at Villa Park. With Vale committed to the attack in the second period, there was always going to be a likelihood that Villa might be able to exploit the space created behind the opposition defence. Villa took just about every chance they created, adding second-half goals through Ian Olney, Stuart Gray (two) and Paul Birch. An easy 6–0 win set up a local clash with West Bromwich Albion at the Hawthorns in the fifth round.

JANUARY 28TH

1911   On the same day as Villa were beating Bradford City 4–1 at Villa Park, William Renneville was becoming the first Villa player to be capped by Northern Ireland in the 2–1 defeat by Wales in Belfast.

1922   The FA Cup second-round clash with Luton Town stretched the record crowd for a cup-tie at Villa Park to 54,000, with Villa winning 1–0.

1938   Derek Dougan born in Belfast. A much-travelled player, he began his career in Ireland with Distillery as a centre-half, switching to the more familiar centre-forward upon signing with Portsmouth in 1957. He joined Blackburn Rovers and was a member of the side that reached the FA Cup final in 1960 and was then bought by Villa as a replacement for the Italy-bound Gerry Hitchens, costing the club £15,000. He spent only two years at Villa, joining Leicester City and then Wolves before retiring as a player. He was chairman of the PFA and later returned to Wolves as chairman and chief executive.

1946 Frank Broome scored a hat-trick in Villa's 9–1 FA Cup fourth-round second-leg win over Millwall. With Villa having already won the first leg 4–2, they advanced to the fifth round 13–3 aggregate winners. As this was the only season in which the early rounds of the FA Cup were decided over two legs, this remains the biggest-ever aggregate win in the competition, as well as Millwall's record defeat in a single game.

1952 Kenny Swain born in Birkenhead. Signed by Chelsea from non-League Wycombe Wanderers, he made 126 appearances for the club before a switch to Villa Park for £100,000 in December 1978. Whilst Chelsea had used him as a striker or in midfield, at Villa he was slotted into defence and helped the club to the League title and European Cup in successive seasons. He left for Nottingham Forest in 1983 and after a spell on loan with West Bromwich Albion became player-coach at Crewe and later took over at Wigan Athletic.

JANUARY 29TH

1949 The FA Cup had served as a welcome break from the rigours of League action for Villa, even if it had taken them three games to get past Bolton in the third round. That brought Cardiff City to Villa Park, a prospect that drew 70,718 on a cold winter's day. The action certainly warmed them up, although it was Cardiff who progressed into the next round 2–1 after managing to shackle Trevor Ford for much of the game.

1955 Villa had taken two games to get past Brighton and Hove Albion in the FA Cup third round, drawing 2–2 at the Goldstone Ground and then winning the replay 4–2 at Villa Park. That brought them head-to-head with Doncaster Rovers, then a lowly Second Division club, at the Belle Vue ground. It turned out to be a classic cup-tie, with plenty of goalmouth action even if no goals, and on the day both sides were evenly matched. They tried again in a replay at Villa Park a few days later and drew 2–2 after extra time, Tommy Thompson scoring both Villa's goals. That required a third meeting at neutral Maine road, and this too finished all square after extra time, 1–1 with Thompson scoring for Villa. They tried a fourth time at Hillsborough and finished goalless. Incredibly, the tie went to a fifth meeting at the Hawthorns where Doncaster finally won 3–1, Johnny Dixon scoring Villa's consolation goal. Not surprisingly this remains the longest cup-tie Villa have been involved in in recent times; seven games and eliminated in the fourth round!

JANUARY 30TH

1929 Aston Villa recorded their best away win with an 8–0 win over Clapton Orient at Millfields in the FA Cup fourth-round replay. The first match at Villa Park had ended 0–0! This result is Orient's heaviest defeat in their history.

1937 Villa came close to going down at home to Doncaster Rovers in the Second Division, recovering in time to force a 1–1 draw. Which was just as well, as not one of the 35 FA Cup and League matches played on the day resulted in an away win!

1974 A crowd of 47,821 were at Villa Park for the FA Cup fourth-round replay between Villa and Arsenal, the two sides having drawn the previous Saturday 1–1 at Highbury where Sammy Morgan had given Villa a first-half lead only for Ray Kennedy to equalise. Morgan repeated the feat in the replay, scoring for Villa in the first half to settle the home side's nerves in a tense and close cup-tie. A goal from Alun Evans in the second period completed the scoring 2–0 in Villa's favour and secured a trip to Burnley for the fifth round.

1990 Having beaten Hull City, Nottingham Forest and Leeds United, Villa had reached the Northern Area Final of the Zenith Data Systems Cup. This brought them a two legged clash with Middlesbrough, with Middlesbrough the visitors to Villa Park in the first leg. A crowd of 16,547 (less than had attended the semi-final!) saw Paul Birch and Bernie Slaven score in the first half to leave the game all square at half-time. A Brennan goal in the second half allowed Middlesbrough to win 2–1 on the night.

JANUARY 31ST

1920 Billy Walker had made his first appearance in the club's colours in the FA Cup first-round match with Queens Park Rangers and instantly proved himself a valuable asset to the club. With him in the side Villa were capable of beating anyone of their day, and he scored both goals in the 2–1 win.

1932 Vic Crowe born in Abercyon. After a spell as an amateur with West Bromwich Albion, he signed professional forms with Villa in 1952 and made his debut in 1954. A member of the side that won the League Cup in 1961 he made over 300 first-team appearances for the club and won 16 caps for Wales. He left Villa Park in 1964 to join Peterborough United but a short while later headed to America to become coach to Atlanta Chiefs. By 1969 he was back at Villa Park and was appointed manager in January 1970, guiding them to the League Cup final in 1971 and the Third Division title a year later. He left in 1974 to coach again in America, later returning to coach in non-League football.

1946 Keith Bradley born in Ellesmere Port. He joined the club as an apprentice and signed professional forms in May 1963, making his debut in February 1965. It was not until 1966–67, however, that he became a regular at right-back and went on to make 116 League appearances for the club and was a member of the side that reached the League Cup final in 1971. He was sent on loan to Peterborough in 1972, the move becoming permanent in November of that year.

1988 The television cameras were at Villa Park to see whether Second Division Villa could pull off a shock and topple the ultimate League champions Liverpool out of the FA Cup fourth round, with a crowd of 46,324 at the ground being joined by millions in their armchairs. Villa were more than a match for Liverpool in the first half, creating chances and hustling Liverpool out of their stride in midfield, but as the second half wore on experience told. A goal from John Barnes effectively won the game for Liverpool, although Peter Beardsley later added a second. Villa tried their hardest to at least grab a consolation effort but found stubborn resistance; Liverpool had now created a new club record of nine games without conceding a goal.

FEBRUARY 1ST

1936 Charlie Phillips made his debut for the club in the 3–1 win at Derby County, scoring one of Villa's goals. He had been signed from Wolves for £9,000 the previous month after six and a half seasons at Molineux and having won ten caps for Wales. He collected another three whilst at Villa Park but made only 22 appearances for the first team and finished his career with Birmingham City.

1959 Simon Stainrod born in Sheffield. Although he supported Wednesday as a schoolboy, he joined United as an apprentice, going on to make 59 appearances for the full League side before a transfer to Oldham in 1979. He spent almost three years with the club before joining Queens Park Rangers in 1980. After a brief spell with Sheffield Wednesday (at last!) he signed for Villa in September 1985 for £250,000 and made 63 League appearances before finishing his career with Stoke City.

1977 Loftus Road was the venue for the first leg of the League Cup semi-final clash between Queens Park Rangers and Aston Villa, and on a cold night 28,739 souls passed through the turnstiles to witness the proceedings. Villa gave a controlled performance on a difficult pitch (hot air balloons costing £12,000 had been used to get the pitch ready for the game!) to earn a goalless draw, confident that they could finish the job off in the second leg in front of their own fans at Villa Park.

FEBRUARY 2ND

1924 Alec Talbot made his only appearance for the Villa team in the current season, helping them overcome Swansea at the Vetch Field 2–0 in the FA Cup second round. He had joined the club in April the previous year, signing shortly after completing a ten hour shift down the pit at West Cannock Colliery. Life above ground proved a better bet, and after gaining a regular place in the side in 1924–25 he made 263 games for the club before departing for Bradford Park Avenue in 1935.

1946 Villa recorded a 5–1 win over Spurs in the Football League (South) match at Villa Park in front of a crowd of 30,736. The end of the Second World War came too late to have resumed normal League football for 1945–46, although the FA Cup was revived, with rounds up to the semi-final being decided over two legs. This was, however, the last season the Football League (South) was in operation, with Villa finishing the season in second place behind Birmingham City on goal average.

FEBRUARY 3RD

1894 Newton Heath (in 1902 they changed their name to Manchester United) were destined to finish bottom of the First Division for the second consecutive season, having survived the Test Matches at the end of the 1892–93 season. Villa helped them on their way with a comprehensive 5–1 victory at Perry Barr, although the Heathens did manage to score one of only seven goals they got on their travels during the season.

1945 With the Second World War all but won, Villa Park was selected as the venue for the international match between England and Scotland, although as this was a wartime game the result was not entered into the records and caps were withheld. There was much work required to get Villa Park ready for the day; the stand seats had been hidden in shelters around the city since the beginning of the war and required dusting and refitting to their rightful place, and on the day of the game 66,000 packed into the ground. England won the game 3–2 thanks to goals from Mortensen (two) and Brown.

1993 After a 1–1 draw at Villa Park in the FA Cup fourth-round clash with Wimbledon, the two sides battled it out for 120 minutes at Selhurst Park in the replay, and with the game still goalless at the end of extra time, a penalty shoot out was required. Here Wimbledon enjoyed the greater share of the luck, winning 6–5 to send Villa out of the cup.

FEBRUARY 4TH

1911 Villa were already involved in a head-to-head battle with Manchester United in the League and there were raised eyebrows when the two sides were paired in the FA Cup second round. Villa had performed admirably in the first round, winning 4–1 at Portsmouth, whilst United had beaten Blackpool at Old Trafford. The meeting between the top two sides was a match worthy of the final itself, but United got the upper hand in front of their own supporters and finally saw off Villa 2–1. If there was any consolation for Villa it was that United were knocked out by West Ham in the next round.

1986 Having drawn 1–1 at Villa Park in the Milk Cup fifth round with Arsenal, few gave Villa's hopes of surviving at Highbury in the replay much more than a cursory glance, especially as they were without Nigel Spink, giving a rare game for goalkeeper Kevin Poole. But Villa put a protective shield around the young goalkeeper, took the lead in the first half thanks to Paul Birch and seemed more than capable of repelling anything Arsenal could throw at them. A second-half goal from Allan Evans effectively ended Arsenal's fight, although they did score a consolation goal from Paul Mariner. Villa were through to the semi-finals to face Oxford United over two legs.

FEBRUARY 5TH

1909 Arthur Cunliffe born in Blackrod. He started his professional career with Blackburn Rovers in 1928 and joined Aston Villa five years later, linking with Ronnie Dix, a team-mate at Ewood Park. He left Villa for Middlesbrough in 1936 and later played for Burnley, Hull and Rochdale, where he ended his playing career in 1946. He was later coach at Bournemouth.

1921 Villa crashed to a 7–1 defeat at Turf Moor against eventual champions Burnley in what was their biggest defeat of the season.

1955 Villa's title hopes took a severe dent after a 6–1 thumping at The Valley against Charlton Athletic. With none of the sides in the top half of the table able to strike consistent form for lengthy spells during the season, Chelsea sneaked through to win the title with one of the lowest points tallies in many a year; only 52 from a possible 84.

1992 FA Cup holders Spurs had been beaten in a replay in the third round and now Villa had to travel to the Baseball Ground to take on Derby County. A superb first-half performance by Villa saw them 4–2 ahead at the break, with Dwight Yorke, who had grabbed a hat-trick, at his clinical best in front of the goal. Villa's other goal had been added by Garry Parker, and although Derby pulled another goal back in the second half to set the match up for a thrilling finale, Villa held on to win 4–3.

FEBRUARY 6TH

1961 Plymouth Argyle had forced a draw in the League Cup fourth round at Villa Park the previous December but when the two sides had met in the replay six days later it had been abandoned. By the time the two sides came to meet for the replay a second time, Villa's form had picked up and they were able to record a 5–3 win at Home Park to reach the fifth round of the competition on their way to winning the trophy.

1990 The second leg of the Zenith Data Systems Cup Northern Area final saw Villa 2–1 down from the first leg at Villa Park and facing a difficult struggle at Ayresome Park against Middlesbrough. A goal from Stuart Gray in the second half forced extra time, but two goals from Slaven and Kerr left Middlesbrough 4–2 aggregate winners and with a passage to the final at Wembley to face Chelsea. The competition had been largely ignored by fans around the country prior to the semi-finals, but 20,806 were at Ayresome Park for the Villa clash and over 76,000 were at Wembley for the final.

FEBRUARY 7TH

1903 The FA Cup first round had paired Villa with one of the most successful sides of the era, a home tie with four times League champions Sunderland. Both Villa and Sunderland were battling with Sheffield Wednesday at the top of the table for the League title, so a 4–1 win for Villa in front of a new record FA Cup crowd of 47,000 enabled Villa to end at least one club's hopes of winning the double. With Wednesday also beaten in the first round, by Blackburn after a replay, it should have left Villa with a clear run towards the final. Unfortunately they were tripped up by ultimate winners Bury in the semi-final.

1931 Huddersfield Town's star, which had shone so brightly during the previous decade, was already showing signs of beginning to dim, but they were still formidable opponents on their own Leeds Road ground. Villa, meanwhile, were battling to keep apace with Arsenal at the top of the table and needed as many points as they could muster. A spirited performance by Villa saw them survive early Town pressure and then go on to romp home 6–1 on the day.

1934 Jimmy Whitehouse died. Born in Birmingham in April 1873, he joined Villa from Grimsby for a fee of £200 and was goalkeeper when they won the double in 1897, leaving to join Newton Heath in September 1900. He remained with the Heathens for almost three years before switching across the city to join Manchester City in February 1903, and he later played for Third Lanark, Hull and Southend before retiring.

FEBRUARY 8TH

1896 Although it was still mathematically possible for Villa to be headed at the end of the season, the 2–2 draw they secured at Derby effectively gave them the title, for the home side had needed to gain both points in order to maintain the pressure on Villa.

1920 Villa's defence of the FA Cup, won at Stamford Bridge the previous season, began with a comfortable 2–0 win over Second Division Bristol City at Villa Park.

1958 Struggling Leicester City inflicted Villa's biggest defeat of the season with a 6–1 win at Filbert Street. Villa conceded 60 goals on their travels during the course of the season, one of the worst in the division.

FEBRUARY 9TH

1889 Preston arrived at Perry Barr protecting an enviable record; in their 21 League matches thus far they had yet to be beaten. The League championship was already theirs, for they were nine points ahead of Villa in second place, and they were to win the FA Cup in the same season, the first such domestic double. But Villa had a record of their own they were keen to protect, for their ten home matches at Perry Barr had all ended with victories to the home side. They had scored 44 goals and conceded just 14 in the process, and apart from Preston only Blackburn Rovers had been similarly unbeaten at home. Something had to give at Perry Barr, where a record League crowd of 12,000 gathered, and it turned out to be the Villa defence, beaten twice on the day as Preston recorded a 2–0 win.

1907　Villa recorded their biggest win of the season with an 8–1 demolition of Sheffield Wednesday at Villa Park.

1982　Ron Saunders resigned as manager of Aston Villa, eight months or so after guiding the club to the League championship and with the club through to the quarter-finals of the European Cup. Assistant Tony Barton was immediately appointed caretaker manager, with the position becoming permanent in April.

FEBRUARY 10TH

1926　Danny Blanchflower born in Belfast. He began his professional career with Glentoran and was transferred to Barnsley in 1949 for £6,500 and six months later won the first of his 56 caps for Northern Ireland. Aston Villa paid £15,000 for his signature in 1951 where he developed into a cultured and stylish midfield player. Three years later he was bought by Spurs for £30,000 and was one of the keys to the double winning side of 1961, a team that then went on to retain the FA Cup and, in 1963, lift the European Cup-Winners' Cup. Troubled by knee injury for some time Blanchflower retired in 1964 and immediately launched into a career in journalism, broken only by spells in charge at Chelsea in 1978 and as Northern Ireland's manager. Footballer of the Year in both 1958 and 1961, he died in 1993.

1948　Jimmy Rimmer born in Southport. Whatever else he achieved in his career, Jimmy will forever be known as the man who won two European Cup-Winners' medals after no more than eight minutes' action. He began his career with Manchester United and was a member of the side that won the FA Youth Cup in 1964, but most of his time was spent as understudy to Alex Stepney. When United won the European Cup in 1968 Jimmy was sitting on the bench, although he collected a medal at the end of extra time. In March 1974 he joined Arsenal and won a cap for England in 1976 whilst with the club, but later fell out with manager Terry Neill and joined Villa in August 1977. Here he was the last line of defence in the side that won the League championship in 1981 and reached the European Cup final the following season, but after only eight minutes he pulled up injured and had to be replaced by Nigel Spink, although once again he collected a medal at the end of the game. He left

Villa for Swansea in 1983 after 285 appearances for the club.

1965 Chelsea made it to the final of the League Cup at Aston Villa's expense. The 1–1 draw at Stamford Bridge was a commendable performance from Villa, but with Chelsea already 3–2 ahead from the first leg it proved not quite enough on the night. Chelsea went through 4–3 on aggregate to face Leicester City in the final (which Chelsea ultimately won).

FEBRUARY 11TH

1961 Aston Villa had been the last club to win the double of FA Cup and League championship in the same season, away back in 1897. There had been numerous occasions in the interim period when the double looked likely, and Villa themselves had ended Newcastle United, Sunderland and Manchester United's dreams along the way, usually with a victory in the FA Cup. By 1961 the latest threat came from Spurs, who were tearing through the League in double-quick time. By chance, they were drawn at Villa Park for the FA Cup fifth round, this match due to be played a week after the two sides met in the League at the same venue! The League game, played first, was probably the more crucial of the two, for Joe Mercer revealed his hand a week too early. Spurs won the League encounter 2–1 and therefore knew what to expect the following week; they won that match too, this time by 2–0 on their way to emulating Villa's feat. The fact that Spurs won the FA Cup semi-final at Villa Park only rubbed salt in the wounds!

1970 Carl Tiler born in Sheffield. He began his career with Barnsley and switched to Nottingham Forest in a deal worth £400,000 in 1991. He cost Villa £750,000 when signed in 1995 but pulled a hamstring on his debut and when he recovered scored his only goal of the season against his former club! Competition for places in the back four led him to sign for Sheffield United for £650,000 in March 1997.

1995 Aston Villa equalled the then Premier League goalscoring record, held by Blackburn and Newcastle, with a 7–1 hammering of Wimbledon at Villa Park. The goals were scored by an own goal from Reeves, Tommy Johnson (three), Dean Saunders (two, one from the penalty spot) and Dwight Yorke in front of a crowd of 23,982. It was Villa's biggest win in the League for 33 years, since they beat Leicester City 8–3 in 1962.

FEBRUARY 12TH

1938 The arrival of Aston Villa for the FA Cup fifth-round clash with Charlton Athletic at the Valley drew Charlton's biggest-ever attendance, 75,031 to witness a 1–1 draw.

1972 A crowd of 48,110 were at Villa Park for the Third Division top-of-the-table clash between Villa and Bournemouth. Bournemouth were enjoying a good season, with their cup exploits against Margate winning them national recognition, and it was Ted MacDougall who gave the visitors the lead in the first half. Villa however never panicked, and goals from Geoff Vowden and Andy Lochhead in the second 45 minutes gave Villa the two points and a strengthened position at the top of the table. Not surprisingly, the attendance was a record for the Third Division and remained so until 1979 when the two Sheffield clubs, United and Wednesday, clashed at Hillsborough.

1986   The four semi-finalists for the Milk Cup were Villa, Liverpool, QPR and Oxford, and if Villa could have stage managed the draw, then they would surely have wanted to avoid Liverpool, with Oxford the preferred choice. Which is exactly what they got, with the home leg at Villa Park first. But Oxford were more than capable of holding their own and put up a spirited performance, scoring twice through John Aldridge. Fortunately Villa also managed two, through Paul Birch and Simon Stainrod, but the 2–2 draw meant Villa would have to win the away leg to qualify for the Wembley final.

FEBRUARY 13TH

1915   The lowest attendance to have witnessed a League match at Villa Park was the 2,900 who saw a goalless draw between Villa and Bradford City. However, with Villa languishing in mid-table and normal League football about to be abandoned at the end of the season owing to the First World War, interest was already beginning to wane.

1937   Plenty of goals at Villa Park as Villa finally won an exciting match against Plymouth Argyle 5–4 in the Second Division.

1992   A 1–0 win at Stamford Bridge against Chelsea was enough to take Villa to the top of the FA Premier League for the first time. Ray Houghton scored the goal that put Villa in the driving seat with just 13 games to play, but unfortunately for Villa it was to prove unlucky.

FEBRUARY 14TH

1920   Tommy Smart made his debut for Villa in the 2–2 draw at home to Everton. Signed from Halesowen Town in January, he went on to play 452 games for the club, helping them win the FA Cup in 1920 and reach the final four years later. He left the club in 1934 to play for non-League Brierley Hill Alliance.

1972   Sasa Curcic born in Belgrade in Yugoslavia. First introduced to English football by Bolton Wanderers, who signed him from Partizan Belgrade for £1.5 million in 1995, he became Villa's then record transfer when switching to the club in August 1996 for £4 million but was subsequently sold to Crystal Palace in March 1998 for just £1 million.

1988   Villa's impressive away form and march up the table, coupled with Middlesbrough's own promotion push, was considered attraction enough for the television cameras to show a Second Division match for the first time. Tony Daley gave Villa the lead in the first half, but Middlesbrough hit back in the second period to win the game 2–1.

1996 The Coca-Cola Cup semi-final draw pitted Villa against Arsenal, thus giving hope that there might still be an all-Birmingham final between Villa and Birmingham City come March time. But Arsenal were in sparkling form in the opening half hour of the clash at Highbury, scoring twice through Dennis Bergkamp. Just as they had had to do two years previously at Tranmere, Villa mounted a recovery, scoring twice through Dwight Yorke to level the game on the day at 2–2.

FEBRUARY 15TH

1945 Lew Chatterley born in Birmingham. Originally signed with the club as an apprentice, he was given a debut in May 1963 and went on to make 164 appearances for the first team in eight different positions. He was transferred to Northampton Town in September 1971 and later played for Grimsby Town, Southampton and finished his career with Torquay United.

1972 With the country in the middle of the miners' strike and the three day week, with evening matches all but banned, it was announced Villa had hired a generator to ensure their floodlight friendly with crack Brazilian club Santos, complete with superstar Pele, would take place as scheduled on the 21st of February.

1977 A night of high drama at Villa Park, where the visit of Queens Park Rangers in the second leg of the League Cup semi-final drew 48,439. The first leg had finished goalless and the second leg looked to be heading the same way until John Deehan scored in the second leg to give Villa the lead. QPR forced an equaliser late in the game to ensure extra time, then John Deehan restored Villa's lead, and when John Burridge saved Don Given's penalty, it looked to be all over. But with time running out for QPR, substitute Peter Eastoe equalised for a second time to force a replay.

1984 Portsmouth, Manchester City, West Bromwich Albion and Norwich had been seen off by Villa in the earlier rounds of the Milk Cup, setting up a two leg clash with Everton in the semi-final. At Goodison Villa's normally reliable defence played under par, with Everton taking advantage with a goal in each half to make the second leg a difficult affair for Villa if they were to make the final.

FEBRUARY 16TH

1889 Villa crashed to the heaviest defeat in their history, going down 8–1 at Blackburn Rovers in the FA Cup third round. Blackburn were something of a bogey side for Villa at the time, for later in the year Villa went to Ewood Park for a League match and lost 7–0!

1934 Mike Pinner born in Boston. He represented seven clubs during his career but only signed as a professional for his last one, Orient, in October 1963. He had begun his League career with Villa in 1954 as an amateur and later played for Sheffield Wednesday, QPR, Manchester United, Chelsea and Swansea, retaining his amateur status throughout.

1938 Willie Hamilton born in Airdrie. He began his career with Drumpelier and joined Villa after giving service to Sheffield United, Middlesbrough and Hibernian, arriving at Villa Park in August 1965. He made 49 League appearances in Villa's colours, scoring nine goals. He won one cap for Scotland during his career but also represented the Football League.

1957 The FA Cup fifth round brought Bristol City and a crowd of 63,099 to Villa Park, where Derek Pace gave Villa the lead only for John Atyeo to equalise. Thankfully Jackie Sewell was on hand to ease Villa's fears with a superb individual goal that took Villa through to the next round 2–1.

1994 Villa were at Prenton Park for the Coca-Cola Cup semi-final first leg and at half-time must have felt like packing up and going home as Tranmere ran them ragged. It was 2–0 at the interval and could have been more, and although Villa recovered somewhat in the second half, scoring through Dalian Atkinson, a third Tranmere goal left them with a 3–1 lead to take to Villa Park for the second leg.

FEBRUARY 17TH

1900 Villa moved another step closer to retaining their League title with a 6–2 win over Notts County at Villa Park. However, the vital game would come in two weeks' time, with second-placed Sheffield United the visitors.

1923 Stoke City were the victims as Villa registered their biggest win of the season, a 6–0 win at Villa Park. However, despite winning 15 of their home matches during the course of the campaign, Villa had been unable to mount a serious challenge for the title, won by Liverpool, because of their poor form on their travels, with only three victories all season. Villa finished in sixth place at the end of the campaign, 14 points behind champions Liverpool.

1990 Irrespective of where either team lay in the League, or even what League they were in, there was still a magical quality about a local derby, with the added incentive of a quarter-final place in the FA Cup increasing both the excitement and pressure surrounding the game between West Bromwich Albion and Aston Villa. Albion were suffering a poor season but had managed to raise their game whenever the cup came around, a welcome respite from the hunt for League points. Villa on the other hand had no such worries; top of the table and battling with Liverpool for the honour of being champions come the end of the season. A crowd of 26,585 were at the Hawthorns for an intriguing battle, with Albion knowing their best chance of seeing off their rivals was on their own ground. A goal from Derek Mountfield for Villa only served to make Albion try even harder to get back on level terms, but a second-half strike from Tony Daley and a convincing performance from David Platt in midfield saw Villa safely home 2–0 winners.

FEBRUARY 18TH

1882 Howard Vaughton and Arthur Brown became the first Villa players to be capped by England when they played in the 13–0 win over Ireland in Belfast. Vaughton scored five of England's goals on the day, the first time any English player had scored as many goals in a single international, although it has to be said that there is still some doubt over this achievement as it was not automatic to record the names of goalscorers. Arthur 'Digger' Brown had first joined Villa in 1878 but left a few weeks later, only to return to the fold in 1880. Sadly, his career was brought to an end owing to ill-health in 1886.

1953 Villa's season of mid-table respectability had meandered on for six months, with their lack of firepower up front being the difference between them and the sides at the top of the table. For the visit of Portsmouth, however, Villa got the result they had been threatening to do for some weeks, recording a season's best in the 6–0 win at Villa Park.

1975 With only two clubs due to be promoted at the end of the season it was vital that Villa timed their run towards the top of the Second Division to perfection, especially with Manchester United far enough ahead of everybody else to make it a four club race to fill the second spot; Villa, Norwich, Sunderland and Bristol City. Villa had hit form at the right time, but maintaining it would require perseverance and luck with injuries. At Portsmouth they had both, and goals from Frank Carrodus, Ray Graydon and Brian Little, even if Portsmouth got two of their own, were enough to collect another two points. Villa were still only fourth in the table, but with Norwich and Sunderland especially dropping points over the past few weeks, Villa were ideally placed to strike.

FEBRUARY 19TH

1881 For the second consecutive season Villa were drawn with Stafford Road of Wolverhampton in the FA Cup, this time in the fourth round. A then record crowd of 5,000 were at Perry Barr to see Stafford Road win 3–2.

1887 Villa had been given another home draw in the FA Cup quarter-finals, being paired with Lancashire rivals Darwen. Villa were in superb form in the first half, powering into a 3–0 lead. At the break, for some reason, the team cracked open the champagne and then proceeded to play so badly in the second half they nearly threw it away, finally squeezing through 3–2.

1921 The FA Cup third round (equal to the fifth round today) pitted Villa against Huddersfield Town at Villa Park. No side this century had managed to retain the cup, but there were many in the 50,627 crowd who went home convinced that Villa might be the first to do it after a 2–0 win that set them up with a clash against Spurs in the next round.

1949 A 2–1 win over Manchester United was witnessed by a crowd of 68,354, at that time the largest to have seen a League fixture. Only one other League game at Villa Park has ever had a higher attendance.

1983 Had Watford's finishing matched their approach play in the match at Villa Park, then Villa would have been staring at elimination from the FA Cup fifth round instead of a scoreline that bore little relation to what went on before. Watford should have been three goals ahead by half-time instead of two down, Gary Shaw and Tony Morley netting for Villa. The second half followed much the same pattern, with Colin Gibson and Gordon Cowans converting Villa's chances and Luther Blissett finally getting Watford on the scoresheet from the penalty spot.

FEBRUARY 20TH

1897 Fred 'Diamond' Wheldon made his debut for England and scored three goals in the 6–0 win over Ireland at Trent Bridge. He went on to represent his country on six occasions.

1904 With Villa drawn away at Spurs in the FA Cup for the second consecutive season there was always likely to be considerable interest in the tie, but few expected a crowd of 32,000 to gather at White Hart Lane, a figure well in excess of what the ground could safely accommodate. As such there were people around the perimeter of the pitch, all eager to view the action. Villa took a 1–0 lead in the first half and looked capable of holding it for another victory at White Hart Lane, but at half-time those on the perimeter wandered on to the pitch to stretch their legs, soon being joined by others from the stands. When the teams came out for the second half it proved impossible to get the pitch cleared and the referee was left with little option but to abandon the game. Spurs were fined £350 and a replay was ordered at Villa Park for the following Thursday. It has often been claimed that this was the first occasion that supporters had invaded the pitch in an effort to get a match their team was losing abandoned, but there is a much simpler explanation; the crowd couldn't get off the pitch once they had got on it!

1926 The crowd at Villa Park topped the 70,000 mark for the first time, with 71,466 in their positions to see the FA Cup fifth-round clash with Arsenal. Arsenal secured a replay with a 1–1 draw and beat Villa 2–0 in the replay at Highbury.

1947 Brian Greenhalgh born in Southport. He began his career with Preston in February 1965, joining Villa two and a half years later in a £55,000 deal that also brought Brian Godfrey to the club. He made 40 League appearances, scoring 12 goals before switching to Leicester City, later playing for Huddersfield, Cambridge, Bournemouth, Torquay and Watford.

1960 Aston Villa helped set the record attendance for a match at Vale Park in the FA Cup fifth-round clash with Port Vale, with 48,745 present to see Villa win 2–1.

FEBRUARY 21ST

1972 A crowd of 54,437 paying receipts of £35,000 turned out at Villa Park to witness the presence of Pele, playing for his Brazilian club side Santos in the friendly match. Villa had hired a generator to ensure everyone had a good view of the game, won 2–1 by Villa.

1990 A 2–0 win at White Hart Lane against Spurs was enough for Villa to replace Liverpool at the top of the First Division as the race for the title hotted up. Goals from Ian Ormondroyd and David Platt meant it was the first time Villa had been top of the table since they had won the League in 1981.

1996 After all the excitement of the first leg of the Coca-Cola Cup semi-final against Arsenal the second leg was never likely to reach the same heights, but a stout defensive display from Villa in front of their own fans, with Villa Park packed with 39,334 inside, was enough to earn a 0–0 draw and a place in the final of the League's cup competition for a record seventh time, a record they now share with Liverpool. Qualifying by away goals was not quite the way Villa fans would have preferred to have succeeded, but come the day at Wembley, how they got there would not matter one bit.

FEBRUARY 22ND

1974 The return clash with table toppers Manchester United drew a crowd of 39,156 to Villa Park. Villa had improved since the sides had met at Old Trafford in November and had won four and drawn one of the last five games, pushing them up to fourth in the table. First-half goals from Ray Graydon and Charlie Aitken put Villa in the driving seat and despite a spirited display from United in the second half, Villa held on to claim a vital scalp in their push for promotion.

1977 Neutral Highbury was the venue for the League Cup semi-final replay between Villa and QPR, with Villa's supporters in the majority among the 40,438 crowd. Two goals in the first half from Brian Little effectively ended the game as a contest, although Villa still kept up the pressure on QPR, mindful of the way the London club had fought back in the previous meeting. A third goal for Little in the second half finished the scoring and ensured Villa were at Wembley for the final, where they were to meet Everton.

1984 Sloppy defending in the first leg at Goodison Park had given Villa a difficult hurdle to overcome in the second leg of the Milk Cup semi-final at Villa Park, with 42,426 looking to see if Villa could retrieve a 2–0 deficit from the first leg. They nearly made it too, a second-half strike by Paul Rideout setting up a frantic finish as Villa searched desperately for the goal that would force extra time, but somehow Everton held on to ensure an all-Merseyside final for the first time, Liverpool having already made it through to the last stage.

FEBRUARY 23RD

1901 The FA Cup third round had been delayed owing to the death of Queen Victoria, with Villa finally beating Millwall Athletic 5–0 at Villa Park. That brought them a home tie with Nottingham Forest and a crowd of 40,000 to see a hard fought and closely contested 0–0 draw. Villa, however, won the replay 3–1 on their way to the semi-finals that season.

1921 Tommy Jackson made his debut in goal for the club in the 1–0 win against Sunderland at Roker Park. He remained with the club for ten years, making 186 appearances for Villa, including the 1924 FA Cup final against Newcastle United. At the end of his playing career he became a teacher.

1972 Villa paid £60,000 to bring Ian Ross from Liverpool to Villa Park.

FEBRUARY 24TH

1906 The FA Cup draw decreed that holders Villa would visit Second Division Manchester United in the third round. Villa did not take their opponents lightly, spending a week on the North Wales coast preparing themselves for the tie, and when they ran out in front of a 40,000 crowd who had paid then record receipts of £1,460, with thousands locked out, they looked ready for battle. But United were not overawed, settled quickly and took the lead after only ten minutes. Villa fought back admirably and soon equalised, but ten minutes from half-time United hit them again to go in at the break 2–1 ahead. The second half was a disaster for Villa; the notorious pitch at Clayton (United would not relocate to Old Trafford until 1910) had begun to cut up badly towards the end of the first half, and whilst United's players were used to playing on the surface, Villa's were not. United kept their feet whilst all about them Villa were losing theirs and went on to rattle in three second-half goals. According to the *Athletic News*, the 5–1 defeat was the biggest drubbing any cup holder had ever received, headlining their report 'Extraordinary Doings at Clayton'. It was certainly the biggest cup upset in years and only partially forgotten when Walsall knocked Arsenal out of the cup some years later.

1943 Tommy Mitchinson born in Sunderland. He joined Sunderland as a junior and rose through the ranks, signing professional forms in

December 1960. After a brief spell with Mansfield he signed for Villa in August 1967 and spent almost two years with the club, making 49 League appearances. He later played for Torquay and finished his League career with Bournemouth.

1965 Wolves and Villa had already drawn 1–1 at Villa Park in the FA Cup fifth round, Tony Hateley scoring for Villa. Four days later they tried again, with nearly 48,000 shoehorned into Molineux to see a match that had all the action of a typical cup-tie if not the goals, for after extra time there had still been nothing between the sides and they would have to try yet again at the Hawthorns.

1996 Manager Brian Little returned to his former club Leicester City armed with his cheque book and paid £1.5 million to take Julian Joachim to Villa Park. Joachim had burst on to the Premiership the previous season, scoring Leicester's first goal in the League in the 3–1 home defeat by Newcastle, although he later endured a two-month spell out of the game with a broken foot. Upon his return he appeared to have lost some of his form, but he would go on to prove a worthwhile acquisition for Villa.

FEBRUARY 25TH

1893 Perry Barr staged its first England international with Ireland the visitors. The game ended with a 6–1 win for England.

1904 Villa entertained Spurs in the FA-ordered replay of a cup-tie that had been abandoned the previous Saturday after the crowd had invaded the pitch with Villa leading 1–0. Justice was not done, for Spurs won 1–0 thanks to a goal from Jack Jones.

1925 The FA Cup third-round replay between Villa and local rivals West Bromwich Albion drew a crowd of 60,015, with the visitors winning 2–1 after the two had drawn 1–1 at the Hawthorns.

1928 Tom 'Pongo' Waring made his League debut for the club, scoring in the 3–2 win at Roker Park against Sunderland. He had begun his League career with Tranmere Rovers where his goalscoring exploits soon attracted the interest of other, bigger clubs. Indeed, when Villa scouts went to run the rule over him, he scored six goals in the 11–1 win over Durham. Signed immediately for £4,700 his first appearance in the club's colours was for the reserve side in the Central League and a crowd of 23,000 turned out to see him score a hat-trick. In the Villa first team his performances were no less impressive, rattling in 167 goals in 226 games, and when he was allowed to leave in November 1935 for Barnsley, a crowd of 5,000 showed themselves against the move by calling for his immediate return. After less than a year with Barnsley he joined Wolves and then went back to Tranmere, finishing his League career with Accrington Stanley. He then played for Bath City before guesting for New Brighton during the Second World War.

FEBRUARY 26TH

1910 Villa swamped Manchester United 7–1 at Villa Park, with Joey Walters scoring a hat-trick and Villa going on to win the title at the end of the season. Born in Prestwich Joey made an impressive start to his Villa career but was prone to losing his form and then having to re-establish himself all over again. In the summer of 1912 he left the club to sign for Oldham and later played for Southend, Millwall, Manchester United (who obviously forgave him for his hat-trick!) and Rochdale. He died from pneumonia at the age of 39.

1944 John Sleeuwenhoek born in Wednesfield. Signed by Villa as an apprentice, he was upgraded to the professional ranks in March 1961 and by the 1962–63 season was first choice centre-half. He remained at the club until November 1967 when he moved across the city to sign for Birmingham for £45,000, later spending a spell on loan with Torquay and finishing his career with Oldham. His father was a Dutch Army paratrooper which accounted for his unusual surname, although John represented England at Schoolboy, Youth and Under-23 level. He died in August 1989.

FEBRUARY 27TH

1904 Villa's best win of the season saw them hand out a 6–1 drubbing to Sheffield United at Villa Park.

1971 Third Division Villa were at Wembley for the League Cup final against Spurs. Having overcome Manchester United in the semi-finals there was little need for Villa to be in awe of anybody at Wembley, and there was also an omen or two in their favour; in 1967 and 1969 Third Division sides (Queens Park Rangers and Swindon respectively) had produced a shock and beaten First Division opposition in the final. Villa gave a good account of themselves against Spurs and might even have won the game; Andy Lochhead shot towards an open goal, the Spurs defence having stopped expecting a free kick for a foul on Pat Jennings, and only Steve Perryman had the presence of mind to race back and clear the line; and later Ian Hamilton hit the bar with a rising shot with Jennings well beaten. Only two late goals from Martin Chivers ended Villa's spirited fight.

1994 Villa had goalkeeper Mark Bosnich to thank when they finally overcame Tranmere in the Coca-Cola Cup semi-final second leg. With Villa 3–1 behind after the first leg things did not seem to be going Villa's way, with Bosnich lucky not to have been sent off following a professional foul and John Aldridge netting from the penalty spot. But goals from Dean Saunders, Shaun Teale and Dalian Atkinson took the game to extra time, and with no further scoring a penalty shoot-out. Bosnich saved three as Villa won 5–4 to book a place in the final against Manchester United.

FEBRUARY 28TH

1953 After seeing off the challenge of Middlesbrough, Brentford and Rotherham United in the previous rounds of the FA Cup, thoughts of Wembley were beginning to form in the minds of most supporters, with 60,658 packing into Villa Park for the sixth round clash with Everton. A single goal from Dave Hickson settled the match in Everton's favour and left Villa fans to dream for another four years at least.

1959 After a superb performance against Everton at Goodison Park in the FA Cup fifth round, where they had won 4–1, Villa were rewarded with a home tie with Burnley in the sixth round. Whilst Burnley were beginning to assemble the side that would soon be challenging for the game's top honours, Villa were in transition. They battled their way to a 0–0 draw at Villa Park before winning 2–0 in the replay.

1998 John Gregory's reign as manager got off to a good start with a 2–1 win over Liverpool at Villa Park. Gregory could hardly have asked for a more difficult start to his tenure, for Villa's next opponents were Athletico Madrid in the UEFA Cup in Spain!

FEBRUARY 29TH

1936 Villa's desperate battle against relegation was beginning to enter the final straight, with every game and point gained vital. They bounced back from a narrow defeat at Bolton by the odd goal in seven with a 3–0 win over fellow strugglers Liverpool at Villa Park.

1940 February had seen feverish activity at Villa Park, even though the Second World War was underway. For the present, the Trinity Road Stand had been refitted as an air raid shelter and the home dressing-room furnished so as to provide a home for the 9th Battalion of the Royal Warwickshire Regiment. But Villa were also planning for the future, and work had been completed on building up the Holte End banking, raising the ground's capacity to around 76,000.

1992 A tally of five points in seven games had dented Villa's hopes of finishing high enough in the table to qualify for European competition, and from a high of fourth they had slipped to eighth. Manchester City, by comparison, were enjoying something of a renaissance and proved just too strong for Villa on the day, scoring through Quinn and White in each half to record a 2–0 win.

MARCH 1ST

1975 Norwich City were making their second appearance in the League Cup final in three seasons, having reached the final in 1973. Then, when managed by Ron Saunders, they had defended for much of the game and were roundly condemned for making the final against Spurs one of the worst witnessed since the final had gone to Wembley. Saunders would be sitting on the other bench in this final, having guided his new team Aston Villa to the final after just nine months in charge. It soon became apparent that Norwich had changed very little since Saunders' departure, for they still showed little attacking inclination in another mediocre final. Not that such matters will have unduly troubled the Villa fans in the 100,000 crowd, for a goal for Ray Graydon was enough to win the cup for the second time in Villa's history. The goal itself was a bizarre one, Graydon watching his penalty being saved by Kevin Keelan, who pushed the shot against a post, but then Graydon reacted quickly and got to the ball to fire it home before anyone else could intervene. For Ron Saunders it was third time lucky; in the two previous seasons he had guided a team to the final only to lose at Wembley, with Norwich in 1973 and Manchester City in 1974.

1978   The arrival of crack Spanish side Barcelona for the UEFA Cup quarter-final first leg drew a crowd of 49,619 to Villa Park, easily their biggest crowd of the competition thus far. However, they were also facing their stiffest opposition in the competition, for Barcelona were seasoned European campaigners and likely to pose a serious threat to Villa's aspirations. The home crowd were silenced in the first half when Johann Cruyff grabbed a goal for the visitors, and despite second-half strikes from Ken McNaught and John Deehan, a second Spanish goal from Zuviria left the score on the night at 2–2. Chief architect of Villa's downfall was Cruyff, and when he was forced to leave the field injured after 82 minutes, he did so to a standing ovation from the Villa crowd.

MARCH 2ND

1888   William McGregor, of Aston Villa, wrote to Blackburn Rovers, Bolton Wanderers, Preston North End, West Bromwich Albion and the secretary of his own club: 'Every year it is becoming more and more difficult for football clubs of any standing to meet their friendly engagements and even arrange friendly matches. The consequence is that at the last moment, through cup-tie interferences, clubs are compelled to take on teams who will not attract the public. I beg to tender the following suggestion as a means of getting over the difficulty: that ten or twelve of the most prominent clubs in England combine to arrange home and away fixtures each season, the said fixtures to be arranged at a friendly conference about the same time as the International Conference. This might be known as the Association Football Union, and could be managed by a representative from each club. Of course, this is in no way to interfere with the National Association; even the suggested matches might be played under cup-tie rules. However, this is a detail. I would take it as a favour if you would kindly think the matter over and make whatever suggestions you may deem necessary. I am writing only to the following: Blackburn Rovers, Bolton Wanderers, Preston North End, West Bromwich Albion and Aston Villa, and should like to hear what other clubs you suggest. I am, yours very truly, William McGregor. P.S. How would Friday, March 23, 1888, suit for the friendly conference at Anderton's Hotel, London?'

1929   Aston Villa booked a place in the FA Cup semi-finals after a slender 1–0 win over Arsenal at Villa Park, watched by a then record crowd of 73,686. Pongo Waring scored the only goal of the game and, unbelievable though it may seem now, put considerable pressure on Arsenal manager Herbert Chapman's position at Highbury, where success had still to be a visitor four years after Chapman took over. Arsenal gained revenge, of sorts; Villa lost the semi-final at Highbury.

1946   The biggest attendance ever to pack into Villa Park was the 76,588 who saw the FA Cup tie with Derby County, generating what were then record receipts of £8,651 2s 6d. With the Football League not yet restored following the end of the Second World War, this was the first and only season in which the rounds up to the semi-final have been decided over two legs. Unfortunately, Villa lost the first leg 4–3.

1957   Villa's train to the FA Cup final at Wembley remained on the right track, but only just. Peter Aldis put through his own net to give Burnley the lead at Turf Moor, but Peter McParland was on hand to equalise on the day and ensure a replay at Villa Park. Villa were mightily relieved to have survived at Turf Moor, for the ground had become something of a bogey for them in recent years. A 2–0 win at home took Villa into the semi-final to face local rivals West Bromwich Albion.

1974   The 100th League meeting between Villa and West Bromwich Albion took place at Villa Park, with a crowd of 37,323 present to see Albion win 3–1, all the goals coming in the first half.

1983   Aston Villa were rocked in the very first minute of their tie with Juventus in the European Cup quarter-final first leg. Although both of the previous visitors (Besiktas and Dinamo Bucharest) had managed to score, it had usually come at a time when Villa were already safely in control of the tie. This time they were not, and despite a Gordon Cowans goal the Italians also added a second to take back to Turin. Villa's grip on the European Cup had effectively been loosened.

MARCH 3RD

1894   Bolton Wanderers inflicted Villa's only home defeat of the season with a 3–2 win at Perry Barr. It was a surprising victory for the Trotters, hovering just above the relegation trap door whilst Villa were battling at the other end of the table and on the brink of lifting the League title for the first time in their history, requiring just two more points to make it safe, but despite the reverse Villa would go on to claim the championship.

1900 Villa and Sheffield United were locked together at the top of the table battling for the championship. A crowd of 50,000, the first to have reached such a figure, saw a 1–1 draw, but at the end of the season it was Villa who had reason to cheer; they lifted the title.

1965 David Norton born in Cannock. He joined the club as a trainee and was upgraded to the professional ranks in 1983, going on to make over 50 first-team appearances before being sold to Notts County for £30,000 in 1988. He later played for Rochdale, Hull, Northampton and Hereford.

1982 Villa resumed the European Cup trail with a convincing defensive performance in Russia, holding the much fancied Dynamo Kiev to a goalless draw in front of 36,000.

1998 With Spanish opponents having been disposed of in the second round, Villa had to return to the country to face Athletico Madrid in the quarter-finals. A single goal on the night from the Spaniards meant a tight match was to come at Villa Park.

MARCH 4TH

1924 Norman Lockhart born in Belfast. Spotted by Swansea whilst playing for Linfield, he was introduced to the Football League in 1946 and made 47 appearances for the Swans before joining Coventry in 1947. He came to Villa Park in September 1952 and made 73 appearances for the club before finishing his career with Bury.

1939 The war clouds may have been gathering across Europe, but at Villa Park there was only one thought; Birmingham must be beaten at all costs! The St Andrews club were having a torrid time of it in the First Division, locked at the bottom of the table with Leicester City and Chelsea in the battle against relegation. Whilst Villa were not much ahead of them, a win against City would dispel most of the fears that they might be sucked into trouble. On the day Villa were rampant, the forward line devastating, and Villa powered to a 5–1 win which made them safe. City ended the season being relegated and had to wait seven years before mounting a campaign to return to the First Division.

1972 Notts County were part of the pack chasing Villa at the top of the Third Division, although with Villa having been beaten only once since the New Year their position was strengthening week by week. Meadow Lane was always going to be a difficult journey for Villa, where Notts County had only lost twice in the season, and County started the first half eager to protect their record. Jim Cumbes needed to be alert throughout the opening 45 minutes but proved more than able when called upon. Villa took over in the second half, taking the lead through Pat McMahon and defending well to protect the advantage. A second goal for McMahon and Ray Graydon rounded off what was an exceptional result in front of County's biggest crowd of the season, 34,208.

MARCH 5TH

1887   Villa were through to their first semi-final in the FA Cup and were drawn to play Glasgow Rangers! The Scottish side had entered the English FA Cup for the first and last time that season and had seen off Everton, Church, Cowlairs (another Scottish side), Lincoln City and Old Westminsters on their way to the semi-final. Villa's route had taken them past Wednesbury Old Athletic, Wolves (a tie that had gone to four games before Villa finally won), a bye, Horncastle and Darwen. The venue for the semi-final was Nantwich Road, the then home of Crewe Alexandra. Whilst this seemed a strange choice for the match, it was chosen simply because of the convenience of the trains, given the distance the Rangers side were having to travel. On the morning of the game Villa got some assistance from an unlikely source; former Rangers player Hugh McIntyre, who was currently playing for Blackburn Rovers, travelled over to Crewe and entertained his former team-mates to a meal, but some of the Rangers players ate too much and their performance in the afternoon was particularly sluggish. Notwithstanding that, Villa scored three times through Hunter (two) and Brown, and made it through to their very first FA Cup final where they would face local rivals West Bromwich Albion.

1892   On the same day as Villa were losing 4–3 at Ewood Park to Blackburn Rovers, Willie Evans was becoming the first Villa player to be capped for Wales in the match against England in Wrexham. England won 2–0.

1921   Villa's reign as cup holders came to an end in the quarter-final at White Hart Lane against Spurs. A crowd of 51,991 saw Spurs gain their revenge for the defeat the previous year with a 1–0 win on their way to winning the cup that year.

1938   A pre-war record crowd of 75,540 were at Villa Park for the FA Cup sixth round clash with Manchester City, paying receipts of over £5,500. With Frank Broome linking well with Frank Shell, the latter in his first season with the club, Villa eased through 3–2 to take their place in the semi-finals for the 14th time.

MARCH 6TH

1920   Villa's progress through the first three rounds of cup competition had been impressive, but then so had Spurs'. Although a Second Division side (Spurs had finished the 1914–15 season bottom of the First Division and when the League resumed in 1919–20 the First Division had been extended. On every previous occasion the two sides due to be relegated had been reprieved; Spurs weren't, voted out in preference to Arsenal!), they were running away with their divisional title and were sure to be a stern test for Villa, especially at White Hart Lane where they were unbeaten all season. It was Villa who had the luck of the game, though they deserved to have won, the only goal of the game being an own goal knocked past his own goalkeeper by Tommy Clay.

1994 Tony Daley scored the only goal of the game in the first half of the Midlands clash with Coventry City at Highfield Road in front of a crowd of 14,323.

1995 Same opponents Coventry City but this time at Villa Park where 28,186 sat through a lifeless performance from both sides, although City could at least claim that as every point was vital in their struggle against relegation, the one gained justified the means.

MARCH 7TH

1903 Spurs had won the FA Cup two years previously (the only time a non-League club has won the FA Cup since the formation of the Football League in 1888) and were a particularly strong Southern League side at the time, but Villa travelled to White Hart Lane confident that they could end Spurs' interest in the competition in the third round. And so it proved, a 3–2 win earning Villa a semi-final clash with Bury, but there the dream was to die in a 3–0 defeat.

1921 George Blackburn made his debut for the club in the match at Bradford City where Villa were beaten 3–0. He had initially signed with the club as an amateur before being upgraded to the professional ranks and went on to make 145 appearances in six years. Capped by England in 1923–24 he joined Cardiff City and won two winners' medals in the Welsh FA Cup, later playing for Mansfield Town.

1963 Aston Villa and Bristol City had first met in the FA Cup third round on 16th January and drawn 1–1, necessitating a replay. Unfortunately, this was postponed 11 times before the two clubs were finally able to meet, with goals from Burrows, Baker and Thomson enabling Villa to win 3–2.

1967 Villa Park staged the replayed FA Amateur Cup fourth-round tie between Highgate United and Enfield. The original meeting between the two sides had been abandoned after 25 minutes when several players were struck by lightning during the game, Tony Allen subsequently dying from his injuries. Villa chairman Norman Smith immediately offered the facilities at Villa Park for the replay, which Enfield won 6–0 on their way to winning the cup that season.

MARCH 8TH

1950 Villa went down 7–0 at Old Trafford against a rampant Manchester United, although three of their goals were scored from the penalty spot, all despatched by Charlie Mitten past a bemused Tommy Jackson.

1980 Villa's reward for beating Blackburn after a replay in the fifth round of the FA Cup was a trip to Upton Park to face West Ham in the quarter-finals. Although West Ham were a slightly better than average Second Division side at the time, they should have held no fears for Villa, already beginning to assemble the side that would win the League in 12 months' time. For much of the game at Upton Park it seemed as though the two sides would have to try again a few days later, as West Ham's defence countered the threat of Brian Little and Terry Donovan, and Villa marshalled Pearson and Cross. There was very little time left when West Ham were awarded a disputed penalty, with Ray Stewart remaining composed enough to send his shot past Jimmy Rimmer and put the Hammers into the semi-final.

1992 Since beating Southampton on December 28th Villa's form in the League had slumped alarmingly; only one win (against Oldham on February 22nd) but more worrying, only two goals scored since the New Year. Whilst they had scored seven in four matches in the FA Cup, each victory had been by the odd goal. The sixth round of the FA Cup had pitched Villa with Liverpool at Anfield, and it was Villa's lack of firepower up front that was to prove their undoing. Michael Thomas gave Liverpool the lead in the second half, but with Villa firing blanks at the other end, Liverpool were seldom troubled on their way to winning the cup.

MARCH 9TH

1889 Villa ended the very first season of League football with a 5–2 defeat at Derby County. Despite only taking one point from the final three games of the season, they still finished the campaign in second place, one point ahead of Wolves but 11 behind champions Preston.

1941 Andy Lochhead born in Millgie. Spotted by Burnley whilst playing for Renfrew Juniors, he spent ten years with the Turf Moor club, scoring 101 goals in 226 League appearances. He then spent a little over a year with Leicester City, helping them reach the FA Cup final before switching to Villa in February 1970 for £30,000. He helped Villa to the League Cup final the following year and then the Third Division title in 1972, finishing at Villa Park in 1973 when he left for Oldham. He finished his playing career in America before turning to coaching. Despite his phenomenal goalscoring record he was not capped for Scotland at full level, winning just one cap for the Under-23 team.

1972 On transfer deadline day Villa paid £75,000 for Chris Nicholl from Luton. He would go on to help the club win the League Cup twice.

1973 Steve Froggatt born in Lincoln. First introduced to the first team in 1991, he performed well at club level and was rewarded with a call up to the England Under-21 side. Injury brought a halt to his run in the first team and he was allowed to join Wolves for £1 million in 1994.

MARCH 10TH

1923 Villa registered one of only three away wins all season with a 5–3 victory at Leeds Road against Huddersfield Town.

1928 The League clash at St James' Park between Newcastle United and Aston Villa resulted in a 12 goal feast, United finally winning 7–5.

1931 Ken Roberts born in Crewe. He joined Aston Villa from the quaintly named Crewe Villa in August 1951 but made only 42 appearances for the club in the League, scoring seven goals.

1964 Shaun Teale born in Southport. He began his career with non-League Weymouth, costing Bournemouth £50,000 when they signed him in January 1989. He soon developed into one of the lower division's better defenders and had a host of clubs queuing for his services. He joined Villa in a £300,000 deal in July 1991 and spent four years with the club, forming an effective partnership with Paul McGrath. He left in 1995 to sign for Tranmere, later spending a spell on loan to Preston.

MARCH 11TH

1908 A 2–0 win over Bristol City at Villa Park kept Villa at the top of the table as they looked to retain the title. Manchester United's 5–0 home victory against Preston kept the pressure on however in a race that would go down to the very last match.

1932 Derek Pace born in Bloxwich. Discovered by Villa whilst playing for Bloxwich Strollers, he was introduced to the first team in March 1951 and scored in the 3–2 win over Burnley. Known as Doc throughout his career he was a reliable goalscorer for the club but had the misfortune to sit out the 1957 FA Cup final, being named 12th man (in an age when substitutes were not allowed) and left for Sheffield United in December 1957. He proved his worth at Bramall Lane, scoring 150 goals in 275 first-team appearances, helping them gain promotion to the First Division in 1961. He then moved on to Notts County before finishing his career with Walsall.

MARCH 12TH

1892 Villa achieved their record League victory with a 12–2 win over Accrington (a side not connected with Accrington Stanley). Villa's goals were scored by John Devey and Johnny Campbell, both of whom grabbed four, Billy Dickson (two), Dennis Hodgetts and Charlie Athersmith.

1938 The race for promotion from the Second Division into the First had developed into a four horse race; Villa, Manchester United, Sheffield United and Coventry City. The clash between Midlands rivals Villa and Coventry at Highfield Road drew a crowd of 44,930 to witness a slender

1–0 win for the visitors as the temperature at the top grew hotter. At the end of the season, Villa and Manchester United were on their way up, whilst Sheffield United and Coventry would have to wait a while longer before taking their places in the top flight.

1958 David Geddis born in Carlisle. He began his career as an apprentice with Ipswich and was signed to professional forms in August 1975 having already won an England Youth cap. After a handful of games on loan to Luton he joined Villa for £300,000 in September 1979 and proved himself a valuable squad member during his time with the club.

1960 Nearly 70,000 spectators were at Villa Park for the FA Cup quarter-final with Preston, a side still inspired by Tom Finney. Fifteen minutes after the game kicked off Gerry Hitchens gave Villa the lead, a goal that served to settle Villa as much as it unnerved Preston. Finney toiled away on the wing but Villa held firm and shortly before the end Peter McParland put the result beyond doubt to put Villa into the semi-final for the 17th time. It would be another 36 years before Villa made it as far again, but for now there was the prospect of a clash with Wolves to look forward to.

1967 Gareth Williams born on the Isle of Wight. He cost Villa £30,000 when signed from Gosport Borough in January 1988, but after only a handful of games was sold to Barnsley for £200,000 in August 1991. He later played for Hull, Wolves, Bournemouth, Northampton and Scarborough.

1977 After taking three games to get past Queens Park Rangers in the semi-final of the League Cup, Villa looked somewhat jaded by the time they got to Wembley for the final against Everton. Everton could have no such excuses, but the two sides cancelled themselves out with a largely uninspiring display that began and ended goalless.

1986 The second leg of the Milk Cup semi-final at Oxford United saw the home side squeeze through to the final, 2–1 winners on the night and 4–3 winners on aggregate.

MARCH 13TH

1899 Villa met Sheffield Wednesday at Hillsborough, although the game only lasted ten minutes; the first encounter between the two sides on 26th November had been abandoned after nearly 80 minutes with Wednesday leading 3–1. The Football League ordered that the remaining ten minutes be played, so Villa had to travel to Sheffield to play the time remaining. Wednesday added one further goal and so the record books are usually written to show a 4–1 win for Wednesday on 13th March 1899. Villa made one change from the side that had played in the original clash, Billy Garraty coming in for Frank Bedingfield, who had left the club for Queens Park Rangers, so this could even be described as the very first substitution in the League's history! Despite this farce, Villa still managed to finish the season as League champions, heading Liverpool by two points.

1918 Leslie G. Smith born in Ealing. Originally an amateur, he was a member of the Wimbledon side that reached the 1935 FA Amateur Cup final subsequently won by Bishop Auckland, and after a spell with Hayes signed as a professional with Brentford. Here he won his only cap for England and at the end of hostilities in 1945 joined Villa for £7,500 in October of that year. He returned to Brentford in 1952 but a short while after was forced to retire owing to injury.

1971 Mighty Halifax Town were the visitors to Villa Park, drawing a crowd of 33,522, one of the best of the season. Fred Turnbull gave Villa a first-half lead but Halifax equalised in the second period.

1977 Andy Gray was named Player of the Year and Young Player of the Year by the PFA (Professional Footballers' Association), the first player to have won both awards in the same season.

1996 It had been 36 years since Villa had last reached the FA Cup semi-finals, although they had gone close once or twice in the interim period. Their opponents in the quarter-finals in 1996 couldn't have been more difficult; Nottingham Forest at the City Ground, where 21,067 were gathered for an intriguing battle. The demands of live television, coupled with Forest requiring three attempts to get past the fifth round before finally doing so with a penalty shoot-out win over Spurs had served only to spread the four ties out over four days. Only Manchester United, looking at their second double in three years, were as yet safely through to the semi-finals, but a first-half goal from Franz Carr was enough to make Villa the second qualifiers for the penultimate stage.

MARCH 14TH

1959 The FA Cup had been a welcome break from League duty, especially as Villa were involved in a battle against relegation, which was ultimately lost. The cup, however, had seen them despatch Rotherham, Chelsea, Everton and Burnley (after a replay) on their way to the semi-final, against Nottingham Forest, a record 16th appearance in the penultimate stage for Villa. But Forest had already won at Villa Park earlier in the season to gain a psychological advantage, and at Hillsborough Quigley got the only goal of the game to earn Forest a place at Wembley.

1993 A crowd of 36,163 were at Old Trafford to see the clash between Premier League leaders Aston Villa and Manchester United. At the end of the game it was Villa who had more reason to cheer, the 1–1 draw (Villa's goal coming from Steve Staunton) keeping them above their nearest rivals for the season's inaugural FA Premier League.

MARCH 15TH

1930 Jack Mandley made his debut for the club in the 5–3 win at home to Huddersfield Town. He joined the club from Port Vale where he had begun his professional career and joined Villa for £7,000 shortly before coming to Villa Park. He remained with the club until 1934, making 112 League and cup appearances before retiring from the game.

1943 Brian Tiler born in Whiston. He made 212 appearances for Rotherham United before joining Villa in December 1968 and went on to help the club reach the League Cup final in 1971 and win the Third Division championship the following year. In October 1972 he joined Carlisle and later played in America before becoming assistant manager of Wigan. He also had spells as coach to the Zambian national side and was in an administrative position with Bournemouth when he was killed in a car crash in Italy in 1990.

1978 A daunting crowd of 90,000 awaited Villa when they came out to face Barcelona at the Nou Camp Stadium for the second leg of the UEFA Cup quarter-final, with Villa facing the added pressure of needing to win to make the next round. Sadly, after John Gidman's sending off in the 23rd minute Villa had too much of a mountain to climb and Barcelona's greater European experience carried them through, Migueli and Asensi scoring for the home side after Brian Little had given Villa the lead. A second Villa goal would have taken the tie to extra time, but the Spanish defence held firm.

MARCH 16TH

1926 Billy Kingdon joined the club from Kidderminster Harriers. Within a month he collected a junior international cap for Scotland but took a little while longer to make his Villa breakthrough, making his debut in the 1926–27 season. He remained at Villa until 1935 when he joined Southampton, having made 241 senior appearances for the club.

1977 A crowd of 55,000 were at Hillsborough for the replay of the League Cup final between Aston Villa and Everton, and after a goalless match at Wembley four days previously, there was at least a couple of goals to cheer. Everton scored both of them, although Roger Kenyon's effort was put through his own net and thus ensured a third game to try and divide the sides.

1983 Aston Villa slipped out of the European Cup quarter-finals, beaten 3–1 in Turin against Juventus and 5–2 on aggregate. Juventus went on to reach the final where they were beaten 1–0 by Hamburg, the first winners from outside England for six years.

MARCH 17TH

1884 Howard Vaughton made his last appearance for England in the international against Wales at Wrexham which England won 4–0, Vaughton's fifth cap for his country. He had joined Villa in 1880 from Wednesbury Strollers and had earned the accolade of being one of the club's first international players, a feat he achieved in the 13–0 win over Ireland in 1882. At club level he was a member of the side that won their very first FA Cup in 1887, a year before injury forced his retirement. However Howard retained his connection with Villa, serving the club as vice-president in 1923 and in February 1933 was made a life member of the club. When he retired in 1888 he started a silversmith business and seven years later in 1895 when the FA Cup was stolen (whilst in Villa's safekeeping!) his was the company charged with producing a new trophy.

1890 A 1–1 draw at Stoke enabled Villa to finish the season in eighth place in the Football League, level on points with Bolton. Under the Football League rules of the time, the last four clubs in the League should have had to apply for re-election, but as Villa and Bolton were level, the rule was suspended, thus saving Villa (and Bolton for that matter) the embarrassment of having to go cap in hand to the Football League. It was quite a slip down the table for Villa, for they had finished in second place at the end of the first season of League football.

1913 Charlie Wallace made his debut for England in the 4–3 win over Wales at Ashton Gate. Charlie had joined Villa in 1907 from Crystal Palace and went on to make 349 appearances for the club, despite losing four seasons to the First World War, and scored 57 goals before leaving for Oldham in 1921. Two years later he returned to Villa Park as a steward, a position he held until 1960. After making his England debut, the year of 1913 turned out to be one of mixed emotions, for the following month he missed a penalty in the FA Cup final, the last to be missed until John Aldridge of Liverpool in 1988, but at least Charlie had the compensation of seeing Villa win the cup.

1934 Having beaten Chesterfield (after a replay), Sunderland, Spurs and Arsenal on their way to the FA Cup semi-final Villa had hopes of making a return visit to Wembley for the final, their first such appearance in the final since 1924. The dreams positively exploded at Leeds Road, Huddersfield, where Manchester City beat them 6–1.

1941 Harry Burrows born in St Helens. He was first associated with the club as a junior and graduated through the ranks before making his debut on Boxing Day 1959 against Hull City, his only appearance of the season. He became a regular in 1961–62 and made 146 League appearances for the club before being sold to Stoke City for £30,000. He made a further 239 appearances for the Potteries club and was then released to join Plymouth, but injury forced his retirement.

1971 The local derby with Walsall in the Third Division at Villa Park drew a crowd of 37,642, although there was little to cheer as the game finished goalless.

1982 An expectant crowd of 38,579 were packed into Villa Park to see whether

Aston Villa could make the European Cup semi-finals at the first time of trying. The team had already drawn with Dynamo Kiev in Russia, but after qualifying from the previous round on away goals Villa were taking nothing for granted and would need to be both clinical up front and careful at the back to overcome such dangerous opposition. Two goals in the first half, courtesy of Gary Shaw and Ken McNaught, eased some of the pressure, and Kiev's challenge evaporated in the second half. With holders Liverpool going out of the competition at the same stage, Villa could now believe they stood a chance of lifting the trophy, for on their night they need fear no one. The European Cup had remained in England for the previous five seasons; it was down to Villa to keep the run going.

1998   Despite a spirited and storming finish to the match with Athletico Madrid, Villa slipped out of the UEFA Cup quarter-finals on away goals. Chasing a 1–0 defeat in Madrid a fortnight earlier Villa attacked from the off but at times it seemed the ball would do anything but enter goal. A killer away goal left Villa with a mountain to climb, but somehow they found the character to keep about their business, scoring through Dwight Yorke to bring the Spaniards in view again. Then Stan Collymore levelled the aggregate scores with some eight minutes to go, but with Villa throwing caution to the wind the elusive third goal would not come and Villa were out on away goals.

MARCH 18TH

1934   Roy Chapman born in Birmingham. He joined Villa in February 1952 from his works side, Kynoch Works, and spent five and a half years with the club, making only 19 League appearances. He was sold to Lincoln in November 1957 and later went to play for Mansfield, Port Vale and Chester and a second spell at Lincoln.

1939   Ron Atkinson born in Liverpool. After being rejected by Wolves he was spotted by Villa whilst playing for the works side BSA Tools as an inside-forward. Unable to break into the first team he was given a free transfer and joined the then non-League Headington United. Southern League champions for two consecutive seasons (by which time they had changed their name to Oxford United) they were admitted to the Football League in place of Accrington Stanley, with Atkinson now at half back and captain. He made 383 League appearances, helping them gain promotion to the Second Division before retiring as a player and moving into management. He started with non-League Kettering and then moved to Cambridge United, guiding them to the Fourth Division title before landing the hot seat at The Hawthorns with West Bromwich Albion. From there he moved to Manchester United, taking them to two FA Cups before being sacked. He returned to West Bromwich before an even briefer stint with Athletico Madrid, although this too ended with the sack and he returned to England to take over at Sheffield Wednesday in 1989. After promotion to the First Division and winning the League Cup he accepted an offer to take over at Villa Park, remaining in charge until October 1995. During that time he won the League Cup in 1994, but it was Villa's inability to mount a sustained League challenge that cost him his job. He went on to Coventry, initially as team manager and then general manager, and then returned to Hillsborough for a second time. His contract was not renewed at the end of the 1997–98 season.

1964   Paul Elliott born in London. First introduced to League football with Charlton Athletic, he was sold to Luton and then Aston Villa for £450,000 where he developed into a highly competent defender. An enquiry from Pisa in the summer of 1987 found him leaning in favour of the Italians but at the end of his contract he went to play in Scotland for Celtic. He cost Chelsea £1.4 million when returning to London but his career was ended in a challenge with Liverpool's Dean Saunders, a tackle that was later the subject of a failed court case.

MARCH 19TH

1892   Aston Villa's second appearance in the FA Cup final was almost a carbon copy of their first; same opponents (West Bromwich Albion), same venue (Kennington Oval) although different score. Whereas Villa's defence had been largely responsible for them lifting the trophy in 1887, so it was their defence that let them down this time around, with goalkeeper Jimmy Warner coming in for particular criticism (and the windows of his public house in Spring Hill were smashed by irate fans!). He was probably only to blame for the third goal, a speculative shot from some 40 yards out that caught Jimmy well off his line, but in truth Villa were well beaten on the day by a better side. The game attracted a then record crowd of 32,810 to the Oval and this was also the first time nets were used.

1960   The only occasion Villa have visited the Old Showground, the home of Scunthorpe United in the League, with Villa winning the game 2–1.

1966   Whilst Spurs were not the great Spurs side of the double era, they could still boast the likes of Jimmy Greaves in their line-up, and in a scintillating first-half display at White Hart Lane, Spurs raced into a seemingly unassailable 4–1 lead. Five minutes after the break, Spurs added another to go 5–1 ahead, but it was then that Tony Hateley got into his stride, giving Spurs defender Laurie Brown the run-around. In the space of four minutes Villa scored three goals, two from Tony Hateley (who thus completed his hat-trick) and one from Alan Deakin to reduce the deficit to a single goal. That was wiped out 11 minutes from the end, Tony Hateley again the scorer, and even at 5–5 that wasn't the end of the drama; Alan Deakin slipped through the Spurs' defence in the 87th minute, rounded Pat Jennings and was confronted with an empty goal. He hesitated long enough to allow a defender to get back on to the line and when he tapped the ball goalwards, Alan Mullery was there to clear it off the line. The 28,371 crowd gave both sides a standing ovation as they left the field.

MARCH 20TH

1897　The FA Cup semi-final draw had paired Villa with Liverpool, and quite by chance the two sides had met in the League the week before at Perry Barr and battled their way to a 0–0 draw. The cup, of course, was always going to be a different matter. For Villa, there was the added incentive of a possible domestic double, for they were already top of the League table and needed only two more points to confirm the trophy would remain their property for a further 12 months. But Liverpool had their own reasons for wanting to reach the FA Cup final, for having avoided Everton in the semi-final (they were drawn with Derby County) there was still the possibility of an all-Merseyside final for the first time. A crowd of more than 30,000 (including over 10,000 from Birmingham) journeyed to Bramall Lane in Sheffield for the clash and whilst Liverpool performed heroically throughout, Villa ran out easy winners 3–0 on the day. Whilst the double dream was still very much alive, the all-Merseyside final would have to wait another 89 years.

1923　Con Martin born in Dublin. He began his professional career with Drumcondra and Glentoran before being brought to England by Leeds United in January 1947. He joined Villa in October 1948 and went on to make 194 League appearances for the side, scoring just once in a match against Charlton, although it has to be said in his defence that whilst he had been signed as a centre-half, 27 of his appearances were in goal! He won a total of 30 caps for the Republic of Ireland and, in an age when it was quite common for Irish players to have dual nationality, six caps for Northern Ireland. In 1956 he left Villa to return home and take up the position of player-manager with Waterford.

1976　Villa drew 2–2 at Filbert Street with Leicester City with Chris Nicholl managing to score all of the goals, for as well as netting two for Villa he also turned two past his own keeper!

MARCH 21ST

1891　A 3–1 win at the Accrington Cricket Club (the Accrington club of the 1800s bore no relation to the Accrington Stanley club who emerged from Peel Park later) enabled Villa to register only their seventh win of the season. This equalled the previous lowest established the previous season, still the lowest number of victories Villa have registered in a single season, although there were still only 22 games that comprised an entire season. In more recent times Villa recorded only eight wins out of a possible 42 in both 1969–70 and 1986–87, both campaigns ending in relegation. However, in 1891 this meant that Villa finished the season in 9th place and had to apply for re-election to the League!

1926 Tommy Muldoon became the first Villa player to be capped for Eire when selected for the international against Italy in Turin. Italy won 3–0.

1929 Portsmouth ended Villa's hopes of returning to Wembley with a 1–0 win in the FA Cup semi-final at Highbury.

1937 Bobby Thomson born in Dundee. An amateur player in Scotland, he began his career in England with Wolves, joining them in August 1954. In five seasons, however, he made only one appearance in the League and was transferred to Villa in June 1959 for £8,000 and promptly scored on his debut! He made 143 appearances for Villa, scoring 55 goals and helped the club reach the League Cup finals of 1961 and 1963. He then moved across the city to join Birmingham City in September 1963 and finished his career at Stockport County.

1940 Colin Withers born in Birmingham. After representing England at schoolboy level he was signed by Birmingham City and made his debut in goal in 1960, conceding six goals as City lost to Spurs. He cost Villa £18,000 when transferred in November 1964 and made his debut in a 4–0 defeat by Spurs! He made 163 appearances for the first team before joining Lincoln City in June 1969, although he played only one game before going to Holland.

1942 Although it does not count in the Villa record books, they did establish their highest ever score in the wartime Birmingham and District League, beating RAF Lichfield 19–2. The difference between them and their opponents can be gauged by Villa's list of goalscorers; Frank Broome 4, Harry Parkes 4, Billy Goffin 4, Albert Kerr 2, Eric Houghton 2, Tommy Cummings 2 and Bob Iverson 1. At the end of the season Villa won the League, its Challenge Cup, the Keys Cup and the Worcester Infirmary Cup.

1968 Dalian Atkinson born in Shrewsbury. He began his career with Ipswich Town and was soon attracting interest from bigger clubs, costing Sheffield Wednesday £450,000 in 1989. A year later he went to play in Spain for Real Sociedad having cost the club £1.7 million, returning to England with Villa for £1.6 million. A member of the side that won the League Cup in 1994 he made over 100 appearances for the first team before resuming his career overseas in Turkey and Spain.

MARCH 22ND

1897 The League title was clinched with a 6–2 win over Bolton Wanderers at Perry Barr. Bolton had begun the match much the brighter side, taking a 2–0 lead before Villa got into their stride and scored the goals required to ensure they could not be headed at the top of the table. They were to finish the season an impressive 11 points ahead of Sheffield United in second place, but already thoughts were beginning to turn to a possible double, for two days previously they had won through to the FA Cup final for the fourth time in their history.

1913 Villa looked capable of lifting the double for the second time, through to the FA Cup final where they would face Sunderland and also closing the gap on the same side at the top of the League. Their title hopes took a dive however, beaten 4–0 at Manchester United.

1929 Jimmy McEwan born in Dundee. He began his career with Arbroath before transferring to Raith Rovers, where he was leading goalscorer for three years. He joined Villa in July 1959 and helped the club to the final of the League Cup in both 1961 and 1963, although he had lost his place in the side by the time of the latter final. After 143 appearances for Villa in the League he was transferred to Walsall, although after only ten games he was appointed trainer.

MARCH 23RD

1888 Following William McGregor's letter to interested parties representatives of Aston Villa, Blackburn Rovers, Burnley, Stoke, Notts County, West Bromwich Albion and Wolves gathered at Anderton's Hotel in Fleet Street on the eve of the Cup final between West Bromwich Albion and Preston North End to discuss the formation of the Football League. Two clubs who did not attend the meeting were Cup finalists Preston and Bolton, although Bolton's secretary John Bentley was the only one to respond to McGregor's original letter. Derby County secretary John Richardson did attend, but only to observe.

1957 The city of Birmingham had three of the four FA Cup semi-finalists in 1957; Aston clashed with West Bromwich Albion at Molineux whilst Birmingham City were facing Manchester United at Hillsborough. No one envied Birmingham City, playing the Busby Babes, reigning League champions and on their way to the European Cup semi-final as well, but Villa had their own problems to contend with. A crowd of 55,549 were at Molineux to see Albion dominate almost all of the game, twice taking the lead only for Peter McParland to peg them back. His second equaliser came with only five minutes left to play. He then got the only goal of the game in the replay at St Andrews in front of 58,067 to set up a final clash with Manchester United, conquerors of Birmingham City in the other semi-final.

MARCH 24TH

1888 Billy Dickson made his one and only appearance for Scotland in the 10–2 win over Ireland in Belfast, even though he scored four of the goals! He was playing for Dundee Strathmore at the time and soon after was bound for Sunderland and then joined Aston Villa in 1889. He was a regular in the side for three seasons and then surprisingly released to sign for Stoke in 1892.

1894　A 2–1 home win over Blackburn Rovers in front of a crowd of 18,000 ensured Villa would finish the season as League champions ahead of Sunderland and Derby, the first time the League trophy would find its way to the club (though not the last by any stretch of the imagination).

1923　Billy Walker scored twice from the penalty spot in the local derby with Birmingham City. Both were awarded after some particularly strong City tackling was rightly punished, and Villa went on to win 3–0.

1938　With Villa on their way to winning the Second Division title thoughts could turn away for a brief moment to think about a possible double, for Villa were through to face Preston in the FA Cup semi-final at Bramall Lane. Villa were more than a match for their First Division opponents, but Preston seemed to have all the luck going, their winning goal in the 2–1 win was scored by George Mutch, but the Villa defence had stopped still certain the Preston player was in an offside position when he scored. The goal was allowed to stand, Villa were out and Mutch went on to score the winner in the final (from the penalty spot, in the last minute of extra time, off the underside of the bar – the gods smiled on him throughout 1938!).

1996　In one of the most one-sided finals seen at Wembley in many a year, Aston Villa beat Leeds United 3–0 in the Coca-Cola Cup, formerly the League Cup. Savo Milosevic gave Villa a first-half lead, but Villa had rarely been troubled and added two more in the second half through Ian Taylor and Dwight Yorke to make the game safe. At the end of the game Leeds' fans gave Villa a sporting ovation, reserving their venom for their own side who were booed off the field.

MARCH 25TH

1893　Villa's third consecutive home game saw them beat Accrington 6–4, thus taking their tally of goals in the three games to eleven. They were at home again nine days later and scored another five.

1905　With Villa too far behind the sides at the top of the League table their only hope of some silverware at the end of the season came with the FA Cup, and after disposing of Leicester Fosse, Bury and Fulham found themselves face to face with Everton in the semi-final at the Victoria Ground in Stoke. Everton were strong opponents, battling Newcastle for the League title (Newcastle had also reached the semi-final of the cup, where they were facing Sheffield Wednesday) and so there were two clubs that might be in a position to emulate Villa's double win of 1897. A crowd of some 35,000 witnessed a close fought affair, a 1–1 draw probably the right result on the day. The replay was scheduled for four days later, at Trent Bridge, Nottingham.

1972   The Third Division's match of the day saw Brighton bring a Villa run of 11 games without defeat to an end with a 2–1 win at the Goldstone Ground.

MARCH 26TH

1951   A stuttering start to the season had left Villa too close to the bottom of the table by the beginning of December. Too many matches were drawn to effectively pull Villa out of trouble and by Easter they were in serious danger of falling through the relegation trapdoor. The climb out of trouble began at Molineux where Villa recorded a much needed win 3–2.

1960   Villa's Cup run had taken them past Leeds, Chelsea, Port Vale and Preston on their way to a semi-final with local rivals Wolves at the Hawthorns. Wolves were chasing the double, a feat last achieved by Villa in 1897, and 55,596 were at the game to see whether Villa could prevent this latest challenge to their pride. Just after half an hour Deeley followed up a shot Nigel Sims could not hold to poke home a goal for Wolves. Villa had plenty of chances in the remaining hour or so, especially in the closing minutes, but Wolves held on to reach Wembley. If there was any consolation for Villa, it was that Burnley would pip Wolves to the title at the very death and put the double out of reach, albeit for only one more season and Spurs.

MARCH 27TH

1886   James Cowan became the first Villa player to be capped for Scotland when selected to play against England at Hampden Park (not the same Hampden Park as at present). The game ended a 1–1 draw.

1920   At the beginning of the season the Football Association had been advised that Crystal Palace, venue for the FA Cup final since 1895, would not be available to them as it had yet to be fully restored following the First World War. The FA duly announced that the 1920 final would therefore be played at Stamford Bridge, the home of Chelsea, and could then only watch in complete horror as Chelsea made it all the way through the competition to the semi-final! There was little the FA could do, since arrangements were already well in hand for the final to proceed at Stamford Bridge, irrespective of whether Chelsea made it or not (even though the FA's own rules of the competition forbade a side playing in the final on their home ground). Under these circumstances, one wonders who was the more relieved when the semi-final result Aston Villa 2 Chelsea 0 came through; the FA or Villa supporters! Villa's goals at Bramall Lane were both scored by Billy Walker who had come into the side in January and galvanised the team, taking them up the table to safety and respectability and reserving his finer moments for the cup campaign.

1943 Emment Kapenge born in Zambia. One of the earliest African players to have appeared in the Football League, he joined Villa in September 1969 along with Fred Mwila with high hopes for his future, but after only three games he returned home again.

1951 Twenty-four hours after taking both points off Wolves at Molineux, Villa did the double over their rivals, winning 1–0 at Villa Park. More importantly, by the time the League table was drawn up Villa had climbed out of the relegation spot, albeit by one place, but they would not occupy either position again for the rest of the season.

1994 Aston Villa joined Liverpool and Nottingham Forest as four-times winners of the League Cup (in its various guises) with a 3–1 victory over Manchester United at Wembley. After taking a 2–0 lead through Dalian Atkinson and Dean Saunders, Villa allowed United to get back into the match with a goal seven minutes from the end but, as Villa relieved the pressure on themselves with an attack in the last minute, United's Russian winger Andrei Kanchelskis handled a goal-bound shot on the line and became the first player dismissed in a League Cup final at Wembley (a United player was also the first to be dismissed in the FA Cup final at Wembley). Dean Saunders netted the resulting penalty. Villa's victory thus deprived United of a possible domestic treble, for at the end of the season they won the Premier League and FA Cup.

MARCH 28TH

1931 With Arsenal all but champions the only race left was to see who could finish in second place, with Villa some way ahead of Sheffield Wednesday. A 4–1 win over Blackpool, destined to be relegated at the end of the season, inched Villa a little closer.

1959 The Easter of 1959 was probably the most crucial of the club's history, for it was their inability to gain more than a single point out of three games which effectively meant they would end the season being relegated. A defeat yesterday at Spurs, themselves in trouble at the wrong end of the table, by 3–2 was followed by a 2–1 defeat at Goodison at the hands of Everton, unbelievably themselves still in some trouble.

1998 After a disastrous start to the season (four games before they scored, five before they had any points in the bag), Villa had started to pull away from trouble during February and were beginning to make contact with the sides at the top of the table, giving renewed hope that Europe might still be a possibility. One of the sides they had left at the bottom, Everton, were still in all kinds of trouble, and Villa's 4–1 victory at Goodison Park only increased the pressure on beleaguered manager Howard Kendall. Villa's goals were scored by Dwight Yorke (two), Julian Joachim and Gary Charles.

MARCH 29TH

1897 Jack Reynolds collected his eighth cap for England in the 4–0 win over Wales at Bramall Lane. Reynolds had originally been capped for Ireland whilst playing for Distillery, collecting five caps between 1890 and 1891. When he arrived in England to play for West Bromwich Albion, it was discovered he had in fact been born in England and was therefore eligible to play for them! He and another Aston Villa player, R.E. Evans, are the only players to have played on both sides of an annual British fixture. Reynolds, known as Baldy throughout his career, began playing with Distillery and then Ulster before signing with West Bromwich Albion in March 1892 and scored one of their goals in their 3–0 FA Cup final win over Villa in the same year. He joined Villa in May 1893 and won two further FA Cup winners' medals as well as two League titles, finishing his career at the club the end of the double year and then going on to play for Celtic, where he won a Scottish League championship medal.

1905 The venue chosen for the FA Cup semi-final replay between Villa and Everton was Trent Bridge in Nottingham, then the home of Notts County, the country's oldest League side. Trent Bridge still exists, although a rather more sedate game takes place there, for it is the home of the county cricket side. Whether Villa found the turf cultivated for the summer game to their particular liking is not recorded, but they were well worth their 2–1 win and a passage into the final to face League champions, Newcastle United.

MARCH 30TH

1912 Manchester United were already injury ravaged before they came to Villa Park for the clash with Villa, missing their regular goalkeeper Hugh Edmonds and several other key players. Their cause wasn't helped when two further players suffered injuries inside the opening 15 minutes, and left to carry on with nine fit men and two passengers, they collapsed to their biggest defeat of the season as Villa ran out 6–0 winners.

1929 Villa recorded their third consecutive win at Ewood Park, winning 5–2 against Blackburn Rovers. It was their best win at the ground since 1896 when they ran out 5–1 winners.

1959 The only point Villa gained over the crucial Easter period came in a 1–1 draw with Spurs at Villa Park in front of a crowd of 34,354, although both points were desperately needed if the club were to climb out of trouble. With just six games left to play, Villa's position now looked perilous.

1960 The enigmatic Bill Shankly had taken over at Anfield the previous December and had belatedly steered Liverpool up the table, although his arrival came too late in the season to seriously threaten Villa and Cardiff at the top of the table. Still, Villa and Liverpool in the Second Division was one of the games of the day, irrespective of the division, and the 4–4 draw at Villa Park was a delight for both sets of supporters. On the same day Chris Price was born in Hereford. He began his career as an apprentice with the local club and made 330 League appearances before moving to Blackburn Rovers, making another 83 appearances for the Ewood Park club. He then joined Villa and slotted into the defence well, helping the club attain the runners-up spot in the First Division in 1990.

1970 The only away game Villa won in a depressing Second Division season came with a 2–0 victory at St Andrew's against Birmingham City. Bruce Rioch and Pat McMahon scored the goals before a sizeable crowd of 41,696, the biggest gathered for an English League match on the day (even though Arsenal, Manchester United and Newcastle United were at home).

MARCH 31ST

1874 Sometime during the month of March, six weeks or so after they had been formed, Aston Villa played their first game. Because there was a lack of football clubs in the area, Villa actually challenged a rugby club to a game! The first half was played under rugby rules, the second under association football. The first 45 minutes therefore saw Villa fielding 15 players, each struggling to come to terms with an oval ball, but they gave a good account of themselves and managed to reach half-time without any score. In the second half the round ball was introduced and midway through the half, Jack Hughes scored the only goal of the game to win it for Villa. The 15 players who represented the club were: W. Scattergood, W.H. Price, W. Weiss, D.J. Stevens, E.B. Lee, F.G. Matthews, H. Matthews, C.H. Midgley, J. Hughes, W. Such, H. Whateley, G. Page, A.H. Robbins, G. Greaves and T. Page. The game was said to have attracted a crowd of around 250, despite the bizarre use of two sets of rules.

1888 Villa's Albert Allen scored a hat-trick for England against Ireland on what was his only appearance for his country, England going on to win 5–1 in Belfast. Allen later became the first Villa player to score a League hat-trick for the club but was sadly forced to retire from the game through illness at the age of 24 and died in October 1899 at the age of 32.

1890 Villa's 3–0 win over Blackburn Rovers at Perry Barr was only their seventh of the season, their worst ever tally and one that was subsequently equalled the following season, although in mitigation it has to be said that the season comprised of only 22 matches.

1928 Jimmy McMullan captained the Scottish side in their astonishing 5–1 win against England, a game that led to the Scottish side being dubbed the 'Wembley Wizards'. He played for Third Lanark, Partick Thistle and

Manchester City during his career and then took over as manager of Oldham in 1933, remaining at Boundary Park for 12 months before accepting the managerial position at Villa Park. Unfortunately, his two years with the club saw Villa lose their First Division status for the first time and in October 1936 he was sacked, being replaced by Jimmy Hogan. McMullan went on to manage Notts County and later had a spell as secretary-manager of Sheffield Wednesday.

1962 Arsenal manager George Swindin had just resigned with the club hovering in mid-table, too far behind the leaders to threaten for the title, too far ahead of the strugglers to worry about relegation. It was the third season that Arsenal had had to settle for mediocrity, and Villa's visit perhaps best summed up their problems; creative up front, with the likes of Skirton able to put chances away, but woeful at the back. Villa took full advantage at Highbury, running out 5–4 winners in a thriller.

1996 At Old Trafford the twin assault on the domestic cups came to an end. With the League Cup having been won the previous week at Wembley, Villa had only to negotiate Liverpool in order to reach the final of big brother, the FA Cup. With the other semi-final having been played earlier in the day, both sides knew Manchester United lay in wait at Wembley, but at Old Trafford the 39,021 only had thoughts for the semi-final. Villa played well throughout, creating plenty of chances and giving the Liverpool defence little time to dwell on the ball. The difference between the two sides on the day, however, was to be found up front; Liverpool took virtually every one of the chances they created, Villa converted nothing. The 3–0 scoreline was something of a travesty in terms of reflecting the contribution Villa had made to the game, but it was Liverpool who now stood between Manchester United and a double double.

APRIL 1ST

1918 George Edwards born in Great Yarmouth. He joined the club from Norwich City in 1938 but his debut was delayed following a chipped bone in his ankle and he had to play with his leg heavily strapped thereafter. During the war he guested for a number of clubs including Aston Villa and resumed his career at Villa Park at the end of hostilities. He made 135 League appearances before leaving the club for non-League Bilston United where he retired in 1955.

1933 Aston Villa were at Highbury for a top-of-the-table clash against Arsenal, lying in second place to the London club but still within striking distance should Arsenal falter. Unfortunately for Villa they didn't, winning 5–0 at Highbury to leave Villa relying on a miracle if they were to become champions.

1941 Tony Scott born in Huntingdon. An England Youth international, he began his career with West Ham and joined Villa in October 1965, making 50 appearances for the club in the League and scoring four goals. He then went to Torquay and later played for Bournemouth and Exeter, where he finished his career.

1982 Caretaker manager Tony Barton, in charge since the departure of Ron Saunders in February, was appointed to the position on a permanent basis with a three-year contract. First-team coach Roy McLaren was elevated to assistant manager at the same time.

APRIL 2ND

1887 Whilst Aston Villa were making their first appearance in the FA Cup final, West Bromwich Albion had been beaten finalists the year previously and were therefore a slightly more experienced side. They could also boast big goalkeeper Bob Roberts, who invariably played in cricket flannels. But Aston Villa were not overawed, even though Albion won the toss and elected to kick with the slope in the first half. Villa defended extremely well in that half, gaining a psychological advantage as Albion were unable to find a way through, and pressed home their advantage in the second half. Roberts made no attempt to save Dennis Hodgett's shot, assuming the winger to be offside and waiting for referee Major Marindin to signal for a free kick. He did not however, pointing to the centre circle to signal a goal. Despite heated protests from the Albion players, the goal stood. Although Albion pressed hard in search of an equaliser, Villa made the game safe two minutes from time with a second goal, captain Archie Hunter pouncing on a back pass to poke the ball past Roberts. A crowd of 15,500 thus saw Aston Villa lift the FA Cup for the first time in their history, 2–0 winners.

1898 The first goal in the Scotland versus England international at Parkhead, the home of Celtic, was scored by Villa's England international Fred 'Diamond' Wheldon, an achievement that won him a bicycle!

1920 Harold Edgley broke his leg in a League match at Stamford Bridge against Chelsea and was therefore ruled out of the next appearance at the same venue, the FA Cup final against Huddersfield Town. Villa lost the game 2–1 and this was to be the last appearance for Edgley for the club, for by the time he regained full fitness he was sold to Queens Park Rangers and later Stockport County. As he had played in every cup round leading to the final, Aston Villa requested permission from the Football Association to present him with a souvenir winners' medal after they had won the trophy.

1938 The Second Division's game of the day brought Manchester United, second in the table, to Villa Park where Villa were top and needing only a handful of points in order to ensure promotion. Villa were irresistible on the day, winning 3–0 against the side that would accompany them back into the First Division at the end of that season.

APRIL 3RD

1887 The triumphant Aston Villa party arrived home from Kennington Oval with the FA Cup at three o'clock in the morning and were greeted by thousands who waited at the station for sight of their heroes.

1915 Liverpool arrived at Villa Park with the previous day's criticism over their performance at Old Trafford still ringing in their ears; they had gone down 2–0 to a Manchester United side battling against relegation. Villa and Liverpool were relatively safe, barring miracles, and Villa added to Liverpool's woe with a convincing 6–2 win. A few weeks later it was revealed that Liverpool's performance at United had less to do with lethargy than with bribery, for players on both sides had agreed in advance to fix the game at 2–0 for United and placed considerable bets on that result. There was no suggestion Villa and Liverpool had a similar arrangement 24 hours later, for Villa had always been beyond reproach, as the Manchester City incident in 1905 had shown, but the Football League commission set up to investigate the United and Liverpool match also looked at a few other games where the results had been surprising.

1932 John Neal born in Silksworth. He began his career with Hull City after being spotted playing for Silksworth Juniors and made 60 appearances for Hull before joining Swindon in July 1957. Two years later he arrived at Villa Park and helped the side win the Second Division title in 1960 and a League Cup winners' medal the following season. He made 114 first-team appearances before finishing his playing career with Southend and then switched to management, with Wrexham, Middlesbrough and Chelsea.

1956 There had been very little for Villa to celebrate throughout the 1955–56 season and going into the Easter matches they occupied bottom place in the table. The day before they had ground out a 0–0 draw at Molineux, fully expecting to capitalise on home advantage at Villa Park. It didn't happen like that, another dour 0–0 draw being the order of the day. Things were looking perilous for Villa.

APRIL 4TH

1893 Aston Villa played five consecutive home games, all in the space of 29 days commencing on 6th March. The first four were all won but they lost the final game, 3–1 to Burnley.

1908 Manchester United were almost home and dry for the title, but Villa, Manchester City, Newcastle, Sheffield Wednesday and Middlesbrough were all competing for second place in the table. Although there was no European competition to aim for, there were still compelling reasons for wanting to finish runners-up; the players would earn 'talent money' or bonuses linked to the placing the club reached. A 5–1 home win over Liverpool kept Villa slightly ahead of their rivals in the race.

1959 As if resigned to their fate, Villa lost at home to fellow strugglers Leicester City 2–1. A brief improvement in form just before Easter had enabled them to close the gap on the clubs above them, who included fellow illustrious names such as Everton, Spurs and Manchester City, but one point from four games had undone all of the good work and left them needing a miracle if they were to stay in the top flight.

1992 After ten minutes of the match at White Hart Lane Villa were two goals behind to Spurs and looking likely to be on the receiving end of something a lot worse. Slowly Villa found their composure, pulled a goal back through Kevin Richardson and then drew level thanks to Ian Olney, and that was all before half-time! Now it was Spurs' turn to be on the ropes and second-half goals from Dwight Yorke, Tony Daley and Cyrille Regis completed the comeback to win the game 5–2.

APRIL 5TH

1902 Such was the demand for tickets for the game between Scotland and England at Ibrox Park that a temporary wooden stand was constructed. It was believed that as Villa's Scottish winger, Bob Templeton, made a dazzling run the crowd strained to follow his progress and caused the stand (already weakened by heavy rain) to split and collapse, sending the occupants through a 70-foot hole. Twenty-five people died and over five hundred were injured, although the majority of people in the ground were unaware that there had been an accident. The game was not considered an official game by the FA as a result of the incident (an interesting development of the disaster was that the FA quickly became a limited company as a protection against personal liability).

1913 On the same day as Villa were going down 3–1 at home to Liverpool, Harry Hampton was scoring the only goal for England in their 1–0 win over Scotland at Stamford Bridge. Whilst the honour afforded Harry Hampton undoubtedly reflected well on Villa, his absence was one Villa could ill afford, for in losing at Liverpool they effectively surrendered the League title to Sunderland at the same time, finally finishing four points behind in second place. It was the second time in three years Liverpool had caused Villa to miss out on the title, for their win by a similar score in 1911 had given Manchester United the title at their expense.

1941 Mike Tindall born in Birmingham. Signed by the club as a junior, he rose through the ranks and signed as professional in April 1958, making his debut in December 1959. He spent a spell on loan in America and returned with renewed vigour, breaking into the first team and holding a permanent place in the side. Unfortunately his run was brought to an end by a broken leg sustained in November 1964, although he subsequently recovered and made a total of 136 appearances for Villa before joining Walsall.

1952 Dennis Mortimer born in Liverpool. Signed by Coventry as an apprentice in 1967, he went on to make 220 first-team appearances before signing for Villa in a deal worth £175,000 in December 1975. He became club captain and guided the side to the League Cup in 1977, the League title in 1981 and the European Cup the following season, remaining at Villa Park until 1985. By this time he had made 404 appearances in Villa's colours, and after leaving Villa went to play for Brighton and then returned to the city to play for a season with Birmingham.

APRIL 6TH

1896 The League championship winning season closed with a 4–1 home win over Wolves, enabling Villa to finish the season four points ahead of Derby County in second place. Villa's title was built on their exceptional home form (only one point dropped out of a possible 30), and although their away form never reached the same heights, they did still manage to take more points than any other side in the division on their travels.

1960 Colin Gibson born in Bridport. Signed by Villa as an apprentice in 1976, he made his League debut in 1978 and battled with Gary Williams to become a permanent fixture in the defence. A member of the side that won the League title in 1981, he made 237 first-team appearances before joining Manchester United in 1985 for £275,000. In 1990 he joined Leicester City for £100,000 after playing 95 games for United.

APRIL 7TH

1894 Since going down 3–0 to Wolves two days before Christmas Villa had not failed to score in any of their following seven League matches, hitting 26 goals in the process. They added another six today, winning 6–3 at Turf Moor against Burnley. It was the second time in their history Villa had scored six away from home, and Burnley had been the first victims as well!

1956 The battle at the bottom of the table had settled into a tense battle between five or six clubs; Villa, Sheffield United, Huddersfield, Spurs and Chelsea and Cardiff if they weren't too careful. Villa were at White Hart Lane to face Spurs and went down to the odd goal in seven to leave them in even more trouble.

1982 Villa's run to the European Cup semi-final had been impressive (the away goals elimination of Dynamo Berlin notwithstanding, although their performance in the first leg had perhaps justified qualification), but then so had Belgian champions Anderlecht's, and a tense and close tussle was anticipated over the two legs. There are those who believe it is better to play the home leg first, build up a commanding lead and then look to hold it in the second leg, whilst others prefer playing away, defending for much of the game and looking for a possible breakaway goal and then finishing the job off at home. Either way, the draw dictated Villa were at home in the first leg, and whilst the need for a goal or two was paramount, the necessity of ensuring nothing was given away at the back was not overlooked. The game was eventually settled by a single goal from Tony Morley in the first half, the 1–0 result perhaps pleasing the Belgians more than it did the English, but Villa had already proved themselves extremely good European travellers; the second leg promised to be interesting.

APRIL 8TH

1899 Villa Park staged its first England international with the visit of Scotland. England, complete with Villa's Jimmy Crabtree and Charlie Athersmith in the side, won 2–1.

1922 Villa Park staged the England and Scotland international, the last time Villa Park has played host to the fixture. Three Villa players were in the England side; Frank Moss, Dick York and Billy Walker, but Scotland won 1–0, their first victory on English soil since 1893. For Frank Moss it was his first cap for his country, even though he had earlier in his career been told he would not play again! He had joined Villa in February 1914 but made only two appearances before the outbreak of the First World War. He enlisted with the 4th Lincolnshire Regiment and saw action in France but was severely wounded in the knee and sent home where he became a PE instructor. By the end of the war he had recovered from his wound and so resumed his playing career, going on to win five caps for England and appearing in 283 games for Villa, later signing for Cardiff City. His son, also called Frank, later served the club with distinction.

1937 Tony Barton born in Sutton. A former England Schoolboy international, he played for Fulham, Nottingham Forest and Portsmouth before switching to coaching, first at Portsmouth and then moving to Aston Villa to become assistant to Ron Saunders. The departure of Saunders in February 1982 saw Barton taking over at the top, guiding the club to the European Cup at the end of the season, but in 1984 he was sacked and subsequently joined Northampton Town. A heart attack brought this position to an end, and although he recovered to assist Chris Nicholl at Southampton, he died in 1993.

APRIL 9TH

1887 A week after winning the FA Cup Villa played host to their Scottish counterparts Hibernian and won a friendly match 3–0 at Perry Barr.

1918 Dick Taylor born in Wolverhampton. After a playing career with Grimsby and Scunthorpe United, he turned to coaching and management before linking up with Joe Mercer at Sheffield United. He was brought to Villa as Mercer's assistant when the latter took over in 1958 and stepped into the manager's seat himself when ill-health forced Mercer's resignation. When Villa were relegated at the end of the 1966–67 season he was sacked from his position.

1938 A week after beating Manchester United at Villa Park in a top of the table clash in the Second Division, Villa were at Bramall Lane against another challenger, Sheffield United. A hard fought goalless draw dented United's hopes (they missed out on goal average to Manchester United at the end of the season) but aided Villa's effort.

1988 After topping the table for all but one week of the New Year, Villa had hit a slump and lost three matches in a row for the only time during the season, allowing Millwall, Middlesbrough and Bradford City to overtake them as the end of season fast approached. The losing streak was brought to an end with a spirited 1–1 draw at Selhurst Park, David Platt giving Villa a first-half lead. From here on in Villa would recover to finish the season in second place.

APRIL 10TH

1891 Frank Barson born in Sheffield. A legendary character within the game, Frank began his playing career with Barnsley having previously been a blacksmith. He cost Villa £2,850 when signing in October 1919 and after three years joined Manchester United following a dispute with the club over his refusal to move to the Midlands. He had already collected an FA Cup-winners' medal whilst at Villa, but it was the FA Cup semi-final in 1926 for which he is best remembered; an alleged foul on Manchester City's Sam Cowan left the City player unconscious, and although the referee had not seen the incident and took no action, the FA later banned Frank for two months. He also spent six months banned whilst at Watford and was alleged to have pulled a gun on his manager whilst at Aston Villa! He left United on a free transfer in 1928 after helping the club attain its First Division status. Indeed, in 1925 Frank was promised a pub if he helped the club win promotion. When they did he was given the keys to a hotel in Ardwick Green, but got so fed up with the flattery being handed out by his customers on the first day he handed the keys to the head waiter and telegraphed his wife to stop the delivery of their furniture! He died in Birmingham on 13th September 1968.

1897 By the time Villa arrived at the Crystal Palace for the FA Cup final against Everton they were on the verge of emulating Preston's achievement of 1889; winning the Football League and the FA Cup double. The League title had already been won, and such was the interest in Birmingham as to whether Villa could achieve the feat, a special works holiday was declared in order that as many fans who wished to travel to London could do so. In the end approximately 20,000 Villa fans were in the crowd of 65,891, and they were to witness one of the most entertaining finals in the cup's history. Villa opened the scoring after 18 minutes through Johnny Campbell, but Everton fought back quickly and equalised through Bell and then took the lead with Boyle. Villa responded to the challenge and got back on level terms with a goal from Fred 'Diamond' Wheldon ten minutes later. The crowd had hardly had time to digest this goal when Villa scored what proved to be the winner, Jimmy Crabtree heading home a corner whilst unmarked in the area. Both sides went close in the second half, but there was no further score and so Villa were crowned double champions. In handing over the trophy Lord Rosebery commented 'I cannot judge the finer points of the game but I can judge the great qualities which both sides have displayed. These qualities we recognise as distinctly British. It was a true Olympian struggle.'

1993 A season's best home crowd of 38,543 were at Villa Park to see the Midlands clash with Coventry City. The resultant 0–0 draw saw Villa headed at the top of the table by Manchester United, a position they were to hold for the rest of the campaign.

APRIL 11TH

1927 Peter Aldis born in Birmingham. Peter initially worked at the Cadbury factory before becoming a professional footballer, signing with Villa in May 1949 and making his debut for the club in March 1951. After overcoming a cartilage operation he became a mainstay in the side and was part of the team that won the FA Cup in 1957 against Manchester United. He was appointed captain in 1958 in his final season with the club and then went into non-League circles, signing for Hinckley Athletic. He later had a spell as manager of Alvechurch.

1903 The game that effectively cost Villa the League title in 1902–03; a 2–1 defeat at Anfield against Liverpool was followed by five straight wins but Villa still finished the season two points behind Sheffield Wednesday at the top of the table. Had Villa won by the same score, they would have lifted the title on goal average.

1990 Successive defeats by Crystal Palace and Manchester City had allowed Liverpool to take over again at the top of the table as the clubs approached the final eight or so games. Villa were at Highbury needing to halt the slump; a second-half goal from Chris Price, his only strike of the season, was enough to secure the three points.

APRIL 12TH

1947 Ernie Callaghan made his last appearance for Villa in the 3–3 draw at home to Grimsby Town and thus became the oldest player to have represented the club in a senior first-team match, being 39 years and 257 days old. It was only his tenth post-war appearance for the club, the Second World War having robbed him of the bulk of his career.

1975 Brian Little scored his sixth goal in three matches, netting a hat-trick in the 5–0 win over Oldham Athletic at Villa Park. Keith Hicks turned through his own net and Chico Hamilton got the other goals for Villa in front of a crowd of 32,748.

1993 Defeat at Norwich at the end of the previous month had allowed Manchester United to take over at the top of the Premier League, but Villa recovered to keep the pressure on Alex Ferguson and his men during the run-in to the title. A Tony Daley goal at Highbury was enough to earn another three points and keep Villa just one point behind, ready should United stumble.

APRIL 13TH

1940 Aston Villa played only their second game of the season, a benefit match for Birmingham's Harry Hibbs at St Andrew's in front of a maximum crowd of 15,000, the receipts amounting to some £650.

1951 Neil Rioch born in Paddington. The younger brother of Bruce, he began his career with Luton and joined Villa in September 1969 in a joint move with Bruce that cost the club £100,000. Whilst Bruce went on to become one of the key players in Villa's history, Neil found it more difficult to hold a regular place in the side and was subsequently sold to York in February 1972. He later played for Northampton and Plymouth where he finished his career.

1970 A crowd of 32,279 were at Villa Park to see Villa close their season with a much needed win, 1–0 over Sheffield United thanks to a goal from Pat McMahon. That left Villa with just 29 points from their 42 matches, and all they could do now was wait and see if that was going to be enough to save them from relegation to the Third Division, with Charlton having to play the following night. On the same day Gary Charles was born in London. He began his career with Nottingham Forest and helped them to the FA Cup final in 1991, switching to Derby County in 1993. He was signed by Villa following the departure of Earl Barrett and was a member of the side that won the League Cup in 1996.

1977 After two draws at Wembley and Hillsborough Everton and Aston Villa met for the third time in the League Cup final at Old Trafford. The crowd of 54,749 knew they were to see the matter finished on the night, for it had already been decided that in the event of another draw after extra time, the match would be settled on penalties. In the event there was no need for such an ending, for both clubs played a more open and attacking game than had been seen in the two previous encounters. Bob Latchford gave Everton the lead in the 38th minute and that seemed for some time to be enough to win the cup, but Villa equalised through Chris Nicholl ten minutes from time and then took the lead a minute later through Brian Little. Everton had little option but to go straight on to the offensive in an attempt to rescue the game, and with time running out were rewarded when Mick Lyons headed home from a corner. That meant energy sapping extra time again, with Everton looking the more tired of the two teams, especially as they were also involved in a marathon FA Cup run at the time. In the closing minutes Brian Little skipped through the Everton defence to convert a centre to clinch the cup for Villa, the third time they had won the competition in their history.

APRIL 14TH

1894 Aston Villa finished the season with a 3–1 home win over Nottingham Forest and thus finished six points ahead of Sunderland at the top of the table. Villa were worthy champions, winning 19 of their 30 matches, losing only five times, one of which was at home, and scoring 84 goals in the process. Sunderland, champions for the previous two seasons, would bounce back to reclaim the title the following season, but Villa were already beginning to emerge as one of the leading sides of the decade, and there were plenty more trophies to be welcomed in the coming years.

1956 Just when it seemed as though Villa were dead and buried the corpse twitched and found new life; Villa recorded a vital win in beating fellow strugglers Sheffield United at Villa Park 3–2 to bring the Yorkshire side within a point of Villa, even if they did still have a game in hand. However, in light of the way results were to go for the rest of the season, the win was to prove vital for Villa, a killer for United.

1970 Charlton's 2–1 home win over Bristol City meant they finished the season with 31 points, two ahead of Villa at the bottom of the Second Division. Aston Villa thus slipped into the Third Division for the first time in their history, accompanied by another of the Football League's founding fathers, Preston North End.

1981 First met second in the top of the table clash between Villa and Ipswich at Villa Park. Villa had suffered just one League defeat all year and had won 12 of their last 16 matches, a run that had carried them to the very top. Ipswich's progress had been no less impressive, although they had lost their last two matches (at Leeds and West Bromwich Albion, the latter no doubt helping out their rivals from across the city!) and been knocked out of the FA Cup at the semi-final stage the previous week. With so much at stake a crowd of 47,495 packed into Villa Park and were stunned into silence when Alan Brazil gave the visitors the lead. The second half was a more even affair, with Gary Shaw scoring for Villa and Eric Gates for Ipswich, but at the final whistle it was Ipswich who had both points in a 2–1 win.

1893 Bob Chatt made his debut for the club in the 1–1 draw at Accrington, who played at the Accrington Cricket Park and who dropped out of the League at the end of the season. Chatt had joined Villa from Middlesbrough Ironopolis who had been trying to get into the Football League – they replaced Accrington the following season – and in the face of stiff competition. He went on to help the club win the FA Cup in 1895 (he scored the first and still the quickest ever goal in a cup final after 39 seconds) and at the end of his Villa career reverted back to amateur status and collected a winners' medal in the FA Amateur Cup with Stockton in 1899. By coincidence, the same years (1895 and 1899) saw the only other instance of a player winning winners' medals in the FA and FA Amateur Cup; Tom Morren helped Middlesbrough to the Amateur Cup in 1895 and Sheffield United to the FA Cup in 1899.

1905 Newcastle United were on the verge of lifting the League championship and therefore stood a realistic chance of emulating Villa's feat of the League and FA Cup double, but Crystal Palace was not to be a happy hunting ground for them; in five appearances at the ground in the cup final they failed to win one, drawing twice and finally winning the trophy in a replay at Goodison Park in 1910. That was in the future, however, for their appearance in 1905 pitted them against a Villa side they had already beaten twice in the League. Villa put these League reversals behind them in the cup final, taking the lead after only three minutes through Harry Hampton and thereafter creating a number of chances that were either saved or squandered. It wasn't until 15 minutes from the end that Villa made the game safe, Hampton following up a shot from Albert Hall that had only been partially saved by Jimmy Lawrence. Captain Howard Spencer collected the trophy from Lord Kinnaird at the end of the game, the fourth time Villa had won the cup.

1922 Tommy Mort made his debut for the club in the 2–1 win over Bolton at Villa Park. Born in Kearsley he began his playing career as a semi-professional with Altrincham in 1921, signing with Villa a few days before his debut. Mort adapted well to the step up to the professional ranks, making 368 appearances for the first team, being capped three times by England, and appeared in the FA Cup final in 1924.

1944 So many people applied for tickets for the League North Cup semi-final clash with Sheffield United that it took many weeks before the money was returned to the unsuccessful applicants! Villa won 3–2 in front of 45,000 lucky enough to get their hands on a ticket.

APRIL 16TH

1897 Perry Barr hosted its last ever match with a Good Friday fixture between

Aston Villa Reserves and Shrewsbury Town in a Birmingham League match. Villa had begun building their new ground on the Aston Lower Grounds, having rented the land from Flowers and Company, a brewer based in Stratford upon Avon for £250 a year, with an option to buy the land at 5s a square yard within 21 years – Villa bought the land in 1911.

1900 Another thrilling finish to the season had seen Villa and Sheffield United neck and neck for the title throughout the season, with United throwing away any advantage they might have held with draws at both Blackburn Rovers and Stoke on successive days. That at least left Villa with a clear indication of what was required of them if they were to retain the title; a victory at Molineux and the League was theirs, anything less and it would all hinge on United's final matches against Burnley and Wolves, although Villa had much the better goal average. A goal from Billy Garraty settled the match in Villa's favour and clinched the title, United's subsequent defeat at Burnley ensuring Villa were two points ahead at the end of the season.

1979 Aston Villa beat Liverpool 3–1, the only time all season that Liverpool (and goalkeeper Ray Clemence) conceded more than one goal. At the season's end they had conceded just 16 goals, an all-time defensive record. Not surprisingly, they ended the season as champions.

APRIL 17TH

1888 Representatives of Aston Villa, Blackburn Rovers, Bolton Wanderers, Burnley, Derby County, Everton, Notts County, Preston North End, Stoke, West Bromwich Albion and Wolverhampton Wanderers met at the Royal Hotel in Manchester and agreed to the formation of the Football League (since the original Football League comprised 12 clubs we can only assume that Accrington were present at the meeting but not listed in the minutes, although as there were only 22 fixture dates available, both Sheffield Wednesday and Nottingham Forest, who wrote asking for membership, were turned down). The move followed concerns that too many friendly games were being cancelled, thereby depriving clubs of gate money, and playing a set number of matches home and away would offset any losses derived from losing friendly matches. Membership was set at £2 2s a year, clubs would be obliged to pay their full-strength team in all matches and William McGregor, the proposer of the Football League, was duly named as chairman, Harry Lockett of Stoke secretary and William Suddell of Preston North End treasurer. There was much discussion concerning the name of the League – McGregor's suggestion of 'Association Football Union' was rejected because of a possible confusion with the Rugby Football Union. McGregor's objections to 'Football League' because he thought it might be confused with the extreme political organisation 'Irish Home Rule League and the Land

League' were overruled. The title was also adopted because it did not limit the competition to English teams; it was believed that Scottish teams might also like to take part.

1897 Villa played their first official match at their new ground, one which has become universally known as Villa Park. Despite heavy rain throughout the day, a crowd of 15,000 attended to see the double champions (Villa had won the FA Cup a week previously and had already sewn up the League championship) win 3–0 against Blackburn. The honour of scoring the first goal at Villa Park fell to Johnny Campbell. He had joined the club from Glasgow Celtic and was to spend two seasons with Villa, winning two League titles and the FA Cup during his time, as well as topping the League's goalscoring charts in 1896. He returned to Celtic at the end of his time with Villa and won a further three winners' medals in both the League and Scottish Cup as well as a further League medal with Third Lanark.

1905 The Villa party who had travelled to London for the FA Cup final had delayed their return to Birmingham until this evening, arriving at Birmingham New Street station after the funeral of the Lord Mayor which had taken place that afternoon. When they arrived they found the station decked out in claret and blue and a huge crowd waiting to greet them. A fleet of charabancs was waiting to take them to the Holte Hotel in Trinity Road for a banquet in their honour.

1933 Villa's last chance of winning the League title all but disappeared, beaten 3–1 at St James' Park against Newcastle United. Villa would finish the season four points behind Arsenal in second place, the first of Arsenal's three consecutive League titles as they set about dominating the English game.

1952 Billy Goffin scored a hat-trick as Villa registered one of their best wins for many a year, beating Chelsea 7–1 at Villa Park.

APRIL 18TH

1892 A 6–3 defeat at Perry Barr to Wolves was not an ideal way to finish the season but it did at least enable Villa to set a record, along with champions Sunderland; they had gone through the entire 26-match programme without drawing a single game, the first time such a feat had been achieved.

1959 Villa lifted themselves to third from bottom with a dour 0–0 draw at home to Burnley, a match the home side should have won. With every point vital in the battle against relegation it was more a case of a point dropped rather than a point gained, especially after two successive defeats.

1993 Manchester United had beaten Chelsea 3–0 24 hours earlier to open up a four point lead at the top of the Premier League; Villa now entertained their rivals Manchester City. Whilst City were safely ensconced in the top half of the table, their supporters knew who they wanted to win the League, draping a 'Good Luck Villa' banner over the seats! The City team were not nearly as benevolent, taking a first-half lead and frustrating Villa's efforts at getting back into the game. Dean Saunders finally found a way through in the second half to level the score, and Garry Parker grabbed the chance to inch Villa ahead from the penalty spot. Ray Houghton added a third before the end and the gap between Villa and United was back down to a single point with three games to play.

APRIL 19TH

1897 Double winners Villa closed their home campaign with a record crowd of 35,000 at Villa Park for the 5–0 win over local rivals Wolverhampton Wanderers, although the football match was coupled with an athletics meeting!

1912 Fred Haycock born in Liverpool. He began his career with Bootle Boys but never meant to pursue football as a career, joining the family's butchery business and only picking football up again whilst on holiday in Ireland. Villa spotted him when he was playing for Prescot Cables and signed him in 1934, although it was two years before he made his debut for the club. He made 110 appearances for the first team before the outbreak of the Second World War and during the hostilities guested for Notts County, Nottingham Forest, Northampton, Plymouth and Wolves. At the end of the war he signed for Wrexham and retired a year later.

1913 Only two players survived from Villa's last appearance in the FA Cup final in 1905, Harry Hampton and Joe Bache. Just as Villa's first three appearances in the cup final had thrown up remarkable coincidences (the same opponents, West Bromwich Albion, in each case), so there were coincidences between 1905 and 1913 – Villa stood between their opponents and the League and FA Cup double. In 1905 two goals from Harry Hampton had denied Newcastle United; in 1913 it was Tommy Barber's turn to deny Sunderland, although Villa were destined to finish in second place in the League and might have lifted the double themselves. It was the first time the top two in the First Division had ever contested the FA Cup final, a fact which guaranteed enormous interest in the game, attracting a record crowd of 120,081 to the Crystal Palace. Villa might have taken the lead after only 15 minutes, being awarded a penalty, but Charlie Wallace allowed nerves to get the better of him and shot wide. Further grief came for Villa when goalkeeper Sam Hardy was carried off with a knee injury, forcing Jimmy Harrop to take over in goal and Harry Hampton slotting into the centre-half position. That signalled a concerted effort from Sunderland to get back on level terms, but all they had to show for their efforts were two shots which hit the post.

Hardy subsequently returned, and with Villa now back to full strength the initiative passed to them, with Barber turning home a corner from Wallace to score the only goal of the game. It was a tough battle between the top two, as best exemplified by the battle throughout between Hampton and Sunderland's Charlie Thomson, any one of which might have earned dismissals in a League match but which were treated leniently by the referee Mr Adams. After the game, however, the FA showed their displeasure by banning both players and the referee for a month! After the game Sunderland's Charlie Buchan revealed that during a lull in the game, Villa's Clem Stephenson told him about a dream he had had the night before; that Villa would win 1–0 with a headed goal from Tom Barber, though quite what Buchan's reaction was when the goal went in isn't recorded!

1960   Stuart Gray born in Withernsea. First introduced to League football by Nottingham Forest, he spent a brief spell on loan to Bolton before joining Barnsley in 1981. Six years later Villa paid £150,000 to bring him to Villa Park and he helped the club win promotion back into the First Division and made 132 appearances for the club before joining Southampton where injury forced him to retire.

APRIL 20TH

1895   Aston Villa and West Bromwich Albion met in the FA Cup final for the third time in eight years, although this time the match was held at the Crystal Palace, where a crowd of 42,560 gathered. It was the first time Crystal Palace had been chosen to host the final and there was considerable confusion at the turnstiles, with the result that many of the crowd missed the only goal of the game! The goal came after just 30 seconds; Charlie Athersmith fired in a centre which was hit towards goal by Bob Chatt, with Joe Reader's attempted clearance cannoning off John Devey's knee into the goal. At the end of the game Devey collected the trophy from Lord Kinnaird, the last player to receive the trophy, for it was later stolen whilst in Villa's possession and never recovered.

1929   Reg Chester scored a hat-trick in the 4–1 win over Huddersfield Town at Villa Park. He had joined the club in April 1925 from non-League Stamford and was to spend ten years with Villa, although first-team opportunities were sometimes difficult to maintain and he made just 97 first-team appearances. He later went to play for Manchester United but then returned to non-League circles.

1954   Villa had been the last club to achieve the double of League and Cup back in the days when Queen Victoria was on the throne. It was an accomplishment that was jealously guarded at Villa Park, and Villa themselves had ensured that Sunderland and Newcastle, both of whom could have equalled the feat over the years, fell by the wayside. They did it again today, thumping West Bromwich Albion 6–1 (just 24 hours after losing 2–0 at the Hawthorns!) to throw a spanner in Albion's League works; at the end of the season they were four points behind Wolves at the top of the table, even if they did win the FA Cup.

APRIL 21ST

1915 When Gavrilo Princip had shot the Archduke Ferdinand in Serbia the previous June and unwittingly hurled the world into the First World War, there were those, not least the British government, who believed the matter could all be sorted out quickly and normal life resumed without too much interruption. Even when diplomatic efforts had failed to resolve the arguments and a British Expeditionary Force assembled and despatched to France, the prevailing mood was still one of 'the boys will be home for Christmas'. But it soon became apparent that this was going to be a war quite unlike any war that had preceded it, and there would be more than one Christmas before the troops were home again. In November 1914, historian A.F. Pollard had written in *The Times* claiming, 'Every club that employs a professional football player is bribing a much needed recruit from enlistment and every spectator who pays his gate money is contributing so much towards a German victory.' Although League football had originally been seen as a way of maintaining morale among the populace, it soon became obvious that it could not continue; the 1914–15 season would be the last until the end of the hostilities. Aston Villa's home match with Manchester City therefore was to be the last witnessed at Villa Park for four years; they signed off with a 4–1 win.

1924 Aston Villa and Newcastle United were due to meet in the FA Cup final at Wembley barely five days after a League clash and so United fielded a considerably weakened side in the League match. Indeed, only one player who played in the League game retained his place for the cup final, a decision that cost United a fine of £750 (then a considerable sum) from the Football Association. As United won the cup, however, they probably had the last laugh.

1956 Another vital game in the battle against relegation, another vital result as Villa won 1–0 to climb out of the bottom two just as the season was drawing to a close. This time the victims were Preston North End, also deep in the mire at Deepdale, where Villa won a tense battle. With just one game left to play, Villa could still save themselves, but everything rested on the last game of the season against West Bromwich Albion, probably the last team to be looking to do Villa a favour after the events of two years previously when Villa had denied them the double.

1962 Bobby Thomson scored a hat-trick for Villa as they hit Leicester City, complete with Gordon Banks in goal, 8–3 at Villa Park.

1964   Kevin Gage born in London. Introduced to League football by Wimbledon (he was their youngest-ever player), he was transferred to Villa in 1987 for £100,000 and at the end of his first season had helped return the club to the First Division. He remained at Villa Park until 1991 when he joined Sheffield United on loan, the deal subsequently becoming permanent for £150,000. He joined Preston in March 1996 on a free transfer.

1982   Aston Villa reached the final of the European Cup with a goalless draw in Brussels against Anderlecht in the semi-final second leg. However, there was fighting between rival sets of supporters during the game and afterwards Anderlecht asked UEFA to expel Aston Villa from the competition. After a week of deliberations, UEFA fined Aston Villa £14,500 but allowed them to remain in the final. Anderlecht were also fined £4,375. Anderlecht subsequently appealed and again insisted on Aston Villa being expelled, but UEFA rejected the move, reducing Anderlecht's fine to £1,458 and ordering Aston Villa to play their next European home match behind closed doors. The actions of the Belgians have always appeared mystifying, for what went on on the terraces had no effect whatsoever on what happened on the pitch, although given the later revelation that Anderlecht had bribed an official to ensure a victory in the UEFA Cup semi-final in 1984 (against Nottingham Forest), perhaps their desire for victory at any cost tells its own story.

1993   Villa's title aspirations took a jolt, beaten 3–0 at Blackburn on the same day as Manchester United were winning at Crystal Palace. With United four points ahead and only two games remaining, Villa were looking for a miracle.

APRIL 22ND

1899   John Welford won a Scottish Cup medal with Celtic as they beat Rangers 2–0 in the final. Whilst numerous Scottish players have won winners' medals in both the English and Scottish FA Cups, John was the only Englishman to have achieved the feat until Gary Stevens and later Paul Gascoigne achieved the Scottish half of this unique double in the 1990s. John Welford had signed for Villa in 1893 and helped win two League titles and the FA Cup before joining Celtic in November 1896. In addition to his Scottish Cup win he also helped Celtic to the Scottish League title and then moved over to Ireland to play for Belfast Celtic. Here he won a medal in the Irish FA Cup, the first player to have won English, Scottish and Irish Cup winners' medals, although the record was later equalled by Jimmy Delaney. On the same day Villa were putting paid to Notts County with a 6–1 win at Villa Park to keep the pressure on Liverpool at the top of the table.

1911   Villa and Manchester United had been neck and neck in the race for the

League all season, although as Easter approached United had held the upper hand; four points clear and with only six games to play. United won their next two matches to maintain their grip at the top, but then the nerves began to appear. Successive draws (against Sheffield United and Sheffield Wednesday), coupled with Villa's relentless pursuit, saw the gap down to a single point. The crunch game was surely Villa versus United on the penultimate Saturday of the season. The importance of the game was reflected by the attendance: 55,000 packing into Villa Park to witness a game that was little more than an ill-tempered battle from the first whistle to the last. United's chances were not helped by having Enoch West sent off, but the match had still to be won and Villa scored four times to United's two in reply to put them on top of the table for the first time since November, a point ahead of United and with two games left to play.

APRIL 23RD

1913 Both Villa and Sunderland had been on course for the double, but a week previously Villa had won the FA Cup at Sunderland's expense, 1–0 at Crystal Palace, with Sunderland all but assured of the League title. As luck would have it, the two were then to meet in the League at Villa Park, with a crowd of 59,740 present to see a close 1–1 draw. Villa ended the season four points behind their rivals in second place.

1932 Aston Villa were scheduled to play Sheffield United in a League match and United's secretary/manager of the past 32 years, John Nicholson, was at the train station to see the team off for the journey to Birmingham. Unfortunately he was knocked down and killed in the yard, and a rather subdued United went down 5–0 at Villa Park during the afternoon.

1960 A 3–0 home win over Rotherham United confirmed Villa as Second Division champions, one season after their relegation from the top flight. With an immediate return to the First Division thus booked, it meant all but three seasons of Villa's battles for League points had been in the highest company.

1975 Sheffield Wednesday were trounced 4–0 at Hillsborough, Villa's goals coming from Keith Leonard, Ian Ross from the penalty spot and two from Brian Little.

APRIL 24TH

1895 Four days previously Villa had won the FA Cup for the second time in their history, beating West Bromwich Albion at the Crystal Palace thanks to an early goal by John Devey. A goodly crowd came to Perry Barr to see the cup being paraded before the last League match of the season against Everton (the fact the game finished 2–2 was somehow lost among the celebrations of the day), although for many it would be their last glimpse of the trophy; five months later it was stolen and never seen again. These were, however, heady days for Villa and their followers, for the previous season they had been League champions and might have mounted a sustained challenge to retain their title had their away form matched that of their home (the Everton result was only the fourth point they dropped at home all season), but Sunderland were to claim their third title in four seasons and Everton finished second, three points ahead of Villa in third place.

1899   Billy Garraty scored a hat-trick in the 7–1 home win over local rivals West Bromwich Albion. He had made his debut in 1898 and remained with the club for ten years, topping the League's top scorer list in 1900, and then left to join Leicester Fosse, returning to Birmingham a month later to sign for West Bromwich. He finished his playing career with Lincoln City.

1911   Having beaten Manchester United to go top of the table two days previously Villa were at last in charge of their own destiny as far as the title was concerned, with at least three points required from their final two games to ensure the title remained at Villa Park. They got one of the points they needed in a tense battle at Ewood against Blackburn Rovers to set themselves up for the final game against Liverpool at Anfield.

1920   Whilst pre-war finals at the Crystal Palace had attracted crowds well in excess of 100,000, the unavailability of the venue and subsequent selection of Stamford Bridge meant only some three quarters of this figure were likely to be accommodated. With the final not an all-ticket affair (it would take the opening fiasco of Wembley in 1923 before such a thought occurred to the FA) many would-be spectators decided before the game that the crush would be too much to bear and so stayed at home. Just 50,018 attended to see a match (albeit paying gate receipts of £10,000) in which Villa were widely regarded as favourites, although Huddersfield were enjoying a good season in the Second Division that would finish with them as runners-up. And Huddersfield proved the critics wrong, defending so well that for the first time the FA Cup final was forced into extra time. It had been announced that should the game finish all square after 90 minutes then a further half hour would be played, but the players were unsure of the arrangements at the end and shook hands and began walking off the pitch, only the referee's intervention ensuring extra time was played. Seven minutes into the additional period came the only goal of the game, Billy Kirton jumping with Huddersfield's Alex Mutch and Tommy Wilson and just getting enough of a touch to watch the ball fly off Wilson and into the goal. In the absence of Jimmy Harrop, Andy Ducat had been named captain and it was he who collected the now familiar trophy (introduced in 1911). It was the sixth time Villa had won the cup, one more than Blackburn Rovers could muster.

1964 Kevin Gage born in Chiswick. First introduced to League action with Wimbledon, he had won a single cap for the England Youth team. He cost Villa £100,000 when signed in 1987 and went on to make 115 League appearances before a £150,000 move to Sheffield United in 1991. He later played for Preston North End.

1972 A goal from Geoff Vowden at Mansfield was enough to earn a 1–1 draw and with it promotion from the Third Division. With two games still left to play Villa stood a good chance of ensuring they went up as champions.

1996 Paul McGrath collected his 51st cap for the Republic of Ireland whilst a Villa player in the match against the Czech Republic in Prague. He is the most capped player in Villa's history. The Czech Republic won the game 2–0.

APRIL 25TH

1931 Villa's 4–2 victory over Manchester City enabled them to finish the season with 128 League goals (they failed to score in the last match at Hillsborough against Sheffield Wednesday), a total that is still the record number of goals scored by one club in a single season in the First Division (only Peterborough with 130 in Division Four in 1960–61 have scored more). They had scored in every home match (a total of 86 goals) and Pongo Waring led the individual scoring lists with 49 goals (a figure which is still Villa's record tally of goals by a single player in a single season), with Eric Houghton weighing in with 30.

1934 Peter McParland born in Newry. He cost Villa £3,880 when signed from Dundalk in 1952 but quickly developed into one of the greatest goalscoring wingers in the club's history. He scored both goals in the 1957 FA Cup final when Villa beat Manchester United and the winning goal in the 1961 League Cup final second leg, netting 120 goals for the club in 340 games. Capped by Northern Ireland on 34 occasions he was part of the side that reached the World Cup quarter-final in 1958. He left Villa for Wolves for £30,000 in January 1962 and finished his League career with Plymouth Argyle.

1936 Aston Villa were clinging to their First Division lives by their very finger tips, second from bottom in the table and two points behind Sheffield Wednesday. Villa were at home to already relegated Blackburn Rovers whilst Wednesday were at home to Liverpool, who were level on points with Wednesday but with a better goal average. A good win for Villa therefore, and victory for either of their two counterparts, could still see them saved, but in a season that had already seen them beaten eight times at Villa Park and 52 goals nestling in the net, Villa played like a side already condemned. A 4–2 win for Blackburn killed off Villa, with Wednesday and Liverpool's 0–0 draw of little or no consequence. The reality was Villa were relegated to the

Second Division for the first time in their history, 48 years after the League had begun.

1959 A tense and at times robust match at Maine Road between two sides battling against relegation from the First Division saw the points shared after a 0–0 draw between Manchester City and Aston Villa. The result meant the matter would go to the final game of the season; Villa at West Bromwich Albion and City at home to Leicester City.

1981 Goals from Gary Shaw, Peter Withe and Allan Evans enabled Villa to close their home campaign with a much needed 3–0 win over Middlesbrough, taking them to 60 points and ensuring that only Ipswich, who still had two games to play, could catch them at the top of the table. A crowd of 38,018 showed at the end of the game that they thought the title was already won, although there was still a final match to play at Highbury before the League trophy could be collected. Withe's goal was his 20th in the League that season making him joint top First Division scorer along with Steve Archibald of Spurs.

APRIL 26TH

1897 The curtain came down on one of Villa's greatest ever seasons, one in which they had lifted the League and FA Cup double for the first time. The League campaign (it was still some time before the FA Cup final was the last match of the season) closed with a 1–0 win at Deepdale over Preston, fitting opponents since it was they who had achieved the very first double in 1888–89. Little did the two teams know, but it would be another 63 years before the feat was accomplished again, although there would be many near misses along the way.

1924 Villa's first appearance at Wembley pitted them against the side they had beaten in the FA Cup final in 1905, only this time the score was reversed with Newcastle United winning 2–0. Following the chaotic scenes at Wembley the previous year when Bolton and West Ham had played in the first FA Cup final at Wembley, it was decided to make the match all-ticket, as has every cup final since. Although the figure for the cup final was usually rounded up to 100,000, the actual attendance for the 1924 cup final was 91,695. The two sides emerged in pouring rain, Villa being led by Frank Moss to be presented to the Duke of York, and it was Villa who looked the brighter side in the early exchanges, hitting the woodwork twice. With five minutes to go the game was still goalless and extra time looked a certainty when Newcastle scored twice in a matter of minutes through Harris and Seymour to take the cup to the North East. United's Walter Hampson achieved the honour of becoming the oldest player to have appeared in the cup final, being 41 years and eight months at the time.

1975 League Cup holders Aston Villa made it a double of sorts, grabbing one of the promotion spots to the First Division after a 2–0 win over Sunderland. Villa Park had expected promotion to be won, with 57,266, the largest crowd of the season, in attendance to celebrate. Goals from Ian Ross from the penalty spot and Brian Little, both in the second half, started the party, and at the end of the game thousands swarmed from the terraces to hail their heroes. Brian Little's goal was his 20th in the Second Division that season, the best tally in the division.

APRIL 27TH

1901 League champions for the previous two years Villa had started the campaign confident that they might be able to clinch a third successive title, but an alarming drop in form had sent them plummeting down the table towards the wrong end. The period after the New Year was especially revealing, for only one match was won (against Sheffield Wednesday in March) and were it not for the points gained earlier in the campaign they might well have been staring relegation in the face! They finished with four straight defeats, including a 4–0 reverse at Manchester City, who therefore gained some revenge for an earlier 7–1 drubbing Villa had handed out.

1941 Geoff Vowden born in Barnsley. Signed by Nottingham Forest in 1958 from the Channel Islands, he made 90 appearances for the club, scoring 40 goals and was then transferred to Birmingham City for £25,000 in 1964. A little over six years later he moved across the city to sign for Villa for £12,500, but after helping the club to the Third Division title he suffered a succession of injuries and retired in 1974 in order to move into coaching.

APRIL 28TH

1915 What was to be Villa's last Football League match for four years saw them go down 4–0 at St James' Park against Newcastle United. With the world at war, it just didn't seem right to be battling for two League points on the playing fields of England when a much deadlier battle was taking place on the fields of France. At the end of the game, players from both sides shook each other firmly by the hand, not knowing what the future held for them, individually or collectively.

1923 Dave Walsh born in Waterford. He began his professional career with Linfield and was spotted by West Bromwich Albion, costing them £3,500 shortly before the start of the 1946–47 season. By the end of the decade he had helped them gain promotion to the First Division but was sold to Villa in December 1950 after netting 100 goals for the Hawthorns club. At Villa his 114 appearances resulted in 40 goals in his four and a half years with the club. He finished his League career with Walsall and also had a spell with Worcester City. He won 20 caps for the Republic of

Ireland and nine for Northern Ireland, six of his appearances coming whilst a Villa player.

1956 The last day of the season and a match at Villa Park that was not one for those of a faint heart. Villa were third from bottom and entertaining local rivals West Bromwich Albion; Huddersfield, their rivals for the second relegation spot were at home to Bolton. Villa held the slight advantage with goal average, but the margin was so slight that only a good win, irrespective of what Huddersfield achieved, would see them safe. Villa duly won 3–0, Huddersfield 3–1, meaning Villa survived by 0.2 of a goal!

1962 Villa fans could be forgiven for thinking that as far as the double was concerned, you wait 64 years and then two come along at once; Spurs had achieved the feat in 1961 and then both they and Burnley stood a chance of doing it all over again in 1962. Ipswich Town's 2–0 win at Portman Road over Villa gave them the title at the expense of Burnley in second place and Spurs third, and Burnley were to finish runners-up at Wembley, beaten by Spurs.

1967 Earl Barrett born in Rochdale. He began his career with Manchester City but after only four appearances and a brief loan spell with Chester was sold to Oldham for £35,000. Here he developed into a solid and reliable full-back and cost Villa £1.7 million when they signed him in February 1992. A member of the side that won the League Cup in 1994 he made over 100 appearances for the club in the League and was surprisingly sold to Everton for £1.7 million in January 1995. He has won three caps for England.

1990 A 3–3 home draw with Norwich City in front of a crowd of 28,988 ended Villa's hopes of winning the League title, for Liverpool beat QPR 2–1 to ensure they could not be headed. Villa, however, were ensured the runners-up spot and with it a place in European competition, the UEFA ban having been ended and England being afforded one place in the UEFA Cup.

APRIL 29TH

1899 In one of the closest of League battles for years, Villa and Liverpool were locked together at the top of the table for much of the season. As luck would have it, the final game of the campaign saw Liverpool visit Villa Park, with the two sides level on 43 points. Liverpool's away form was impressive, with seven victories recorded on their travels, but Villa had yet to lose at home during the campaign and had already netted 53 goals in front of their own supporters. A crowd of over 41,000 packed into Villa Park to see the head-to-head, including a fair contingent from Merseyside, but it was they who were to go home empty-handed as goals from John Devey (two), Fred Wheldon (two) and Jim Crabtree gave Villa a 5–0 win and the title for the fourth time in their history. It was their home form that had made them so irresistible, dropping only two points out of 34; the fact they could only win four times on their travels mattered little in the final analysis.

1905 After Aston Villa had beaten Manchester City 3–2 in an extremely bruising affair (Alex Leake and Sandy Turnbull were involved in a stand-up fight midway through the game) it was revealed the Villa players were approached on several occasions before and during the game by City players and officials offering inducements to 'throw' the game. This had come a week after City had been involved in another battle with championship challengers Everton, and therefore the Football Association was duty bound to investigate the two matches, with their announcements being made on August 4th 1905.

1911 Another close finish to the season had seen Villa and Manchester United see off the challenge of Sunderland to enter the home stretch neck and neck. Villa had beaten United a week previously to put themselves in the driving seat, then taken a point off Blackburn to leave themselves in sight of the finishing line. They needed only a point at Anfield to be sure of the title, but even then United had to win at home to third-placed Sunderland to stand any chance of overtaking them. Certainly United thought their chance had gone, for only 10,000 were at Old Trafford to watch their game, whilst Anfield was packed to its limits, even if Liverpool, the home side, were languishing in mid table. With little or nothing other than pride to play for, Liverpool tore into Villa, catching them unawares with the ferocity of their tackling and general play. Knocked out of their stride, Villa fell to a 3–1 defeat, a defeat they could ill afford. The players then trooped off the field to try and find out what had happened at Old Trafford; had Sunderland saved them? With no Radio 5 Live or BBC teleprinter to relay the scores around the country, we can but wonder how the news finally made its way into the Villa dressing-room at Anfield, but when it did, it meant heartbreak; United had won 5–1 and so taken the title from Villa's grasp.

1944 When the Second World War broke out Villa Park had been closed for football and given over to the military, with Villa going off to play at Solihull Town's ground in the Birmingham and District League. After two seasons Villa Park was returned and they could compete in the various regional leagues and cups, beating Stoke City, Coventry, Bath and Sheffield United on their way to reaching the League North Cup. All of these ties had been decided over two legs, as was the final, with Villa facing Blackpool at Bloomfield Road in front of a crowd of 28,000. Villa took the lead two minutes after half-time thanks to Billy Goffin, only for Jock Dodds to equalise eight minutes from time after Tommy Pearson, guesting from Newcastle United on the day, put him through. The crowd had barely time to recover their breath when Dodds scored again, but Villa would be a different proposition on their own pitch. There was considerable controversy over the number of guest players who took part in the game, especially for Blackpool. Whilst Villa numbered only one in their line-up (Potts of Doncaster), Blackpool had no fewer than six; Savage (Queen of the South), Pope (Hearts), Kinsell (West Bromwich Albion), Stanley Matthews (Stoke), Dix (Spurs) and Pearson (Newcastle).

1959 On the last day of the season the final relegation position was between two sides, Aston Villa and Manchester City, with Portsmouth already down. Villa were at West Bromwich Albion, where only a win would do. City meanwhile were entertaining Leicester City, who had only recently saved themselves from the drop, a win at Villa Park pulling them clear. Villa knew the enormity of their task and took the game to Albion, taking the lead and holding it until just two minutes from the end when Ronnie Allen slipped through to equalise. The news that Manchester City had won 3–1 meant Villa were out of the First Division for the first time since 1937–38 when they won the Second Division title. All but two seasons of their League life had been spent in the top flight. Villa vowed to make it an immediate return.

1972 Villa clinched the Third Division title with a 5–1 home win over Torquay United at Villa Park in front of a crowd of 37,582. Goals from Geoff Vowden (two), Andy Lochhead, Brian Little and an own goal ensured the trophy.

APRIL 30TH

1898 George Johnson made his debut for Villa in the 2–0 home win over Nottingham Forest. He had begun his career with West Bromwich Albion but was unable to break into the side, leaving for Walsall, where he made his reputation and then signing for Villa in August 1897. He went on to help Villa win the title in 1899 and 1900, and scored 47 goals in 108 appearances for the club. Sadly his career was brought to an end by a serious leg injury sustained in 1906.

1910 Despite a 2–0 defeat at Anfield against Liverpool, Villa were already assured of their sixth League title, finishing the season five points ahead of Liverpool in second place. Whilst Liverpool could boast a much better away record (Liverpool won eight times, as opposed to Villa's six), no one in the division could live with the men in claret and blue at Villa Park, where they had lost just 32 times in the League in the previous ten years. Unfortunately, it would be another 70 years or so before the League trophy was to make a return visit to Villa Park.

1949 Alun Evans born in Bewdley. After just 22 League games for Wolves Bill Shankly paid £100,000 in 1968 to take him to Anfield, the first teenage player to have cost such a fee. The tag weighed heavily on him and his career at Liverpool seldom matched his debut when he scored against Wolves. Four years later he joined Aston Villa for £72,000 and made 72 appearances, scoring just 17 goals and was sold to Walsall. After three seasons he went to America and then Australia before retiring in 1980, his career never having reached the potential promised in 1968.

MAY 1ST

1940   Brian Godfrey born in Flint. He began his career with Everton but made only one appearance for the side before being sold to Scunthorpe United. In 1963 he was sold to Preston and spent almost four years with the club and was then bought by Aston Villa, along with Brian Greenhalgh for £55,000, making 139 League appearances and scoring 22 goals. In 1971 he was swapped with Ray Graydon of Bristol Rovers and finished his career with Newport County. A full Welsh international he won three caps for his country.

1942   Charlie Aitken born in Edinburgh. Signed by Aston Villa in August 1959, he made his debut for the club in the final game of the 1960–61 season and then went on to become one of the finest servants the club has ever had, being an ever-present for five seasons. He helped the club to the final of the League Cup in both 1963 and 1971, won a winners' medal in 1975, collected three caps for Scotland at Under-23 level and holds the appearance record for Villa, having made 561 League appearances. He was granted a testimonial in 1970 and finally left the club in 1976, going on to play in America.

1943   Trevor Hockey born in Keighley. He began his career with Bradford City and arrived at Villa Park for £38,000 in June 1973 having played for Nottingham Forest, Newcastle United, Birmingham City, Sheffield United and Norwich City. He made 24 League appearances for Villa before heading back to his first club Bradford City. He won nine caps for Wales during his career.

MAY 2ND

1931   Tom 'Pongo' Waring had already scored 49 League goals during the season, easily Villa's best individual record (and second only to Dixie Dean as the highest individual tally in the First Division), but missed out on hitting the magical 50 mark thanks to the woodwork twice and some magnificent saves by Wednesday goalkeeper Breedon. Villa went down 3–0 in the match at Hillsborough.

1937   Tommy Ewing born in Swinhill. He joined Villa from Partick Thistle in February 1962 for £20,000 and made just 39 appearances for the League team, scoring four goals from the outside-right position. He won two caps for Scotland during his career and also represented the Football League.

1981 An estimated 20,000 Villa fans swelled the Highbury crowd to 57,472 as Villa chased their first League title in over 70 years. Arsenal's own title aspirations had only recently ended, so only Ipswich (at Middlesbrough on the same day) stood between Villa and the title. On the day it was Arsenal who played more like champions, scoring twice in the first half through Young and McDermott and preventing desperate Villa attacks at the back. At half-time the position looked bleak, for in addition to their own problems the news that Ipswich were ahead was hardly likely to cause much glee. Villa took up the challenge in the second half but were still unable to find a way through a stubborn Arsenal defence. Then Villa found an unlikely hero; Bozo Jankovic scored twice for Middlesbrough to turn the game around at Ayresome Park and bring Ipswich's hopes of a League title and UEFA Cup double to an end. At Highbury, the news that Villa were champions was greeted by a huge outpouring of emotion as thousands of Villa fans swarmed on to the pitch to celebrate. If the finale was not quite that which had been anticipated or expected before the game, the relief at having at last won the title after so long more than made up for it.

1988 The Second Division's biggest crowd of the season, 36,423, was at Villa Park for a match vital to both Villa and their opponents Bradford City. It was Villa's last home match of the campaign and all three points were required if they were to stand a chance of making an immediate return to the First Division, although Bradford were also in contention for a promotion place. The game was settled by just one goal, David Platt scoring with a header for Villa after 23 minutes. Thereafter Villa held out as Bradford went looking for an equaliser and took all three points. Bradford were to miss out on automatic promotion by one point and were then beaten in the play-offs.

1993 A 1–0 home defeat by an Oldham side desperately battling against relegation ended Villa's interest in the FA Premier League title, for Manchester United could not now be caught. According to legend, United manager Alex Ferguson was on a golf course at the time Villa were playing Oldham; Villa's below-par performance gave him the championship!

MAY 3RD

1900 Villa Park staged the international between England and Scotland. The England side contained Villa's Billy George and Albert Wilkes and the match finished a 2–2 draw.

1902 Villa Park again staged the England and Scotland clash, although this game was effectively a replay of the match the previous month at Ibrox which had seen part of a stand collapse and over 20 people lose their lives. That game was later declared unofficial, hence the match at Villa Park which was drawn 2–2.

1942 Malcolm Beard born in Cannock. He joined Villa in July 1971 after making over 350 appearances for Birmingham City, but after a handful of outings for Villa he retired from the game.

MAY 4TH

1944 Jim Cumbes born in Manchester. After learning his trade with Tranmere Rovers, he cost West Bromwich Albion £33,350 in 1969 and soon became established as their first choice goalkeeper. A fee of £36,000 brought him to Villa Park in 1971 and he went on to make 157 League appearances for the club, helping them back into the top flight and winning a League Cup medal. After a brief spell with Portland Timbers, where he linked up with former Villa player Vic Crowe, he returned to play for Southport in non-League football. He was also an accomplished cricketer, especially as a fast bowler and, given his goalkeeping experience, a solid fielder!

1957 Once again Aston Villa were the last line of defence between a side winning the League and FA Cup double, and just as they had done in 1905 and 1913, Villa were in a mood to protect a feat they had been the last to achieve. The game effectively turned in favour of Villa as early as the sixth minute, Roy McParland crashing into Manchester United keeper Ray Wood with such force that Wood broke his cheekbone and was forced off the field. There is no doubt that the incident would not be allowed today, but many were of the opinion that Wood could equally have got out of the way and thus prevented such an injury. With no substitutes allowed, Jackie Blanchflower had to take over in goal but he could do little to prevent McParland scoring twice in five minutes in the second half to give Villa an unassailable lead. Although Wood later returned and Tommy Taylor reduced the deficit, Villa were able to hold on to claim their seventh FA Cup final win, a then record. If the circumstances surrounding their win were marred, it did not show on the faces of either the team or their fans as the FA Cup was paraded around Wembley. It was the seventh time Villa had won the FA Cup, more than any other club at the time.

MAY 5TH

1951 A 6–2 home win over Stoke City enabled Villa to finish the season in 15th place, a respectable position given the trouble the club were in earlier in the season. Indeed, it wasn't until Easter that Villa had begun to climb out of trouble, leaving Everton and Sheffield Wednesday to be relegated. With the departure of Everton, Villa now took over as the First Division's longest residents, having spent all but two seasons in the top flight.

1972 A crowd of 45,567 was at Villa Park to bid farewell to the Third Division, with Chesterfield the visitors (Villa had opened their Third Division campaign the previous season against the same opponents). Prior to the game League president Len Shipman presented the Third Division championship trophy to captain Bruce Rioch. A goal from Ian Ross, his only strike of the season, was enough to win the game (Villa's 32nd of the season, a new club record) and thus take Villa to 70 League points for the season, their record under the old system of two points for a win. The win was Villa's 32nd of the season out of a possible 46 and therefore another divisional record.

MAY 6TH

1944 The second leg of the League North Cup was played at Villa Park in front of a crowd of nearly 55,000, all anxious to see if Villa could overturn a 2–1 deficit from the first leg. It took less than a minute for Villa to level the tie, Bob Iverson passing to Frank Broome (who looked to be offside), although Blackpool got their revenge when they equalised through a similarly offside looking goal from Dix. That the officials might have missed the incidents is not surprising; at the start of the war the Football League Management Committee had given referees permission to wear spectacles if they so wished! Villa went back into the lead with a goal that looked to have been handled by George Edwards before going in. Blackpool levelled a second time but Villa began to pull away, scoring first through Eric Houghton and then Frank Broome to wrap the game up at 4–2 (5–4 on aggregate) and set up a meeting with Charlton, winners of the League South Cup in a play off match. Villa later donated the trophy they had won in the League North to the Red Cross and this was auctioned off for charity.

1974 Villa manager Vic Crowe was sacked by the club after taking charge in 1970. Although he had taken the club back into the Second Division in 1972, it was an inability to maintain the progress and restore them to the First Division which effectively cost him his job at Villa Park.

MAY 7TH

1927 Jimmy Gibson made his debut for Villa in the goalless draw against Huddersfield Town. He had cost Villa a then record fee of £7,500 when joining the club from Partick Thistle and went on to become a regular fixture in the side for the next nine seasons or so, injuries apart. He won four of his eight Scottish caps whilst with Villa and made 225 appearances for the club before finishing his career in April 1936.

1938 A 2–0 home win over Norwich City ensured Villa finished the season four points ahead of Manchester United at the top of the Second Division table and promoted back into the top flight after an absence of just two years.

1988 Villa ended the season with a goalless draw at the County Ground,

Swindon, and thus ensured they finished in second place and were promoted back into the First Division. Unlike previous seasons, it was their away form which won them promotion instead of their form at Villa Park. Six clubs had visited Villa Park and returned home with all three points, whilst a further seven had taken home one point; Villa won only nine games in front of their own supporters. Away from home they had the best record of the division; 13 victories and five draws and only four defeats. Had their home form matched that of their travels, they would have finished the season as champions. As it was, promotion in manager Graham Taylor's first season in charge was warmly welcomed by everyone connected with the club. At the end of the first hundred years of League football, Villa could claim a record that read: Played 3,504, Won 1,501, Drawn 782, Lost 1,221, Goals For 6,051, Goals Against 5,260. Only Burnley, Derby, Notts County and Wolves had played more games, because they had spent more seasons in the lower divisions. Nobody, however, had scored more goals than them, indicative of the attacking traditions of the club.

1994 The curtain was brought down on the Holte End for the last time, for by the start of the following season it would be replaced by an all-seater stand capable of accommodating 13,462 seats. The farewell attracted 19,210 fans, all of whom were given a certificate to signify they were present at the last game, a 2–1 win over Liverpool!

MAY 8TH

1982 A goal from Pat Heard was enough to settle the local derby with West Bromwich Albion at the Hawthorns in front of a crowd of 19,615.

1987 Billy McNeill was sacked as manager of Aston Villa after less than eight months in charge at the club. He had joined the previous September from Manchester City, with Villa bottom of the table. At the end of the season their position hadn't changed and they had been relegated to the Second Division, along with his former club Manchester City! McNeill's assistant Ron Wylie was also dismissed, and Villa were looking for their fourth manager in three years.

MAY 9TH

1966 Manchester United heaped more misery on Villa, trouncing them 6–1 at Old Trafford in the penultimate game of the season.

1993 Villa's season came to a close with their third successive defeat, this time by 2–1 at Queens Park Rangers, leaving Villa ten points adrift of Manchester United at the top of the table. Compensation, of sorts, was that Villa had again qualified for European competition the following season in the UEFA Cup.

MAY 10TH

1977 Birmingham City won a fiery derby match at St Andrew's 2–1, the vital goal a penalty converted by Trevor Francis, with John Deehan getting Villa's goal. After the game Ron Saunders gave vent to his fury. 'Francis continually conned the referee. He got Leighton Phillips sent-off, and forced a penalty decision which was a joke. If Brian Little got as much protection from referees, he would be the world's best striker.'

1998 Arsenal had already won the title and perhaps had one eye on the FA Cup final, which they were also to win, thus becoming only the second side to have achieved a double double. Villa meanwhile had marched up the table on the back of eight wins out of ten games and still stood a chance of clinching a place in the UEFA Cup for the following season, but they needed to beat Arsenal to keep ahead of Blackburn. There was only one goal in the game, Dwight Yorke converting a penalty, but it was the way Yorke struck the ball that caused amusement among the fans and anger from his manager; he chipped the ball to where David Seaman in the Arsenal goal had been standing, with Seaman diving one way and watching with a smile on his face as the ball gently floated over him! With Villa having won the game, the European dream now rested on Chelsea.

MAY 11TH

1954 John Gregory born in Scunthorpe. He began his career as an apprentice with Northampton, signing professional forms in January 1973. After 187 League appearances he was transferred to Villa in June 1977 for £40,000, making his League debut in a 2–1 win at QPR in August the same year. After 65 appearances he was sold to Brighton for £250,000 in July 1979, later joining QPR in a deal worth £300,000 and helping them to the FA Cup final in 1982. By November 1985 he had racked up over 160 outings in the League team and was transferred to Derby County, helping them to the Second Division title in 1986–87 during the course of his 103 League games. When he retired he moved into coaching and management, replacing Alan Smith as manager of Wycombe Wanderers in October 1996 and then accepting an offer to take over from Brian Little at Villa Park midway through the 1997–98 season.

1968 Villa had begun the season with a new manager (Tommy Cummings) and high hopes that they might make an immediate return to the First Division after relegation at the end of the previous campaign. Whilst they stayed in the division, at the end of the day it was almost in the other direction they were headed, for a run of four games without defeat, even if only one of those had been won, just before the end of the season pulled them out of trouble. The visitors on the last day of the season were

Queens Park Rangers, themselves needing the points to ensure promotion, and they grabbed a 2–1 win that took them up with Ipswich. Whilst Villa could only watch with envy, QPR were taking their place among the elite. Villa meanwhile had to endure the depths of despair before they were again to enjoy life at the very top.

MAY 12TH

1984 The curtain came down on a disappointing season for Villa, with no European qualification and tenth place in the League. Ipswich beat them 2–1 at Portman Road in what was to be Tony Barton's last League match in charge.

1987 A Villa move to appoint Arthur Cox and Roy McFarland was turned down by Derby County, the club where the pair were then in control. It was now believed Villa would turn their attentions to Watford manager Graham Taylor who had recently announced he was looking for a change after ten years in charge at Vicarage Road.

MAY 13TH

1967 After four seasons of continual struggle, putting together enough points in the closing weeks of the season to pull clear of the trapdoor, relegation came almost as a relief to Villa. It would allow them to regroup, to put together a side capable of challenging for the game's top honours, rather than battle it out at the bottom. Already relegated by the time they came to play the last game of the season at Southampton (three straight defeats having killed off any chance of a last gasp escape), the Saints hammered the final nail with a 6–2 victory. Villa had been relegated twice before; on the first occasion their Second Division sojourn had lasted two seasons, the second time barely one. Their stay in the Second Division this time would last three seasons, but when they left the League, it was in the wrong direction.

1989 A 1–1 home draw with Coventry City gave Villa 40 points from the season, just one above the relegation trapdoor and an immediate return to the Second Division. Thankfully, Middlesbrough, West Ham and Newcastle had not managed to acquire so many points and Villa were saved.

1998 A single goal from Gianfranco Zola, 24 seconds after he had come on as a substitute for Chelsea, sent Aston Villa into Europe the following season; Chelsea winning the European Cup-Winners' Cup meant there was an English vacancy in the UEFA Cup which Villa would now fill.

MAY 14TH

1938 Frank Broome of Aston Villa made his first appearance for England in the international against Germany in Berlin. This game, of course, is infamous for the English players being advised to give the Nazi salute prior to the start of the game on the instructions of the Foreign Office and the British Ambassador, Sir Neville Henderson. Henderson later made amends, offering Hermann Goering his binoculars and telling him 'You really must watch these goals [as England score], they're delightful' as England won 6–3.

1983 A 2–1 win over Arsenal at Villa Park ensured Villa finished the season in sixth place and qualified for the UEFA Cup the following season. Goals in each half from Gary Shaw and Colin Gibson wrapped up the points.

MAY 15TH

1914 John R. Martin born in Birmingham. He joined Villa from Hednesford Town and made 57 post-war League appearances, scoring 13 goals for the club.

1933 Peter Broadbent born in Ellerington. He began his career with Brentford but made his name with Wolves, making 453 League appearances for the Molineux club between 1951 and 1965 and earning seven caps for England. After a brief spell with Shrewsbury he was signed by a Villa side desperate for some firepower up front, although the club's problems at the time he signed lay more with the defence! He spent three years with Villa before winding down his League career with Stockport County.

1938 Frank Broome made a return appearance to the Reichssportfeld, this time playing for Villa in a friendly against a German Select XI, but all the Villa players refused to give the Nazi salute. Broome scored twice and Frank Shell once as Villa won 3–2.

1963 Leicester City were beaten 3–1 at Villa Park as Villa continued to pull away from the lower reaches of the table.

1979 A trip to Maine Road for the game against Manchester City brought the season to an end, Alex Croply, Dennis Mortimer and John Deehan scoring the goals that enabled Villa to sign off with a 3–2 win.

1982 With the European Cup final only 11 days away, interest in the League had all but disappeared, with only 20,446 present for the 2–1 home defeat by Everton.

MAY 16TH

1934 Joe Beresford collected his first cap for England in the 2–1 defeat in Prague. He had joined Aston Villa from Mansfield Town in 1927 and went on to make 251 first-team appearances, scoring 73 goals, including a hat-trick in only his second appearance for the club. He was surprisingly sold to Preston where he helped them to the FA Cup final in 1937.

1966 Villa recovered from the 6–1 mauling against Manchester United with a final day 2–0 win at Stamford Bridge against Chelsea.

1977 A 1–0 home win over Stoke City was Villa's fifth game in under two weeks, and there were still two games to go! Andy Gray scored the only goal from the penalty spot in the second half.

MAY 17TH

1919 Villa goalkeeper Sam Hardy guested for Nottingham Forest when they won the Victory Shield against Everton 1–0 at the City Ground. He had begun his career with Chesterfield and signed for Liverpool in 1905, spending seven years at Anfield before joining Aston Villa in 1912. A member of the side that won the FA Cup in 1913, the First World War cut across his Villa Park career but he did manage to make 183 first-team appearances. He joined Forest in August 1921 and helped them to the Second Division title in his first season, but his career was brought to an end by injury in October 1924, by which time he was 41 years of age.

1969 Villa had ended the season escaping relegation to the Third Division for the first time in their history by the skin of their teeth and then departed for a brief tour of North America. A spirited 2–2 draw with Spurs in Atlanta may have been little more than an exhibition game, but it gave Villa hope that if they could live with the likes of Spurs, then the forthcoming season in the Second Division would hold no fears.

MAY 18TH

1916 Ambrose Mulraney born in Wishaw. He began his career with Celtic but began to make a serious impact when he joined Ipswich in 1936, and but for the Second World War could well have gone on to earn international recognition. In 1945 he joined Birmingham City and switched to Villa in September 1948, but after only 12 League games suffered an Achilles tendon injury that forced his retirement.

1987 Villa appointed Graham Taylor as manager in succession to the recently departed Billy McNeill. Taylor had spent ten years with Watford, guiding them from the Fourth Division to the First and into the FA Cup final for the first time in their history in 1984. He had recently announced he wanted a change after ten years with one club, and following Derby's rejection of a Villa approach for Arthur Cox and Roy McFarland Taylor was seen as the ideal man for the job of restoring Villa to the First Division after relegation at the end of the season.

MAY 19TH

1987 Graham Taylor took over at Villa Park and his first job was to open negotiations with Chelsea over the possible sale of defender Tony Dorigo to the Stamford Bridge club. The move finally went ahead for a fee of £475,000.

MAY 20TH

1944 Stamford Bridge was the venue for the meeting between the winners of the League North and League South Cups, Aston Villa and Charlton Athletic respectively. Honours ended even with a 1–1 draw, Revell scoring for Charlton and Eric Houghton firing home for Villa in front of a crowd of 38,540.

1983 Villa paid £175,000 to Everton for tigerish midfield player Steve McMahon. He remained with Villa for the next two years before a £375,000 move took him to Anfield and Liverpool.

MAY 21ST

1963 Two days before they were due to meet Birmingham City in the first leg of the Football League Cup, Villa closed their League campaign with a 1–1 draw at Ipswich Town.

1982 Villa warmed up for their forthcoming European Cup final against Bayern Munich with a 3–0 win over Swansea City in the final game of the season. Although the final was only five days away, Villa resisted the temptation to rest key players, putting out the strongest possible side. Goals from Tony Morley, Des Bremner and Peter Withe won the game.

MAY 22ND

1974 Graham Fenton born in Wallsend. Another graduate of Villa's youth scheme, he made 39 appearances for the club and was also loaned to West Bromwich Albion to gain experience before being sold to Blackburn Rovers for £1.5 million in 1995.

1980 Villa paid their then record transfer fee of £500,000 to bring Peter Withe to the club from Newcastle United. The purchase was to be a vital one for Villa, galvanising the club and making Villa potential title challengers, and the fact that Withe was also being chased by Leeds United and Everton was indicative of how Villa's fortunes had by now changed.

MAY 23RD

1946 Graham Parker born in Coventry. He joined Villa as an apprentice and made just 17 League appearances for the club before being allowed to join Rotherham in December 1967. He later played for Lincoln, Exeter and Torquay United.

1963 One of the worst winters in recent memory had totally thrown the League season into chaos, with Villa having been without a game of any kind between January 19th and February 13th, with other clubs hit even harder. The result was the League and the various cup competitions had to be extended, with Villa meeting Birmingham City at St Andrew's in the first leg of the League Cup final, the competition Villa had won in its first season. Whether Villa were jaded after such a long and drawn out campaign remains unknown, but the form that had taken them past Peterborough, Stoke, Preston, Norwich and Sunderland in the previous rounds deserted them in the final. Goals from Leek (two) and Bloomfield against one from Bobby Thomson gave Birmingham a 3–1 win they were well worth in front of a crowd of 31,850. It left Villa with a mountain to climb in the second leg.

1977 Chris Nicholl scored once and Andy Gray grabbed a hat-trick as Villa romped to an easy end of season win over West Bromwich Albion at Villa Park. For Gray the season had been a delight, his 25 goals in the League making him the division's top goalscorer, the first time a Villa player had headed the First Division scoring charts since the great Pongo Waring in 1931.

MAY 24TH

1941 Cammie Fraser born in Blackford. Signed by Villa from Dunfermline in October 1962, he made only 17 appearances for the League side, scoring one goal, before switching across the city to join Birmingham in February 1965. He was capped twice by the Scottish Under-23 side.

1994 The court case brought by former Villa star Paul Elliott against current Villa player Dean Saunders was continuing at the High Court, having opened the day beforehand. The case referred to an incident in which Saunders, then playing for Liverpool, launched a tackle which effectively ended the career of Elliott, then playing for Chelsea. The hearing heard opinions from the likes of Terry Butcher and Dennis Wise, both of whom stated that they thought the challenge to be 'over the top'.

MAY 25TH

1976 Ian 'Chico' Hamilton was reported to be joining American club Minnesota Kicks for £30,000, although within two months he was sold to Sheffield United.

1994 Wimbledon's Vinnie Jones was subpoenaed to give evidence at the Elliott versus Saunders court case, but his evidence merely consisted of the opinion that only Saunders knew if the challenge was malicious or not!

MAY 26TH

1947 The latest date that Villa have played a League match, with Villa going down 1–0 at home to Stoke City. This had followed a particularly harsh winter, with some clubs still playing into the following month and the League title not settled until June 14, when Stoke were beaten by Sheffield United!

1982 Perhaps the greatest night in Villa's long and illustrious history. Having

LEFT: William McGregor, the man who came up with the idea for the Football League

BELOW: Villa Park as it was just after the Second World War

F. WHELDON

OGDEN'S CIGARETTES

ASTON VILLA

A. HALL
ASTON VILLA F.C.

VAL ,,FOOTER'' GUM

PRINTED IN HOLLAND

F. BIDDLESTONE
Aston Villa

2

CLOCKWISE FROM TOP LEFT: cigarette cards of Fred 'Diamond' Wheldon, Villa, Albert Hall and Fred Biddlestone

ABOVE: John Devey, captain of the
side during the 1890s

LEFT: Pongo Waring scored 49
League goals for Villa in
1930–31, a record tally for a
single season

ABOVE: Villa come out before the start of the 1924 FA Cup final at Wembley, only the second final to be played at the stadium. Unfortunately, Newcastle won 2–0

LEFT: Charlie Athersmith

The 1982 European Cup winners

Peter Withe scores the only goal of the 1982 European Cup final against Bayern Munich

Peter McParland and Ray Wood have just collided during the 1957 FA Cup final between Villa and Manchester United. The incident left Wood badly injured and gave Villa the initiative to win the Cup

Peter McParland scoring for Villa in the same match against Manchester United. Villa went on to win the 1957 FA Cup final 2–1

Brian Little scores the winning goal in the 1977 League Cup final
second replay against Everton

The League champions of 1980–81, Villa's first championship
success in 71 years

Villa Park as it was in 1990, before redevelopment was completed

survived and prospered through four rounds of enthralling European competition, overcoming Icelandic, East German, Russian and Belgian competition along the way, with UEFA officials perhaps the closest to putting them out of the cup, Aston Villa were playing in the European Cup final for the first time. Their opponents couldn't have been more difficult, West German champions Bayern Munich, three times winners of the very same trophy and one of Europe's premier clubs. The final was held on Feyenoord's ground in Rotterdam, with thousands of Villa fans making the journey across the North Sea to take their place in the 46,000 crowd. After only eight minutes Villa were hit by a disaster, goalkeeper Jimmy Rimmer having to go off injured and being replaced by Nigel Spink, making only his second first-team appearance! If the very last line of defence was inexperienced, then the same could not be said for the ten players in front of him, and with the likes of Dennis Mortimer marshalling events and a 'they shall not pass' attitude prevailing, Villa weathered some fierce German attacks in the first half. With 22 minutes of the second half played Tony Morley slipped past German defender Augenthaler and headed for the by-line, with Peter Withe making for the middle area. Morley's cross found Withe completely unmarked in the box and the ball hit the net via the post for the only goal of the game. There were still one or two scares to come, but when the final whistle blew the ground seemed to explode into a sea of claret and blue. Manager Tony Barton, in charge for seven weeks, gave up trying to stem the tears and Nigel Spink was hailed the hero of the hour. But they were all heroes, for everyone had played their part in taking Villa to the pinnacle of the European game. Special thoughts were also reserved for the luckless Jimmy Rimmer; 14 years earlier he had sat on the bench when Manchester United won the European Cup and collected a winners' medal with a minimum of effort. Tonight he collected a second, his injury ensuring the energy expounded was only just more than on the first occasion.

1994 Dean Saunders was called to give evidence in the ongoing court case involving Paul Elliott. Saunders claimed he lifted his feet instinctively to avoid getting seriously hurt himself.

MAY 27TH

1963 With both sides showing no changes since their first meeting four days previously, Villa took on Birmingham City in the League Cup final second leg at Villa Park in front of a crowd of 37,920. Despite creating many chances throughout the game against a Birmingham side content to sit on their 3–1 lead from the first leg, Villa couldn't find a way back into the tie and thus lost 3–1 on aggregate. There would, however, be other great nights for Villa in the competition.

1992 Ian Olney was sold to Oldham for a fee of £700,000.

MAY 28TH

1909 Tom Gardner born in Huyton. He began his career with Liverpool, making his debut in 1930, but was transferred to Grimsby after only four games. A year later he joined Hull City and in February 1934 moved on again and joined Aston Villa. His performances during the rest of the season earned him the first of two caps for England. He remained with the club until 1938 when he joined Burnley and finished his career in 1946. During the war he guested for a number of clubs including Blackpool and he died in 1970.

1991 Dr Jozef Venglos resigned as manager of Aston Villa after just one season in charge. Heralded as a brave but adventurous appointment when he had taken over before the previous campaign, it was Villa's inability to mount a sustained challenge for the League title which had caused him to resign.

MAY 29TH

1925 Dennis Parsons born in Birmingham. He began his career with Wolves but was spotted by Villa whilst playing non-League football for Hereford United, signing at Villa Park in September 1952. He went on to make 36 appearances in goal for the club before returning to the non-League game.

1971 Villa signed goalkeeper Tommy Hughes from Chelsea. He had joined Chelsea from Clydebank as cover for Peter Bonetti but eventually grew frustrated by the lack of first-team opportunities and jumped at the chance of joining Villa. Unfortunately he found it just as tough at Villa Park and after only 16 League appearances switched to Brighton. Here he had three games, subsequently finding his mark with Hereford for whom he made 226 appearances.

1985 Liverpool fans rioted before the European Cup final at the Heysel Stadium in Belgium, which left 39 fans dead, and in the immediate aftermath English clubs were banned from European competition indefinitely by UEFA. Although there were a number of half-hearted attempts by the Football Association to get the ban lifted or at least have an expiry date set, it would not be until the beginning of the 1990–91 season that English clubs were readmitted, with Aston Villa and Manchester United being the first English clubs to return.

MAY 30TH

1906 The Football League meeting at the Holborn Restaurant in London rejected a proposal put forward by Villa and seconded by Everton to abolish the maximum wage for players. The timing could not have been more ironic, for on the same day punishment was being handed out to Manchester City for flaunting the very same rule!

1966 Lee Butler born in Sheffield. He was first spotted by Lincoln City whilst playing in goal for Haworth Colliery and joined City in 1986. His performances for the Sincil Bank club soon alerted the attention of other clubs and Villa paid £100,000 to sign him in August 1987. Stiff competition at Villa Park restricted his appearances and he was sent on loan to Hull, later joining Barnsley for £165,000. He later played for Scunthorpe and Wigan.

MAY 31ST

1949 Frank Carrodus born in Manchester. He began his career with non-League Altrincham before signing with Manchester City in 1969 but found first-team opportunities limited at Maine Road. He joined Villa in the summer of 1974 for £95,000 and in five years made over 150 League appearances and won two League Cup winners' medals. He left for Wrexham in December 1979 and later had spells with Birmingham City and Bury before going off to play in non-League circles again.

JUNE 1ST

1983 Aston Villa paid £200,000 to Swindon for former England Schoolboy, Youth and Under-21 international Paul Rideout. He had broken through the ranks at Swindon two years previously and went on to make 54 League appearances for the club before being sold to Italian club Bari for £400,000 in 1985. On the same day Gordon Cowans scored England's second goal in a 2–0 win over Scotland as they claimed the Home Championship. The news was tempered by Peter Withe's withdrawal from the squad to tour Australia.

JUNE 2ND

1964 Mark Walters born in Birmingham. First associated with Villa as a schoolboy at the age of 14, he was taken on to the groundstaff as an apprentice in 1980 and joined the professional ranks two years later. That same year he made his first-team debut and quickly became established as one of the brightest wing talents in the game and made 225 appearances for the club. He was sold to Glasgow Rangers in December 1987 for £500,000, winning three League titles and two Skol Cups during his time at Ibrox. He was then sold to Liverpool in 1991, even though his middle name is Everton, costing the Anfield club £1.25 million and won an FA Cup winners' medal in 1992. After loan spells with Stoke and Wolves he joined Southampton in 1996 and six months later switched to Swindon.

JUNE 3RD

1921 Reg Beresford born in Walsall. He was associated with Villa during the

Second World War but when the hostilities ended signed with Birmingham, subsequently joining Crystal Palace two years later without having made a first-team appearance! His stay at Selhurst Park was only slightly more fruitful, appearing seven times in the first team before going into the non-League game.

1994 Wolves paid £1.25 million for winger Tony Daley, offering him a four-year contract, although because of injury he was already one year into his term before he made his debut!

JUNE 4TH

1968 Ian Taylor born in Birmingham. He began his career with Port Vale after costing them £15,000 from Moor Green in 1992, moving on to Sheffield Wednesday for £1 million in July 1994. After only a handful of games for the Hillsborough club he joined Villa in a further £1 million move in December and was a member of the side that won the League Cup in 1996, scoring one of the goals in the 3–0 win over Leeds.

1974 Ron Saunders was appointed manager of Aston Villa in place of Vic Crowe. Saunders had begun his managerial career with non-League Yeovil Town in 1968 and taken over at Oxford United 12 months later. Appointed manager at Norwich City he had taken them to the First Division and the final of the League Cup in 1973 before resigning after a poor start to the 1973–74 season. He then had five months in charge at Maine Road with Manchester City before taking over at Villa Park.

JUNE 5TH

1913 George Cummings born in Thornbridge. He began his career with Partick Thistle and was already a full Scottish international when he was signed by Aston Villa in 1935 for £9,350. Unfortunately the Second World War cut right across his career but he did manage to make 232 first-team appearances before his retirement in 1949.

1971 Bristol Rovers striker Ray Graydon joined Villa having hit 13 League goals the previous season.

1986 Villa paid £450,000 for Sheffield Wednesday striker Garry Thompson who had scored just nine goals in 44 first-team appearances. Although his strike rate improved at Villa Park, netting 19 goals in 70 appearances, he was sold to Watford in 1988.

JUNE 6TH

1938 Barry Stobart born in Doncaster. He joined Wolves as a junior and rose through the ranks, signing professional forms in December 1955. He spent nine years at Molineux but was never a regular in the side and joined Manchester City in August 1964. Three months later he came to

Villa Park for £30,000 and made 45 appearances in the League, scoring eight goals. He left for Shrewsbury in October 1967.

1963 Dariusz Kubicki born in Warsaw in Poland. A £200,000 signing from Legia Warsaw in 1991, he made 34 appearances for the club at right-back before moving on to Sunderland in 1994 for half the fee Villa had paid. A full Polish international with 49 caps to his credit.

1973 Welsh international Trevor Hockey joined Villa from Norwich City, although at the end of the season he was on his way again, this time to join Bradford City.

1988 Villa manager Graham Taylor signed Derek Mountfield from Everton for £450,000. Mountfield had captained Everton to their recent glories of two League titles, an FA Cup and the European Cup-Winners' Cup and his experience was going to be vital to Villa if they were to avoid an immediate return to the Second Division following their recent promotion.

JUNE 7TH

1991 Ron Atkinson was appointed manager of Aston Villa, 32 years after being given a free transfer from the club as a player. Villa had previously targeted the larger than life character as manager, once when he was manager at Manchester United, but this time he said yes to an approach from Doug Ellis and resigned as Sheffield Wednesday manager in order to take over at Villa Park.

JUNE 8TH

1996 Gareth Southgate was a member of the England side that kicked off the European Championships with a 1–1 draw against Switzerland at Wembley. Alan Shearer gave England the lead after 23 minutes, but with seven minutes left England conceded a penalty. Of course, it was penalties that were to end England's interest in the competition...

JUNE 9TH

1986 Aston Villa paid £200,000 to Arsenal to bring Martin Keown to Villa Park. The Arsenal defender had been unsettled by his inability to hold a regular spot in the first team and slotted straight into the Villa side. He later went to play for Everton, where he won his first cap for England and then returned to Highbury in 1993.

1987 Steve Sims was transferred from Watford to Villa having made 171 League appearances for the Hornets in two spells with the club. The defender had also played for Leicester City and Notts County.

JUNE 10TH

1966 David Platt born in Chadderton. After being shown the door by

Manchester United, he joined Crewe Alexandra and developed into a workmanlike midfielder and was snapped up by Aston Villa in 1988. He made his England debut in 1990, just in time to stake a place in the World Cup squad, where his performances grew with each successive game, not least his appearance off the substitutes bench against Belgium to score the winner in the last minute of extra time. In 1991 he was signed by Bari for £5.5 million and a year later moved on for a similar fee to Juventus. After a further move within Italy (to Sampdoria) he returned to England with Arsenal in 1995, retiring from the game in the summer of 1998.

1994 Dean Saunders was cleared in the High Court of making a reckless challenge on Paul Elliott during a match between Liverpool and Chelsea. In addition to losing out on a claim for compensation after his career was ended by the tackle, Elliott was also facing a possible legal bill for £500,000. In his summing up Mr Justice Drake said that whilst he felt players should have the right to seek redress from the courts for career-wrecking injuries as a result of foul play, he was satisfied in this instance that Saunders had made an honest attempt to play the ball.

1996 Villa Park staged the European Championship group match between Holland and Scotland, with the game finishing a goalless draw.

JUNE 11TH

1915 Frank Broome born in Berkhamsted. He was discovered by Villa whilst playing Spartan League football for Berkhamsted Town and given a trial, coming through this successfully and being offered professional forms. He made his debut in 1935 as an inside-forward but was later converted to outside-right and went on to earn seven caps for England. At the end of the Second World War he made just one appearance in the League before being transferred to Derby, making over 100 appearances for the Rams and then another 105 for Notts County. He finished his League career with Crewe Alexandra after a brief spell with Brentford, and finished playing altogether with Shelbourne in Ireland. He turned to management, taking over the reins at Exeter City and Southend United, coached in Australia and then had a second spell in charge at Exeter.

JUNE 12TH

1965 After 196 League appearances for Villa, Ron Wylie was sold to Birmingham City, thus leaving Villa Park for the first time. However, he would later return as coach, reserve-team coach and Community Liaison Officer, thereby spending four different spells with the club.

JUNE 13TH

1941 Tony Hateley born in Derby. First introduced to League football with Notts County, he scored 77 goals in just 131 League appearances and was transferred to Villa in August 1963 for £23,000. At Villa he showed he was capable of scoring goals at the highest level, netting 68 in 127 appearances before a £100,000 move to Chelsea in October 1966. At the end of the season, having helped them to the FA Cup final he was sold to Liverpool in another £100,000 move. After a year at Anfield he was sold to Coventry, remaining just less than a year before joining Birmingham City. After a second spell with Notts County he ended his career with Oldham Athletic. His son Mark also enjoyed a highly successful football career.

1975 Ricardo Scimeca born in Leamington Spa. Signed by Villa as a trainee, he was upgraded to the professional ranks in 1993. He had won five caps for England at Under-21 level.

1996 Villa Park staged the European Championship group match between Switzerland and Holland, with the Dutch winning 2–0.

JUNE 14TH

1968 After 146 League appearances goalkeeper Colin Withers was sold to Lincoln City, although he made only one appearance for the Imps before going off to play in Holland with the Go Ahead club.

JUNE 15TH

1996 Whilst Paul Gascoigne's goal grabbed most of the accolades, the England defence, including Gareth Southgate, performed heroics in the European Championship match against Scotland at Wembley. England went on to win 2–0.

JUNE 16TH

1987 Dean Glover was transferred to Middlesbrough after only 28 League appearances for Villa. He had also spent a brief spell on loan to Sheffield United prior to being sold to the Ayresome Park club.

JUNE 17TH

1960 Gary Williams born in Wolverhampton. Originally signed by the club as an apprentice, he made his debut in 1978 and enjoyed an extended run in the side until a bad injury brought his career to a temporary halt. He proved he had fully recovered during a loan spell with Walsall, during which he helped them gain promotion to the Third Division, and returned to Villa Park in time to help the club win the League title for the first time in 71 years. The following season he was a member of the side that won the European Cup and seemed on the verge of international recognition when selected for the England Under-21 side, but injury forced him to withdraw and he was not picked again. After 302 appearances for the Villa first team he was transferred to Leeds United, playing a handful of games before moving on to Watford and then Bradford City.

JUNE 18TH

1928 Stan Lynn born in Bolton. He began his League career with Accrington Stanley, making 25 appearances before switching to Villa for a fee of £10,000 in March 1951. A member of the side that won the FA Cup in 1957 and the League Cup in 1961 (although he only played in the first leg) he went on to make 323 appearances for the first team before switching across the city to Birmingham in 1961. There he helped them win the League Cup (against Villa!) before retiring in 1965.

1982 It was announced that Doug Ellis, the former Villa chairman and Birmingham director, had been appointed Wolves chairman, with debts at Molineux in the region of £2.5 million.

1984 Aston Villa manager Tony Barton was sacked from the club after being in charge since 1982. He had originally taken over as caretaker when Ron Saunders left the club and had guided them to the European Cup at the end of the season when it was announced he had been given the job on a permanent basis. However, results since then had slipped and the club had suffered early exits from both domestic cup competitions as well as finishing no higher than 10th the previous season. Barton's assistant Roy McLaren was also dismissed from the club at the same time.

1996 Villa Park staged the European Championship group match between Scotland and Switzerland, with the Scots winning 1–0.

JUNE 19TH

1910 Eric Houghton born in Billingborough in Lincolnshire. After playing as an amateur for Billingborough and Boston Town Eric was signed by Aston Villa as an amateur in August 1927 and upgraded to the professional ranks a year later. He made his debut in 1930 and went on to become a permanent fixture in the side for the next 16 years, although all he had to show for his efforts was a championship medal from the Second Division in 1938. However, he did score 170 goals in 392 appearances, an exceptional ratio. He finished his playing career with Notts County and returned to Villa Park in 1953 to take over as manager, guiding the team to the FA Cup in 1957. He was sacked in November 1958 and replaced by Joe Mercer.

1983 Nigel Spink made his debut for England in the 1–1 draw with Australia in Melbourne. Nigel was hardly at fault for the goal England conceded; it was turned past him by Phil Neil!

JUNE 20TH

1972 Alun Evans, the first teenager to change hands for £100,000 when Liverpool bought him in 1968, was now a 23 year old 'veteran' when Villa paid £72,000 to sign him from the Anfield club.

1979   After 100 appearances for Burnley Tony Morley joined Villa for a fee of £200,000. He had begun his career with Preston North End and after 99 first-team outings cost the Turf Moor club £100,000 when signed in February 1976. He remained with Villa for four and a half years, helping them win the League title and European Cup in successive seasons before moving across the city to West Bromwich Albion in December 1983 for £75,000.

JUNE 21ST

1944   John Dunn born in Barking. He joined Chelsea as an apprentice and graduated through the ranks, signing professional forms in February 1962. After a spell at Torquay he arrived at Villa Park in January 1968 and went on to make 101 League appearances in goal before finishing his career with Charlton.

1964   Dean Saunders born in Swansea. He joined the local club and made appearances on loan to Cardiff City before moving to Brighton and then Oxford United where he made his name as a regular goalscorer. He then joined Derby County, scoring 42 goals in 106 appearances before a £2.9 million move to Liverpool. After 42 appearances, during which time he scored 11 goals and won an FA Cup-winners' medal he moved on to Aston Villa for £2.3 million in 1992. He later played in Turkey before returning home and signing with Nottingham Forest and later playing for Sheffield United. He has made over 40 appearances for Wales, scoring 12 goals.

JUNE 22ND

1930   Billy Myerscough born in Bolton. He joined Walsall from non-League Ashfield in 1954 and switched to Villa Park in July 1955, going on to make 64 League appearances and scoring 15 goals for the club. He left in 1959 for Rotherham and later played for Coventry, Chester and Wrexham where he ended his career.

1944   Alan Baker born in Tipton. A former England Youth international, he turned professional with Villa in 1961 and spent five seasons with the club, moving on to Walsall in 1966. He retired from the game in 1972.

1980   Villa paid their then record fee of £500,000 for Newcastle United striker Peter Withe. He, perhaps more than any of the players purchased at the time, turned Villa into potential champions, not least because of his previous experience with Nottingham Forest where he had already won a championship medal. In 1982 he helped Villa achieve the highest accolade, European champions, by scoring the winning goal in the final against Bayern Munich.

JUNE 23RD

1972 Hereford United, newest members of the Football League at three weeks (they were elected at the annual meeting of the League on June 2nd) were drawn against one of the oldest in the first round of the League Cup; an away tie at Villa Park against Aston Villa.

1996 Villa Park staged the European Championship quarter-final between the Czech Republic and Portugal, with the Czechs winning 1–0. The game also produced the highest receipts from a match at Villa Park, £1,196,712.

JUNE 24TH

1959 Bobby Thomson was transferred from Wolves to Aston Villa after making only one appearance for the Molineux club! He had more joy at Villa Park, scoring on his debut and going on to help the club to two League Cup finals.

JUNE 25TH

1956 After 39 League appearances for Villa, right-half Larry Canning was sold to Northampton Town. He made only two appearances for Northampton, however, and then became a broadcaster for the BBC.

1963 Also on the move was Derek Dougan, off to London Road to join Peterborough United. He had made 51 League appearances in Villa's colours and would subsequently play for Leicester City and Wolves, later becoming chief executive at Molineux.

JUNE 26TH

1970 Three weeks after he had joined Birmingham City as Public Relations Officer, Ron Wylie resigned in order to take up the post of coach with Aston Villa!

1996 England and Germany played out an entertaining 1–1 draw in the semi-final of the European Championships at Wembley. With no goals in extra time, the game was settled by a penalty shoot-out. Gareth Southgate had his penalty saved and Germany went through 6–5, later winning the tournament with a 'golden goal' in extra time.

JUNE 27TH

1974 Trevor Hockey left Villa after 24 League appearances in order to rejoin his first club Bradford City.

1978 It was announced in the *Daily Express* that Villa had been awarded a government grant of £150,000 in order to develop facilities at Villa Park 'that can be used by the local community, integrating the playing staff. The money is to be used to develop outside pitches, floodlighting and general sports halls and to pay staff – called motivators – to organise and co-ordinate activities. The long-term repercussions of the project, simply called "Football and the Community", were spelled out by the game's top administrator League secretary Alan Hardaker. "What it means is that the State have at last accepted that the local professional soccer team can be the fulcrum on which a successful community can work. It is the greatest step forward that has taken place in football in the 20 years that I have been associated with the game."' Villa were one of 18 clubs to have been awarded a grant, ranging from the £5,000 given to Wolves and West Bromwich Albion to the full £150,000 awarded to Aston Villa.

JUNE 28TH

1977 Defender Chris Nicholl was sold to Southampton for £60,000 after five years at Villa Park, during which time he had helped the club to two League Cup wins. In his first season with Southampton he helped them gain promotion to the First Division.

JUNE 29TH

1977 Villa signed Northampton defender John Gregory for £40,000, who would go on to make 65 appearances for the club before joining Brighton and Hove Albion. He returned to Villa in 1998 as manager in place of Brian Little.

JUNE 30TH

1990 Former Villa player and Bournemouth chief executive Brian Tiler was killed in a car crash in Italy, an accident that also left then Bournemouth and now West Ham boss Harry Redknapp seriously injured. Brian had made 106 League appearances for the side between 1968 and 1972 and had been a member of the sides that reached the League Cup final in 1971 and won the Third Division title the following season.

JULY 1ST

1985 Italian Serie A club Bari paid £400,000 for Villa striker Paul Rideout. He had been with the club for two years following his transfer from Swindon and would spend three years in Italy before coming home with Southampton.

1995 Aston Villa accepted an offer of £2.35 million for striker Dean Saunders from Turkish side Galatasaray. He had joined Villa in February 1992 for £2.9 million from Liverpool, where he had won an FA Cup winners' medal, adding to his haul with Villa in the League Cup in 1994. The move to Turkey reunited him with Graeme Souness, his former manager at Liverpool. The money Villa received barely had time to clear the bank, for on the same day Villa paid £2.5 million to bring Gareth Southgate from Crystal Palace. Although Palace had been relegated after only one season in the Premier League, Southgate's performances in midfield had not gone unnoticed by the bigger clubs, prompting a Villa swoop to land their man.

JULY 2ND

1977 Ray Graydon left Villa after 193 League appearances for Coventry City, although his contract with the Highfield Road club was cancelled the following March and he went to play in North America.

JULY 3RD

1946 Bobby Park born in Edinburgh. He joined Villa as an apprentice and was upgraded to the professional ranks in July 1963, going on to make 73 League appearances and scoring seven goals for the club. He left in May 1969 for Wrexham and later played for Peterborough, Northampton and Hartlepool.

1954 Gordon Smith born in Glasgow. A Scottish youth international, he began his career with St Johnstone and had won four caps for the Scottish Under-23 side by the time Villa bought him for £80,000 in August 1976. He won a winners' medal in the 1977 League Cup, albeit as a substitute, but struggled to command a regular place in the side. He was sold to Spurs for £150,000 in February 1979, by which time he had made 79 League appearances for the club, and after finishing his League career with Wolves went to play in South Africa and North America.

1979 Brian Little agreed to move from Aston Villa to Birmingham City in a deal worth a reported £160,000, with Villa having already earmarked the money for a swoop on Grimsby's Terry Donovan. Although Donovan eventually joined the club, the money had to come from elsewhere; Brian Little failed a medical examination and the move to Birmingham fell through.

1987 Chelsea paid Villa £475,000 for defender Tony Dorigo. He had originally joined the club as an apprentice and made 111 League appearances for the club before Chelsea signed him, and he later went on to represent England despite having been born in Melbourne, Australia.

JULY 4TH

1962 Alfie Hale was sold to Doncaster Rovers after just five appearances for Villa. He was spotted by the club whilst playing in Ireland for Waterford and signed for Villa in June 1960, but found a first-team place difficult to come by at Villa Park. No such problems at Belle Vue however, for he made 119 appearances at inside-forward, scoring 42 goals. He later played for Newport County and won 13 caps for the Republic of Ireland.

JULY 5TH

1916 Ivor Powell born in Bargoed. He first turned professional with Queens Park Rangers in 1937 and remained with the club throughout the war before signing for Villa in December 1948. He went on to make 79 appearances for the club in the League as well as earning four caps for Wales. He was injured in October 1950 and unable to regain his place in the side, prompting a move to Port Vale in the summer of 1951. After only six games for the Vale Park club he joined Bradford City as player-manager.

1993 Gordon Cowans returned to Villa on a free transfer from Blackburn Rovers, so beginning his third spell with the club.

1995 Mark Draper signed for Aston Villa in a £3.25 million deal with Leicester City. Villa manager Brian Little had tried to sign the player before the transfer deadline day for a fee of £3 million but that bid had been turned down by the Filbert Street club. The extra three months or so wait to get their man cost the club an additional £250,000.

JULY 6TH

1946 Fred Mwila born in Zambia. One of the earliest African players to have appeared in the Football League, he joined Villa in September 1969 along with Emment Kapenge with high hopes for his future, but after only one game he returned home again.

1984 Manchester United manager Ron Atkinson revealed he had been offered the job of manager of Aston Villa but had decided to remain at Old Trafford. Villa had recently parted company with manager Tony Barton and were eventually to replace him with the former Shrewsbury manager Graham Turner.

JULY 7TH

1998 David Platt announced his retirement as a player in order to pursue a career in management. The former England and Villa player still had a year left to run on his contract with Arsenal but announced that he intended travelling around the world for the next 12 months or so observing coaching techniques at first hand. He also said that he had already been offered a couple of player-manager roles but had turned them down in order to gain experience that would serve him in good stead come the millennium – what price a future return to Villa Park?

JULY 8TH

1994 Steve Froggatt joined Wolves in a deal worth £1.5 million, having been with Villa since 1991.

1998 Stan Collymore reported back from training ahead of his team-mates on the advice of manager John Gregory. Aside from a disappointing season with Villa Collymore had endured a nightmare during the summer, being heavily criticised for publicly assaulting his girlfriend Ulrika Jonsson in Paris during the World Cup tournament. Gregory had already stated that Collymore had around a month to prove he had a future at Villa Park; if Collymore wasn't in the starting line-up for the opening game against Everton, then questions would be asked!

JULY 9TH

1979 John Gregory was sold to Brighton for a fee of £300,000, then a record for the Goldstone Road club. John had made 65 League appearances for Villa since his transfer from Northampton and would later play for Queens Park Rangers in the 1982 FA Cup final. He returned to Villa in 1998 as manager in place of the recently resigned Brian Little.

JULY 10TH

1979 Villa banked a further £150,000 with the sale of Tommy Craig to Swansea City, a then record fee for the Vetch Field club. Tommy had made 27 League appearances for Villa since joining the club from Newcastle United and proved to be an important acquisition for Swansea as they looked to consolidate their Second Division status.

JULY 11TH

1925 Eddie Lowe born in Hawne. Signed by Villa in the summer of 1945, he made 104 appearances for the League side, winning three caps for England (he was the first Villa player to be so honoured after the Second World War) before switching to Fulham in 1950. He then made 474 appearances for the Craven Cottage club and finished his League career with Notts County in 1964 where he was also player-manager. His brother Reg was also on Villa's books at one point but left for Fulham without having played for the Villa first team.

1991 Aston Villa paid £1.7 million to Real Sociedad in order to bring Dalian Atkinson back home to England. Atkinson had spent a year with the Spanish club and went on to help Villa win the League Cup three years later.

JULY 12TH

1991 After just two substitute appearances for West Bromwich Albion, where he has been since signing as a trainee, Ugo Ehiogu was signed by Aston Villa for £40,000. His subsequent development into one of the best defenders in the game proved the money to have been well spent.

JULY 13TH

1934 Gordon Lee born in Hednesford. Originally signed by Villa in 1955, he had to wait until he had completed his National Service before making his debut in 1958. He went on to make 142 first-team appearances before switching to Shrewsbury in 1966 as player-manager. In 1968 he went to Vale Park as manager of Port Vale, later spending spells in charge at Blackburn Rovers, Newcastle United, Everton, Preston North End and Reykjavik in Iceland, subsequently becoming assistant to David Pleat at Leicester. He took over as caretaker when Pleat left, but was subsequently sacked.

1966 Villa Park staged the World Cup Group 2 match between Argentina and Spain which was won by the Argentines 2–1 on their way to the quarter-finals in front of a crowd of 42,738.

1979 Terry Donovan was transferred from Grimsby Town to Aston Villa.

JULY 14TH

1988 Gordon Cowans arrived back in Birmingham after a £250,000 transfer from Bari. He had spent three years with the Italian side after helping Villa win the First Division title and European Cup in successive seasons at the start of the decade, and with Villa due to start the coming season back in the First Division, his experience would be vital.

1994 Dariusz Kubicki's transfer to Sunderland was made permanent, the Roker Park club paying a fee of £100,000 for the Polish-born player. Kubicki had gone on loan to Sunderland in March.

JULY 15TH

1943 Evan Williams born in Dumbarton. He joined Wolves from Third Lanark and spent a brief spell on loan to Villa during the 1969–70 season, appearing in goal on 12 occasions.

1950 John Robson born in Consett. Spotted by Derby whilst playing for Birtley Youth Club, he was signed as a professional in October 1967 and went on to make 171 League appearances for the Rams before switching to Villa in 1972 for £90,000. Although originally signed as a defender he was successfully converted to midfield and helped the club win the League Cup in 1975 and seemed assured of a lengthy career at Villa Park until he was diagnosed as suffering from multiple sclerosis and forced to retire.

1985 Former Villa player Andy Gray returned home, signed from Everton where he had just helped the club win the League title and European Cup-Winners' Cup the previous season.

JULY 16TH

1966 Villa Park staged the World Cup Group 2 match between Argentina and West Germany, with the game finishing goalless in front of a crowd of 46,487. However, the main controversy surrounded the dismissal of Albrecht of Argentina for repeated dangerous play, with the Argentinians (and later the Uruguayans) claiming that there was a European conspiracy against South American sides!

JULY 17TH

1987 Wimbledon defender Kevin Gage joined Villa in a move worth £100,000. Over the next four years he proved himself a solid and reliable performer for the club, making 138 first-team appearances before a £150,000 move to Sheffield United.

1995 Brian Little paid £3.5 million to Partizan Belgrade of Yugoslavia for striker Savo Milosevic, even though he had not seen him play, relying on a video produced by the player's agent! Although he took time to settle at Villa he finished his first season with a winners' medal in the League Cup, scoring the first goal in the game against Leeds United at Wembley.

JULY 18TH

1984 Aston Villa appointed Graham Turner as manager in succession to Tony Barton who had recently left the club. Villa had originally approached Ron Atkinson, then manager of Manchester United but been turned down and had then targeted Turner, the manager of Shrewsbury Town. His ability to operate on a shoestring at Gay Meadow had not gone unnoticed by the bigger clubs, and when Villa offered him the position he had little difficulty accepting.

JULY 19TH

1991 Tony Cascarino was sold to Celtic for a fee of £1.1 million, whilst Barnsley handed over a slightly smaller cheque for Lee Butler at £165,000.

1994 After 57 first-team appearances for the Villa Neil Cox was transferred to Middlesbrough for a fee of £1 million. He had been with the club since February 1991 having joined from Scunthorpe United.

JULY 20TH

1885 The Football Association agreed to allow professionalism. This was to be an important step, not least for the likes of Villa and Preston, because it now allowed them to attract the best players and reward them for their efforts. There were restrictions however, and no player could play in an FA Cup match before he had resided in the local area for at least two years.

1966 Villa Park staged its last World Cup Group 2 match with West Germany beating Spain 2–1 in front of a crowd of 45,187.

1976 After 249 appearances in Villa's colours Ian 'Chico' Hamilton was released to sign for Sheffield United.

1947 Ray Graydon born in Bristol. After joining Bristol Rovers as an apprentice he was upgraded to the professional ranks in 1965 and went on to make 132 League appearances for the club before switching to Villa Park. In six years with the club he won two League Cup winners' medals and left in 1977 to join Coventry City. After only one season he went to play in America, returning in November 1978 to finish his League career with Oxford United.

1963 Kevin Poole born in Bromsgrove. A product of Villa's youth scheme, he found competition for the number one spot at Villa particularly keen and had a spell on loan to Northampton before being released by the club and subsequently joined Middlesbrough.

1977 Chris Nicholl moved on from Villa Park to Southampton for a fee of £90,000. He had joined Villa in 1972 from Luton and helped the club win two League Cups.

1988 Frank Brett died in Chichester. Born in Kings Norton on 10th March 1899, Frank arrived at Old Trafford in February 1921 having been spotted playing for Redditch. A fee of £300 was agreed, but it then transpired that he had earlier signed amateur forms with Aston Villa, with whom United were unable to come to terms over his transfer. The matter was subsequently put before the FA, who fined United ten guineas for having registered him before his transfer from Villa had come through. In August 1922 Frank returned to Villa but had little success, later moving on to Northampton Town and then Brighton and Hove Albion.

1970 Despite being relegated to the Third Division for the first time in their history, Villa still managed to announce a profit for the season of £35,695, with gate receipts up by £50,000 over the course of the campaign.

1991 Aston Villa and Bari completed the transfer of David Platt for £5.5 million, the then record transfer fee involving a British player.

1963 Andy Townsend born in Maidstone. After spells with non-League Welling United and Weymouth he was introduced to the League with Southampton, although he had to go to Norwich in order to gain regular football. He joined Chelsea in 1990 for £1.2 million (he had cost Southampton £35,000 and Norwich £300,000 on his previous travels) and developed into a highly respected midfield player and motivator, and in 1993 he joined Villa for £2.1 million. A member of the side that won the League Cup in 1994 and 1996, he also represented the Republic of

Ireland on numerous occasions whilst with Villa and in 1998 made a return to Wembley with Middlesbrough in the Coca-Cola Cup.

1990 Villa's new manager in place of the England-bound Graham Taylor, 54 year old Jozef Venglos, began work at Villa Park. He had previously been manager of the Malaysian, Austrian and Czech national sides (he had guided Czechoslovakia to the World Cup quarter-finals earlier in the summer), Slovan Bratislava, Sporting Lisbon and Kuala Lumpar and was seen as an adventurous appointment by Villa, one of the first non-British managers to be given the top job at one of the biggest clubs in the country.

JULY 24TH

1966 Martin Keown born in Oxford. Signed by Arsenal as an apprentice, he rose through the ranks to become a first-team player but his inability to hold a regular spot in the first team led him to request a transfer, signing for Aston Villa in 1986 for £200,000. He made 133 games for the club before a £750,000 deal took him to Everton, where he earned his first cap for England in 1992. He returned to Highbury in 1993 for a fee of £2 million and helped them to the double in 1998.

1991 Villa paid £350,000 to Charlton Athletic for midfield player Paul Mortimer, but after only 14 first-team appearances he was on his way to Crystal Palace, finally arriving back at Charlton in 1994.

JULY 25TH

1991 After glowing reports of the form of Shaun Teale, Villa handed over a cheque for £300,000 to bring him to Villa Park. He had begun with non-League Weymouth and cost Bournemouth £50,000 when signed in January 1989, quickly developing into one of the best defenders in the lower divisions. He was to spend four years with Villa before switching to Tranmere Rovers.

JULY 26TH

1982 Brian Little was appointed youth team coach at Villa Park. In 1994 he was appointed first-team manager.

1993 Chelsea midfield player Andy Townsend joined Villa for a fee of £2.1 million and would go on to help the club lift two League Cups during his seven years at Villa Park.

1996 Aston Villa paid Sporting Lisbon of Portugal £1.75 million in order to bring midfield player Fernando Nelson to Villa Park. A full Portuguese international player he made his debut for Villa in the third game of the following season against Derby and quickly settled into the side.

JULY 27TH

1987 Alan McInally joined the club from Celtic, having started his career with Ayr United. In his first season at Villa Park he scored only four goals in 25 League appearances.

JULY 28TH

1992 Ray Houghton signed for Aston Villa for a fee of £900,000 after nearly five years at Anfield with Liverpool. During his time with Liverpool he won the League twice and the FA Cup twice, and two years after joining Villa would collect his second League Cup winners' medal, the first coming with Oxford in 1986.

JULY 29TH

1959 Villa signed Raith Rovers' leading goalscorer for the previous three seasons, Jimmy McEwan, for £8,000. At the end of his first season with the club he had helped them back into the First Division and the following season to the final of the League Cup. He remained at Villa Park for seven years before joining Walsall.

JULY 30TH

1987 After 240 League appearances for Villa, defender Gary Williams was transferred to Leeds United, later playing for Watford and Bradford City.

JULY 31ST

1960 Jimmy Cantrell died in Basford at the age of 78. Born in Sheepbridge, near Chesterfield on May 7th 1882, he had represented Chesterfield Schools and then gone on to play for Bulwell Red Rose and Bulwell Whitestar before joining Hucknall Constitutional FC. Spotted by Villa whilst playing for this club he was signed in July 1904 and played for the club for four seasons as centre-forward, leaving in March 1908 for Notts County. Four years later he joined Spurs where he helped them win the FA Cup in 1921 and later played for Sutton Town before retiring. He then became a professional golf player.

AUGUST 1ST

1917 Tommy Southren born in Sunderland. He was playing for Peartree Old Boys when spotted by West Ham and joined the London club in December 1949. Five years later he came to Villa Park and went on to make 63 appearances on the wing for the club, subsequently leaving for Bournemouth in October 1958.

1993 Villa paid Portsmouth £1.2 million for striker Guy Whittingham. The former soldier (he had bought himself out of the army in order to pursue a career in professional football) had scored 88 goals for Portsmouth in 160 League appearances but was ultimately to find the going somewhat tougher at Villa Park and was sold to Sheffield Wednesday for £700,000 in 1994 after a loan spell with Wolves.

AUGUST 2ND

1976 Villa paid £80,000 to Scottish club St Johnstone for defender Gordon Smith. He would remain with the club for two and a half years before moving to Spurs.

AUGUST 3RD

1989 One of the greatest pieces of transfer business Villa have ever conducted; a fee of £400,000 brought Manchester United defender Paul McGrath to Villa Park. United manager Alex Ferguson believed Paul to be too prone to injury, but whilst he frequently missed training through stress or strain, he was never found wanting on the field when it mattered. He confounded all of his critics, spending seven years with Villa and twice helping the club win the League Cup, and went on to become Villa's most capped player with 51 appearances for the Republic of Ireland to his credit. When he left in 1996 he went to Derby, and even then Villa fans thought he'd been shown the door too early!

AUGUST 4TH

1905 Following violent incidents in the games between Manchester City and Aston Villa and Manchester City and Everton, both of which occurred at the end of the 1904–05 season, and an FA Commission which looked into matters relating to these matches, the FA announced that Billy Meredith, Manchester City's captain, was to be suspended for one season for attempting to bribe his Aston Villa counterpart with £10. The case, understandably, was a sensation, not least because Meredith took no part in either game! Nor was this the end of the matter, for later the following season Meredith was reported to the FA by Manchester City for attempting to obtain his normal wages. When Meredith was brought before the FA he revealed a letter written by a Manchester City director which indicated that the original bribery attempt was made with the blessing of the club and that Meredith would be looked after in the event anything went wrong. This time the FA came down like a ton of bricks; City were fined £250, the secretary and chairman suspended from football for life, the other directors ordered to resign, 17 players suspended until 1st January 1907 and forbidden ever to play for City again. Billy Meredith denied the charge of bribery at the time, claiming he was being made a scapegoat, although he later admitted to having made the attempt, saying he had been asked to do so by a City director. He was lucky he was not banned from football for life, a fate that befell Enoch West when he was found guilty of similar activities in 1915 (in a match that Meredith also played in!).

1956 Steve Hunt born in Birmingham. His first spell at Villa Park was not a success and he left to join New York Cosmos for £50,000, helping them win the NASL Championships in 1977 and 1978, returning to England with Coventry in September the same year. An £80,000 transfer took him to West Bromwich Albion in 1984 and he won two caps for England during his time at the Hawthorns. He returned to Villa in a £90,000-plus-Darren-Bradley deal and he finished his career with the club when injury forced his retirement in 1987.

AUGUST 5TH

1944 With the successful completion of the Normandy invasion, some of the travel restrictions that had been in force earlier in the war were relaxed (when Singapore had fallen, the resultant drop in the availability of rubber had caused a shortage of footballs!) and Villa were able to travel to Edinburgh to play an Edinburgh Select XI which ended in a 4–4 draw.

1972 Villa Park staged the FA Charity Shield between Villa and Manchester City, with the First Division visitors winning 1–0 thanks to a goal from Francis Lee from the penalty spot in the first half.

AUGUST 6TH

1933 Ron Wylie born in Glasgow. Signed by Notts County from Clydesdale in September 1950, he made 227 games for the Meadow Lane club and cost Villa £9,250 when he joined in November 1958. Settling into the inside left spot he formed an effective partnership with Peter McParland and helped the club win promotion in 1960 and the League Cup the following year. In June 1965 he joined Birmingham City after 245 appearances in Villa's colours, and when his playing career ended he returned to Villa Park in the capacity of coach. He then had spells coaching with Coventry and in Cyprus and Hong Kong. He was appointed manager of West Bromwich Albion in 1982 and when he lost this job returned to Villa Park a third time to coach the reserve side. Although this job came to an end following the appointment of Graham Taylor, Ron Wylie made a fourth return to Villa as the club's Community Liaison Officer.

1957 John Deehan born in Birmingham. A member of the side that won the League Cup in 1977, he made over 100 appearances for the first team before being sold to West Bromwich Albion in September 1979. A little over two years later he was on the move again, joining Norwich City and helping them to the League Cup in 1985. He later played for Ipswich Town, Manchester City and Barnsley and then switched to management and coaching, returning to Carrow Road as manager in 1994. He resigned in 1995 and took over the reins at Wigan Athletic.

1991 Villa paid £450,000 to Real Sociedad to bring Kevin Richardson back to English football after one season with the Spanish side. He went on to make 170 appearances in Villa's colours before a £300,000 move to Coventry in February 1995.

AUGUST 7TH

1989 A fee of £750,000 took Villa defender Martin Keown to Everton. He had been with Villa since June 1986 and was a regular member of the Villa defence during his time with the club, having made 133 appearances for the first team.

1991 Coming in from Merseyside was Liverpool defender Steve Staunton who cost Villa £1.1 million from the Anfield club. A surprise sale by Liverpool, Staunton had helped the club win the FA Cup in 1989 and the League title the following year, as well as being a regular in the Republic of Ireland side. However, he had been unable to gain a regular place in the Liverpool side, appearing in six different positions during the last campaign.

AUGUST 8TH

1958 Nigel Spink born in Chelmsford. He joined Villa from Chelmsford City in 1977 and made his debut in 1979. In May 1982 he was thrown into the spotlight when called upon to replace the injured Jimmy Rimmer eight minutes into the European Cup final in Rotterdam, but he performed heroics to ensure a Villa victory. By 1982–83 he had made the goalkeeper's position his own and at the end of the season won his only cap for England. He helped the club win the League Cup in 1994 before losing his place to Mark Bosnich and was subsequently allowed to join West Bromwich Albion on a free transfer in 1996.

AUGUST 9TH

1914 Joe Mercer born in Ellesmere Port. He joined Everton as a youngster and won a League championship medal with them before the war as well as establishing himself as a regular member of the England side. If the Second World War had not interrupted his career there might have been no end to the honours he picked up, but he resumed his career in 1946 with Everton, despite a knee injury, until December 1946, when Tom Whittaker paid £7,000 to take him to Arsenal (although Mercer was allowed to continue training with Everton and travel down to London on match days). With Mercer's experience the guiding light, Arsenal won two League championships and he made one winning and one losing appearance in the FA Cup final until a broken leg in 1954 finished his career at the age of 40. He moved on to management, taking over at Sheffield United and then replacing Eric Houghton at Aston Villa in

December 1958, restoring them to the First Division, winning the League Cup in 1961 and making the final in 1963. He suffered a stroke in 1964 and was forced to retire, but returned with Manchester City, where, in tandem with Malcolm Allison, he led them to the League title in 1967–68, the FA Cup in 1969 (thus becoming the first man to have captained and managed an FA Cup winning team at Wembley) and the European Cup-Winners' Cup and League Cup in 1970. He became general manager in 1971 before retiring in 1972, although he was briefly caretaker manager of England. A former Footballer of the Year in 1950 he died in August 1990.

1931 Nigel Sims born in Cotton-in-Elms. He spent eight seasons with Wolves but was unable to displace England international Bert Williams from goal and so moved to Villa in March 1956 in search of a regular spot in the side. He helped the club win the FA Cup in 1957 and the League Cup in 1961 and made 309 appearances for the side before moving to Peterborough in September 1964. A short while later he headed for Canada, returning to England after six years.

1953 Villa kicked off the new season with a 1–0 defeat by Spurs at White Hart Lane, but manager George Martin had already departed, the victim of boardroom unrest. He had been a player before the Second World War with Hull City and Everton, helping the latter club to the League title in 1930–31, before taking over as manager at Luton Town. He then led Newcastle to the Second Division title in 1948, but was unable to settle in the North East and joined Villa in December 1950. He later returned to management with Luton after a spell as scout, but was undoubtedly a man of many talents, making a number of records in the 1940s and also earning a reputation as a sculptor!

AUGUST 10TH

1968 A 3–1 defeat at Bramall Lane against Sheffield United seemed to set the scene for the rest of the season; only two games were won away from home and only ten points picked up on their travels, with the result that Villa were involved in the relegation dogfight for most of the season. A final placing of 18th in the Second Division was the lowest in Villa's history, although it got worse before it started to get better.

AUGUST 11TH

1917 Albert Kerr born in Lancaster. He joined Villa in 1936 and made his debut at the beginning of the 1936–37 season. He was a regular in the side in 1938–39 until a hip injury allowed Frank Broome to take his place and Albert Kerr was unable to get back into the side. Unfortunately the Second World War cut right across his career and in the 1946–47 season he made just one appearance when injury forced him to retire. He died in 1979.

AUGUST 12TH

1972 After an absence of two years Villa returned to the Second Division, winning 1–0 at Deepdale against Preston thanks to a second-half goal from Willie Anderson in front of a crowd of 17,371.

AUGUST 13TH

1997 The new season saw Villa full of confidence, having qualified for Europe the previous campaign, and Stan Collymore arriving to link with Savo Milosevic and Dwight Yorke in one of the most potent strike forces in the Premiership. Despite a 1–0 defeat at Leicester on the opening day, the first game at Villa Park saw a crowd of 37,112 looking forward to the coming months. Blackburn brought them back down to earth with a bump, winning 4–0 with Chris Sutton scoring a hat-trick.

AUGUST 14TH

1964 Paul Rideout born in Bournemouth. After graduating through the ranks with Swindon he was transferred to Aston Villa in 1983 for £200,000 and spent five years at Villa Park before a £400,000 move to Bari. He returned to play for Southampton and had a brief spell with Notts County before he was surprisingly sold to Glasgow Rangers for £500,000, spending seven months in Glasgow before joining Everton for a similar fee. Scorer of the goal that won the FA Cup in 1995, he later went to play in China.

1971 What was to be Villa's championship-winning season in the Third Division kicked off with a 3–1 win over Plymouth Argyle (the first visitors to Villa Park the previous season, Villa's debut in the Third Division) with the goals coming from Geoff Vowden, Pat McMahon and a Willie Anderson penalty. A crowd of 26,327 were present for the start of a momentous season.

1995 After four years with Aston Villa Shaun Teale was sold to Tranmere Rovers for £450,000. He had joined Villa in 1991 from Bournemouth for £300,000 and made 153 first-team games before his transfer.

AUGUST 15TH

1970 Villa kicked off their first season in the Third Division with a 3–2 win at Chesterfield thanks to goals from Pat McMahon and Bruce Rioch who scored twice. The novelty of having them in their division saw many clubs register attendances well above average whenever Villa were in town, with 16,750 at the Recreation Ground for the opening day of the season.

1987 Six years previously, Villa and Ipswich had been locked in battle for the First Division title; today they both kicked off the season in search of

Second Division points. A 1–1 draw at Portman Road gave them one apiece, but at the end of the season it was Villa who were headed back to the top, promoted in second place.

AUGUST 16TH

1972 The League's newest members Hereford United kicked off their League Cup campaign at the home of one of the oldest; Villa Park, where 32,314 saw Villa win easily enough 4–1 thanks to goals from Bruce Rioch, Ray Graydon, Geoff Vowden and Alun Evans.

1975 After an absence of eight years, Villa Park embraced First Division football again with the visit of the previous season's European Cup finalists Leeds United. A crowd of 46,026 saw Leighton Phillips score the goal all Villa fans had dreamed about during the dark days of the Third Division, but two strikes from Peter Lorimer brought them back down to earth with a bump. The coming nine months were at times a struggle as Villa tried to adapt to life in the top flight, but thankfully they found their form at the right time and pulled clear of trouble.

1980 The start of one of the most glorious seasons in Villa's history kicked off with a convincing 2–1 win at Elland Road against Leeds, Tony Morley and Gary Shaw scoring the goals that gave hope for the future months.

AUGUST 17TH

1928 Pat Saward born in York. After a spell with Crystal Palace as an amateur he joined the professional ranks with Millwall in July 1951 and enjoyed four years at The Den before joining Villa for £7,000 in 1955. He remained at Villa Park for six years, helping the club win the FA Cup in 1957 and the Second Division title in 1960 as well as collecting 13 of his 18 caps for the Republic of Ireland. He joined Huddersfield in 1961 after 152 appearances in the Villa League side and became player-coach at Coventry in 1963. After a spell in charge at Coventry he later coached in Saudi Arabia.

1974 What was to become the season that Villa restored themselves to their rightful place in the First Division began with hardly the most auspicious of starts, a 1–1 draw at Bootham Crescent against York, Villa's goal coming from Ray Graydon.

1991 When the fixture list decreed that Aston Villa should visit Sheffield Wednesday for their opening game of the season, the choice could hardly have been worse, for Villa's new manager Ron Atkinson had resigned from Wednesday in order to take over at Villa Park! He was assured of a hostile reception from the home fans among the 36,749 crowd but fortunately Villa soon quietened them, winning an entertaining game 3–2.

AUGUST 18TH

1951 A topsy turvy season began with a 5–2 drubbing at Burnden Park against

Bolton Wanderers, although Villa would recover and finish the campaign in sixth place, albeit ten points off champions Manchester United.

1971 Despite having reached the final of the League Cup the previous season Villa's status as a Third Division side still dictated that they enter the competition at the first-round stage, and they received a home draw with Wrexham. They were held on the night too, Andy Lochhead and Willie Anderson from the penalty spot scoring Villa's goals in the 2–2 draw in front of a crowd of 24,552.

AUGUST 19TH

1970 As a result of relegation to the Third Division Villa were required to enter the League Cup at the earliest possible stage, the first round. This brought them a clash with the oldest Football League club Notts County and 17,843 were at Villa Park for the tie. County's chances weren't helped by having John Hobson sent off, and goals from Willie Anderson, Pat McMahon, Bruch Rioch and Chico Hamilton gave Villa an easy 4–0 win and the start of a run that would lead all the way to Wembley and the final.

1972 Second Division football returned to Villa Park with the visit of Huddersfield Town attracting a crowd of 34,843. Having won their opening game of the season (at Preston) Villa were in a confident mood and goals from Geoff Vowden and Ray Graydon ensured the 100% record was maintained in a 2–0 win.

AUGUST 20TH

1915 Vic Potts born in Birmingham. He joined Spurs in 1934 and was sent to the club's Northfleet nursery club but began his League career with Doncaster Rovers, spending one season with the club before the outbreak of the Second World War. His work brought him back to the Midlands during this time and he guested for Villa during the war, subsequently signing permanently at the end of the hostilities. He made 72 appearances for the first team before being forced to retire owing to injury, going on to become reserve-team coach at Notts County and then Walsall.

1943 George Cummings' *sine die* ban from the game was lifted after only seven months and within a year he was representing Scotland.

1960 Villa announced their return to the First Division with a 3–2 win over Chelsea at Villa Park.

1961 Steve McMahon born in Liverpool. He graduated through the ranks at Everton and made over 100 appearances for the club until sold to Aston Villa for £175,000 in 1983. At Villa Park he made 87 appearances for the first team before he returned to Merseyside, this time with Liverpool, in 1985 for £375,000 and won a host of honours and medals, including 17 caps for England. He then moved on to Manchester City in 1991 and became player-manager at Swindon in 1994.

AUGUST 21ST

1976 West Ham put up a spirited first-half display to thwart Villa in the opening game of the season at Villa Park, watched by a crowd of 39,012. Villa responded to the challenge in the second half, forcing open the Hammers defence time and again, finally running out 4–0 winners thanks to a brace of goals apiece from Andy Gray and Ray Graydon, one of Graydon's goals coming from the penalty spot.

1991 After a fine win at Sheffield Wednesday on the Saturday, the visit of Manchester United held no fears for the first game of the new season at Villa Park. A crowd of 39,995, what was to be the biggest of the season at Villa Park went home deflated when Steve Bruce converted a penalty in the first half for the visitors to register the only goal of the game.

AUGUST 22ND

1959 Villa's first Second Division match since 1938 saw them at the Goldstone Ground to face Brighton and Hove Albion, and despite a late goal from Jackie Sewell in the 2–1 win, they did not look comfortable with life in the lower League. Over the next nine months however, they would prove themselves too good for the rest of the opposition.

1961 Aston Villa had been one of the few First Division clubs to have welcomed the introduction of the Football League Cup, although their progress had at times belied their status. They made it to the final of the 1960–61 final, the two games being held over until the beginning of the following season owing to a fixture pile-up. The first leg of the first final was held at Rotherham, with the lowly Second Division club recording a 2–0 win in front of only 12,226 spectators.

1964 By the time Villa kicked off the new campaign with a 2–1 home defeat by Leeds United, Dick Taylor had been confirmed as the club's new manager. He had taken over on a caretaker basis the previous January following Joe Mercer's resignation through ill-health and had then steered the club away from relegation. His reward was the job on a permanent basis.

1970 Villa's first Third Division match at home drew 29,205 (one of the biggest gates of the day!) to Villa Park for the visit of Plymouth Argyle, with Pat McMahon scoring in the first half to earn a 1–1 draw. Despite the dropped point Villa were still expected to be challenging for promotion at the end of the season.

1982 League champions Villa were at Wembley for the annual curtain raiser to the new season, the FA Charity Shield against FA Cup holders Spurs. In a closely fought and evenly matched game, both sides had their own heroes, Peter Withe for Villa and Mark Falco for Spurs, both players scoring twice to ensure the shield was shared for six months apiece.

AUGUST 23RD

1971 After being held to a 2–2 draw at home to Wrexham in the League Cup first round the action switched to the Racecourse Ground. Another draw, this time 1–1 after extra time, meant a third meeting between the two sides. The selection of West Bromwich's Hawthorns ground meant it would be almost a home game for Villa.

1975 Villa were left still searching their first win back in the First Division after an entertaining but fruitless game at Norwich, Villa going down 5–3. Charlie Aitken scored the last of his 16 League goals for the club and there were two strikes for Ray Graydon, the club's top scorer that season with 12, but it was Villa's defence that let them down on the day.

1997 Another blank sheet on the 'goals for' column as Villa went down 1–0 at St James' Park against Newcastle United. It was their third defeat in a row and left Villa anchored at the bottom of the table when the media compiled the first of the campaign; come next May they'd qualified for Europe.

AUGUST 24TH

1928 Tommy Docherty born in Glasgow. After a distinguished playing career with Celtic, Preston, Arsenal and Chelsea he began his managerial career with Chelsea, guiding them to finals of the League Cup and FA Cup after taking over from Ted Drake. He left Chelsea in 1968 in order to take over at Rotherham United, Queens Park Rangers and then Aston Villa, all in the space of six weeks! Appointed at Villa Park in December 1968 he made the promise he would take them out of the Second Division – he did; they were relegated to the Third Division for the first time in their history. By then Docherty had already left, and after a spell managing in Portugal he was appointed manager of Scotland. He then accepted the position of manager at Old Trafford and guided them to the FA Cup but was dismissed after admitting to having an affair with the wife of the club's physiotherapist. After other managerial positions he became an after-dinner speaker.

1991 Villa bounced back from the disappointment of a home defeat by Manchester United with a convincing 3–1 win over the League champions Arsenal at Villa Park. Steve Staunton from the penalty spot, Gary Penrice and Tony Daley scored the goals that spiked the Gunners.

AUGUST 25TH

1934 Jimmy Allen made his debut for the club in the opening game of the season, a 2–1 defeat at Birmingham City. He joined Villa at the end of the previous season (during which he helped Portsmouth to the FA Cup final), costing a then record fee of £10,775 for a player who had already collected two caps for England. He went on to make 160 appearances for the first team before the outbreak of the Second World War, during which he guested for Birmingham City, Fulham and Portsmouth.

1958 Villa Park switched on its floodlights for the first time and the crowd were able to see goals from Myerscough, Dixon and McParland overcome Portsmouth. The official inauguration of the lights did not take place until November with a visit from Hearts for a friendly match.

AUGUST 26TH

1939 Villa kicked off the new season with a 2–0 home win over Middlesbrough. This was also the first time players wore numbers in the League, a move which had been passed at the League's annual meeting during the summer.

1954 Tony Morley born in Omskirk. Signed by Preston as an apprentice, he made 99 first-team appearances for the Deepdale outfit before a £100,000 move took him to Burnley in February 1976. His form at Turf Moor soon had bigger clubs in the hunt for his signature and a £200,000 fee saw him signing for Villa in June 1979. A member of the side that won the First Division title in 1981 and the European Cup the following season, he remained at Villa Park until December 1983 when he joined West Bromwich Albion for £75,000. He was unable to settle at the club and had loan spells with Birmingham City and FC Seiko in Hong Kong before being sold to Den Haag in Holland. He later returned to West Bromwich for a second spell.

AUGUST 27TH

1980 Tony Morley scored the only goal of the game in the first half in the League Cup second-round first-leg match against Leeds at Villa Park.

1983 An entertaining start to the new season as Villa beat local rivals West Bromwich Albion 4–3 at Villa. Astonishingly, six of the goals were scored in the first half, so the two teams had obviously spent the pre-season working on their defence! Goals from Allan Evans, Mark Walters, Gary Shaw and a second-half strike from Brendan Ormsby won the game for Villa.

1997 Villa finally scored their first goals of the season at the fourth attempt but still went home pointless. Spurs took a fifth-minute lead at White Hart Lane, although Villa should have been level a minute later when Steve Staunton smashed a free kick against the underside of the bar. Stan Collymore then went close with a curling shot before Dwight Yorke netted following a quick break. Collymore scored his first of the season, blasting home from short range and Villa seemed to have the game sewn up. Two goals from Spurs in ten minutes turned the game upside down, but Villa had done enough to have deserved a point at least.

AUGUST 28TH

1920 A masterful display from Villa enabled them to thump five past Arsenal with no reply.

1921 Amos Moss born in Birmingham. He joined Villa as a junior and rose through the ranks, playing for the club during the war and making 109 post-war League appearances at wing half, scoring just five goals.

1939 Aston Villa maintained their unbeaten start to the season but dropped a point in the 1–1 draw with Everton.

1946 Fred Turnbull born in Wallsend. Fred was playing for Centre 64 FC when he was invited for a trial at Villa in 1966, subsequently signing professional forms in September the same year. After making his debut in 1967–68 he was a member of the side that reached the League Cup final in 1971 and won the Third Division championship the following season, although he was already beginning to be troubled by a number of injuries. In 1974 he was forced to retire and in 1976 the club held a testimonial for him.

1954 There were nine goals at Hillsborough but Villa managed only three of them, going down 6–3.

1974 This time it was Villa's turn to hit six, demolishing Hull City 6–0 at Villa Park. The first three games of the season had all ended in draws, so a 6–0 win was a superb way to register their first win. The goals were scored by Sammy Morgan, who scored a hat-trick, Ray Graydon, Brian Little and Chico Hamilton.

1975 Gareth Farrelly born in Dublin. He joined Villa as a trainee and rose through the ranks, signing as a professional in 1992. He spent a spell on loan with Rotherham and whilst first-team opportunities at Villa Park were limited, he did break through to the full Republic of Ireland side.

1979 It had been decided to have the first two rounds of the League Cup played over two legs, the object being to give the lower League clubs the chance of two bites of a money-making tie with a big club. Villa were drawn at Colchester's Layer Road ground for the first leg and two goals from Gary Shaw effectively ended the contest.

AUGUST 29TH

1925 Len Capewell scored five of Villa's ten goals in the opening day of the season victory over Burnley to equal the individual record for the most number of goals in a game by a single player, jointly held by Harry Hampton and Harold Halse. It was, of course, the first day that the new offside rule came into operation; whereas before three players had to be between the attacker and the goal, now only two were required, and Villa adapted to the rule far better than their opponents, winning the match 10–0.

1936 Villa kicked off the season in unfamiliar surroundings; relegated at the end of the previous season for the first time in their history they were at Vetch Field for the Second Division match against Swansea Town. Despite a 2–1 win, life in the Second Division was not going to be easy for Villa, with mid-table respectability all that was achieved after a gruelling campaign.

AUGUST 30TH

1930 Villa kicked off the new season with a 4–3 win at Old Trafford, Pongo Waring having scored all four goals for Villa. By the end of the season he would have scored another 45 and the team 124!

1951 Peter Withe born in Liverpool. After an unsuccessful start to his career with Southport and Barrow he went to America and South Africa in order to restore his confidence, arriving back in England in November 1973 and signing for Wolves. After just 12 games he was sold to Birmingham City, remaining at St Andrew's for a year before Brian Clough signed him for Nottingham Forest. Here he linked with Tony Woodcock and inspired the club to promotion from the Second Division and then the First Division title the following season. By the time Forest won the European Cup Peter had already left, signed by Newcastle United in August 1978. Villa paid their then record fee of £500,000 to sign him in May 1980 and he proved the catalyst for the championship-winning side, netting 20 goals during the course of the season. The following year he scored the winning goal in the European Cup final and also collected five caps for England in his five seasons with the club. After Villa he had spells playing for Sheffield United, Birmingham City and Huddersfield before returning to Villa Park as Jozef Venglos's assistant. He later managed Wimbledon in his own right but was sacked and returned once again to Villa Park to serve the club as chief scout.

1958 After a fairly bright start to the season, with a draw and win at home against Birmingham City and Portsmouth respectively, Villa were brought back down to earth with a bump with a 7–2 mauling at Upton Park by newly promoted West Ham. This match effectively set the scene for the rest of the season, for five successive defeats sent them down to the bottom of the table and staring a nine month struggle to remain in the First Division.

AUGUST 31ST

1946 After a seven-year absence, League football returned to Villa Park. The fixtures for 1946–47 were exactly those of the abandoned 1939–40 season, which meant Middlesbrough were the visitors, with a crowd of 50,572 in attendance. Whereas Villa had won the 1939 clash 2–0, this time they went down 1–0 to a goal from Wilf Mannion. The Villa side included only three players that had played in the corresponding fixture seven years previously; Cummings, Callaghan and Broome.

1971 Villa finally got past Wrexham in the League Cup first round second replay, but once again it was a close run thing. Goals from Andy Lochhead (two), another Willie Anderson penalty and an own goal finally saw off Wrexham in a 4–3 thriller. The crowd of 20,697 at the Hawthorns meant 57,362 spectators had seen the three clashes.

1987 A 1–1 draw at home to Manchester City left Aston Villa bottom of the Second Division after four matches had been played. Villa would recover, climbing the table over the next eight months and finishing second and promoted.

SEPTEMBER 1ST

1894 Aston Villa and Birmingham City met in the League for the first time, although Birmingham were still known as Small Heath, with Smith and Gordon scoring the goals at Perry Barr that enabled Villa to register a 2–1 win in front of a crowd of 20,000.

1909 Billy Gerrish made his debut for the club, scoring a hat-trick in the 5-1 win over Woolwich Arsenal. Signed from Bristol Rovers during the summer as a partner for Harry Hampton, Gerrish won a League title medal at the end of his first season but was then blighted by injuries, subsequently leaving to play for Preston North End and then Chesterfield. At the outbreak of the First World War he enlisted with the Footballers' Battalion Middlesex Regiment and was killed in action in France in 1916.

1919 The Armistice of 1918 came too late in the year for normal League football to be resumed for 1918–19 and clubs continued with their regional war Leagues, eagerly anticipating September of the following year when the League could begin in earnest. All sides bore the scars of the war; Villa had lost Tommy Barber and Arthur Dobson, killed in action, whilst time had done for Joe Bache, Harold Halse and Tom Lyons, but Villa Park was packed for the first game of the season against Derby County, the game ending a 2–2 draw. Whilst a dreadful start in the League was to cost Villa dear as far as their title aspirations were concerned, come the turn of the year and the FA Cup, the new side were beginning to gel together.

1950 Villa beat Sunderland 3–0 at Villa Park, with one of the goals being scored by Peter Aldis, a header from 35 yards! Not surprisingly, this feat is considered the record distance from which a player has scored with a header. Quite by chance, the previous record of 30 yards was achieved by a Villa player, Frank Barson, but Aldis' achievement was even greater, for it was his first goal for the club!

1962 Tony Cascarino born in St Paul's Cray. He was spotted by Gillingham whilst playing for non-League Crockenhill and was transferred in exchange for a team kit! Although he was playing in the Third Division he earned the first of his 51 caps for the Republic of Ireland and was transferred to Milwall in 1987, linking with Teddy Sheringham to form an effective strike partnership. He was sold to Villa for £1.5 million in 1990 but found it tough going at Villa Park, netting just 11 goals before a move to Celtic in 1991.

SEPTEMBER 2ND

1893　What was to be Villa's first League championship kicked off with a surprisingly close 3–2 win over West Bromwich Albion at Perry Barr. Albion had been expected to be one of the chief challengers for the title, but though they could raise their game for the clashes with rivals Villa, indifferent form on the rest of their travels put paid to any sustained thoughts of the title. Not so Villa, who were to show sparkling form for much of the campaign, losing only five games out of thirty and finishing worthy champions.

1895　Just as they had done two years previously, Villa began what was to become a championship-winning campaign with a home win over West Bromwich Albion, this time an even closer run affair at 1–0. Whilst Albion had yet to enjoy any kind of success in the League (they were to finish the season bottom of the table) they were always likely to raise their game whenever Villa were in opposition, as three close FA Cup finals between the two sides bear testament. This was also the game in which Jimmy Crabtree made his debut for the club. He had joined during the summer from Burnley and went on to win four League titles and the FA Cup as well as 11 caps for England and a total of 14 in all. He joined Oreston Rovers in 1902 but moved on to Plymouth a year later, rejoining Oreston in August 1904.

1896　Villa kicked off the defence of their title with a 2–1 win over Stoke at Perry Barr in front of a crowd of 6,000, their goals being scored by John Cowan and John Devey. This was to be the season that Villa won the coveted double, a feat not achieved since Preston had emerged triumphant in 1889, the very first season of the Football League. In the interim period, however, the feat had become much harder to accomplish, with eight more League games to play during the course of a season, tougher opposition being encountered in both competitions and football beginning to catch hold across the entire country.

1912　Andy Ducat made his debut for the club in the 1–0 win over Chelsea. Andy joined the club during the summer from Woolwich Arsenal for £1,000 but then broke his leg four games into the season and was forced to sit out as the club made the FA Cup final at the end of the season. He had to wait seven years before fortune smiled on him; Jimmy Harrop was injured before the 1920 final and Andy Ducat captained the side at

Stamford Bridge. He was one of the few players to have been capped by England at both football and cricket, and when he left Villa in 1921 it was to sign for Fulham so that he could be nearer Surrey Cricket Club. He later managed Fulham and also played as an amateur for the London Casuals. He died whilst batting for Surrey Home Guard in their match against Sussex Home Guard at Lord's in July 1942.

1939 Villa stumbled to their first defeat of the season, beaten 1–0 at Derby. However, the following day the British government declared war on Germany and the Football League was immediately abandoned, with all results expunged from the records. When normal League football resumed in 1946, many of the faces and names who had taken part in 1939 were long gone.

1973 Savo Milosevic born in Bijeljina, Yugoslavia. Brian Little was shown a video of Savo playing for Yugoslavian side Partizan Belgrade in 1995 and on the strength of it paid £3.5 million to bring the giant striker to Villa Park. Although he took a while to settle at the club he finished his first season with a winners' medal in the League Cup, although towards the end of the 1997–98 season he fell foul of the Villa supporters after an alleged spitting incident at a game against Blackburn Rovers.

SEPTEMBER 3RD

1898 Albert Wilkes made his debut for the club in the 3–1 home win over Stoke. He had begun his career playing for Oldbury Town and was spotted by Walsall whilst playing against Villa in the Birmingham Charity Cup final and offered professional terms. At Villa he helped the club win the League title twice and was rewarded with five caps for England, the first coming against Scotland in April 1900. After 157 games for Villa the wing half was allowed to leave, joining Fulham and later Chesterfield. He returned to Villa in 1934 when elected on to the board of directors.

1906 Chris Buckley made his debut in the 2–0 win at Stoke. The brother of Major Frank Buckley, later a highly successful manager with Wolves, Chris had joined Villa in 1906 from Brighton and Hove Albion and went on to make 143 first-team appearances for the club. He overcame a broken ankle to win a League championship medal and joined Woolwich Arsenal in 1913. He returned to Villa in 1936 as a member of the board and was later elected chairman.

1932 Villa would end the season in second place behind Arsenal, helped in no small measure by a 6–1 win achieved over Bolton Wanderers at Villa Park.

1935 Stan Crowther born in Bliston. Stan had joined Villa in August 1955 from Bliston and was a member of the side that won the FA Cup in 1957 against Manchester United. Indeed, it was his performance on the day that was indirectly to lead to a piece of history the following year; in the aftermath of the Munich air disaster United were short of players and were given special permission by the FA to sign players irrespective of whether they had already played in the competition that season. Stan actually signed the transfer forms at United less than an hour before the kick off against Sheffield Wednesday and went with them all the way to Wembley. After just 13 appearances for United in the League however, he joined Chelsea and finished his career with Brighton.

1970   Gareth Southgate born in Watford. He joined Crystal Palace as a trainee and was upgraded to the professional ranks in 1989, helping the club win promotion to the top flight in 1994. At the end of the following season when they were relegated back, Southgate was transferred to Villa for £2.5 million and was switched from midfield to the defence, subsequently forcing his way into the England side. He bounced back from a missed penalty in the European Championships semi-final in 1996 to retain his place in the side and was the foundation upon which Glenn Hoddle built his 1998 World Cup side.

1971   The FA Disciplinary Committee handed out a £3,000 fine suspended sentence until the end of the 1972–73 season.

1980   Villa completed a 4–1 aggregate win over Leeds United with a 3–1 win at Elland Road thanks to goals from Peter Withe and two from Gary Shaw.

SEPTEMBER 4TH

1897   Fred Wheldon scored a hat-trick for the second successive match, following up an opening day haul of three in the 5–2 home win over Sheffield Wednesday with three against West Bromwich Albion, in a clash Villa won 4–3 at home. He had joined Villa at the start of the previous season from Small Heath (now Birmingham City) for £100 plus the proceeds of a testimonial and had scored 22 goals in 37 appearances in the double-winning side. The 1897–98 campaign was even better, for he netted 23 goals in just 28 games and was top goalscorer for both the club and League. Known throughout his career as 'Diamond', he helped the club win the League title three times in just four seasons and also collected four caps for England. After 138 appearances for the Villa first team (scoring 78 goals) he was transferred to West Bromwich Albion, later going on to play for Queens Park Rangers, Portsmouth and Worcester City, finally ending his career with Coventry City. As well as his exploits on a football field he was also an accomplished cricketer for Worcestershire, smashing 4,869 runs during his career.

1899   Villa had begun their defence of their title with a 1–0 win at Sunderland and now played their first home match of the campaign. Poor Glossop were the opponents as Villa rattled in nine goals without reply on their only visit to Villa Park in the League.

1976 A 2–0 win at Everton the previous week had put Villa top of the First Division table after only three games. They retained top spot with a 5–2 win over Ipswich at Villa Park thanks to goals from Brian Little, Ray Graydon and an Andy Gray hat-trick.

SEPTEMBER 5TH

1912 Ronnie Dix born in Bristol. Discovered by Bristol Rovers, he signed as a professional in 1929, by which time he had already made his League debut. Indeed, in scoring on his debut at the age of 15 years 180 days he became the youngest ever scorer. He joined Blackburn Rovers in 1932 and a year later Villa swooped to take him and his left wing partner Arthur Cunliffe, with Dix making his debut in the last game of the 1932–33 season. He moved on to Derby where he won his only cap for England and in 1939 joined Spurs, finishing his career with Reading in 1949.

1927 Portsmouth were the victims as Villa registered their biggest win of the season with a 7–2 victory at Villa Park.

1961 Villa were chasing a two-goal deficit from the first leg of the League Cup final against Rotherham and had to wait until the 67th minute for their initial breakthrough, finally scoring through Alan O'Neill. Four minutes later Harry Burrows levelled the aggregate score and sent the game into extra time, where, in the 19th minute, Peter McParland scored the winner to make Villa the first side to have won the League Cup. Villa's attendance of 30,765 was their biggest in the competition to date and although Gerry Hitchens did not score in either leg of the final he did finish the competition's top scorer with 11 to his credit.

SEPTEMBER 6TH

1930 West Ham became the first club to be hit for six during the season, going down 6–1 at Villa Park. By the end of the campaign Villa had also scored six against Huddersfield twice, seven against Manchester United and eight against Middlesbrough. Although Villa didn't win the League, finishing second behind Arsenal, they did register their highest ever tally of goals in a season, 128.

1947 Bruce Rioch born in Aldershot. He began his career with Luton Town and soon proved a stylish midfield player, making 148 League appearances before he and his brother Neil were sold to Villa for a combined fee of £100,000 in July 1969. He helped the club to the final of the League Cup in 1971 and the Third Division championship the following season, although in 1974 he was sold to Derby for £200,000. After a brief spell with Everton he returned to Derby in 1977 and later had spells with Birmingham City, Sheffield United and Torquay as well as playing in America. He then turned to management with

Middlesbrough and has since had spells in charge at Millwall, Bolton and Arsenal before becoming assistant manager at QPR. He is currently in charge at Norwich City.

1980 Villa had opened the campaign with three victories and a draw in their first four games and were making the early running in the race for the title. Villa slipped to their first defeat of the season with a 1–0 reverse at Portman Road against Ipswich, the side that was to prove Villa's most relentless pursuers over the next nine months.

SEPTEMBER 7TH

1895 Local rivals Small Heath were beaten 7–3 at Perry Barr on the way to a Villa title triumph.

1959 Des Bremner born in Aberchider. He began his professional career with Hibernian and helped the Easter Road club reach the finals of both the Scottish League and Scottish FA Cup prior to a £250,000 move to Villa Park in 1979, with Joe Ward making the opposite journey as part of the deal. In his five years with the club he helped them win the League and European Cup in successive seasons and was sold to Birmingham City in 1984, later playing for Fulham and Walsall.

1965 Garry Parker born in Oxford. He began his career with Luton but was unable to command a regular place in the side and so was sold to Hull for £72,000 in 1986. Here he developed into a tigerish midfield player and earned a move to Nottingham Forest in 1988, this time costing £260,000. He helped them win the League Cup twice and reach the FA Cup final before a £650,000 move to Villa Park in 1991. He spent four years with Villa, making 99 appearances in the first team before switching to Leicester, helping them in the Premier League and then their first major honour in the game, the League Cup in 1997.

SEPTEMBER 8TH

1888 The very first League match Villa played, with a crowd of some 2,500 present at Dudley Road to see Wolves against Aston Villa. Wolves took the lead in the first half through an own goal from Gershom Cox (the very first in the Football League), although Villa replied through Tommy Green shortly before the interval. Although both sides had their chances in the second half, the game ended in a draw. It was not until a few weeks later that it was decided that both teams would receive one point apiece in the event of a draw! Gershom Cox meanwhile recovered from his early mistake and went on to make 98 first-team appearances for the club and later played non-League football before being forced to retire after sustaining a broken leg. He then joined the police force and was often on duty at Villa's home games.

1894 Liverpool had entered the Second Division at the beginning of the 1893–94 season and won the League without losing a game. However, since automatic promotion and relegation had yet to be introduced, they were required to play in the Test Matches, beating Newton Heath (now known as Manchester United) to gain promotion. They had then drawn their first two games in the First Division, a run of 31 games without defeat that was finally brought to an end by a 2–1 win for Villa at Anfield. Villa had previously been responsible for ending Preston's unbeaten run from the start of the Football League in 1888.

1919　Arthur Dorrell made his debut for the club in the 1–0 defeat by Derby County. He won a winners' medal in the FA Cup at the end of the season, deputising for Harold Edgley who broke his leg three weeks before the game. He went on to make 390 first-team games, and won four caps for England before winding down his career with Port Vale.

SEPTEMBER 9TH

1893　Villa had opened their League campaign with a home win over West Bromwich Albion and now faced as stern a test for their first away match as they could imagine: champions Sunderland at their then ground at Newcastle Road. Villa showed remarkable spirit in gaining a 1–1 draw to give credence to their hopes they might topple a Sunderland side that had won the title for the previous two seasons.

1899　West Bromwich Albion were the only club to win a League match at Villa Park during the course of the season, winning 2–0 in the third game of the season. Villa recovered from the setback, however, going on to win the title at the end of the campaign.

1901　Joe Bache made his debut for Villa in the 2–0 win over Notts County at Villa Park. He went on to make 473 appearances for the first team, scoring 185 goals and forming an extremely effective partnership with Albert Hall. He later captained the side and won two FA Cups and one League championship medal during his time with the club. The outbreak of the First World War brought his League career to a close, becoming player-manager of Mid Rhondda in 1920. He later coached Grimsby Town and returned to Villa Park as reserve-team coach in 1927. He won seven caps for England while with Villa.

1945　Pat McMahon born in Glasgow. He began his career with Celtic, the club he supported as a schoolboy, but was released in 1969 after playing only three League games. Snapped up by Villa that summer he made 149 first-team appearances, scoring 30 goals, and was a member of the side that reached the League Cup final in 1971. He left Villa in 1976, going to play in America for Portland Timbers.

1970　Villa's first First Division scalp in the League Cup competition. Burnley were the visitors to Villa Park where a crowd of 28,341 saw second-half goals from Chico Hamilton and substitute Lionel Martin give Villa a 2–0 win in the second round.

1975 The defence of the League Cup began with a second-round 2–0 home win over Oldham Athletic thanks to goals from Keith Leonard and Chris Nicholl in front of a crowd of 23,041. The win set up a home clash with Manchester United in the third round.

1996 A goal from Tommy Johnson after 14 minutes seemed to have settled Villa in their UEFA Cup first-round first-leg match against Helsingborg, but nine minutes from time, with Villa having been unable to add to their tally, the visitors grabbed a vital away goal and levelled the score.

1895 The FA Cup trophy, which was on display in the window of William Shillcock's boot and shoe manufacturers shop at 73 Newton Row, Birmingham, was stolen sometime during the night or early next morning. Despite the offer of a £10 reward for information it was never recovered, although in 1958 Harry Burge, then aged 83, claimed that he had been responsible for the theft and that the cup had been melted down to make counterfeit florins. Aston Villa, the holders, had insured the cup for £200 and proposed that this sum should be spent on a replacement in gold. However, the Football Association decided that the next trophy should be as close to the original as possible and, after one was provided by Vaughtons Ltd at a cost of £25, fined Aston Villa this exact sum. The Vaughton's company was the very same silversmith's started by former Aston Villa player Howard Vaughton on his retirement from playing!

1971 Brighton and Hove Albion were to be one of Villa's rivals for promotion from the Third Division, finally finishing the season in second place and accompanying Villa in the Second Division. The meeting at Villa Park drew a crowd of 25,809 and they were treated to a clash that lived up to its billing. The two defences cancelled each other out during an enthralling first half, but Villa finally found a way through thanks to Ray Graydon to open Brighton up a little. A second Villa goal, scored this time by Chico Hamilton, wrapped up the points.

1974 Villa's League Cup campaign began with a visit from First Division Everton to Villa Park, but the home side were not overawed by the size of their task, taking a first-half lead through Chris Nicholl to put pressure on Everton. Bob Latchford equalised in the second 45 minutes and it was Everton who went home happiest, convinced they would be able to finish the task off back at Goodison Park.

1892 The actions of Villa goalkeeper Dunning during the match between Stoke and Aston Villa ensured a major change in the rules. With just two minutes of the game left and Villa leading 1–0, Stoke appeared to have the perfect opportunity of gaining a point when they were awarded a penalty. Whether he disagreed with the decision or was simply wasting time will never be known, but Dunning picked the ball up and booted it out of the ground! By the time the ball could be retrieved, the referee signalled the end of the game, thus denying Stoke their chance of an equaliser. As a result of this, the rules were amended to allow time for penalties to be taken.

1928 Tom Cummings born in Castledown. A solid and reliable centre-half for Burnley for some 14 years, he finished his playing career with Mansfield and then switched to management, taking over at Mansfield Town. In the summer of 1967 he replaced Dick Taylor in charge at Villa Park but his time at the club was not successful and he was sacked in November 1968 with the side at the bottom of the Second Division.

1931 Grimsby had the Division's worst defence when on their travels, conceding 70 goals during the campaign. A tenth of them came at Villa Park as Villa registered their biggest win of the season, 7–0. They did score another seven later on in the season, beating Middlesbrough 7–1 over Christmas.

SEPTEMBER 13TH

1902 Alex Leake made his debut for the club in the 2–0 defeat at Nottingham Forest. He had begun his career with Small Heath and made 199 appearances for the club before switching to Villa in the summer of 1902. He went on to become an important member of the side that won the FA Cup in 1905 and won five caps for England during his time with the club. He made 141 first-team appearances before leaving for Burnley in 1907, later playing for Crystal Palace in 1912. Even though he was by now 40 years of age, he was still selected for England, although he did not play.

1939 Villa Park staged its first game in the Birmingham and District League, with Villa taking on RAF Hednesford. Villa would later switch to using Solihull Town's ground in the competition.

1961 With the final of the 1960–61 League Cup held over to the following season, Villa had been holders for just eight days before they were required to start their defence of the trophy! A 4–3 win at Valley Parade took them safely into the second round.

1967 Warren Aspinall born in Wigan. He began his career with his local club, Wigan Athletic, graduating through the ranks and earning a £150,000 move to Everton in February 1986, although he was immediately loaned back to Wigan for the rest of the season. His time at Goodison was not entirely successful and a further move to Aston Villa followed in 1987 for a fee of £300,000. He made 44 League appearances for Villa before being sold to Portsmouth for £315,000 in 1988 and has since gone on to play for Bournemouth, Swansea and Carlisle United.

1966 Local rivals West Bromwich Albion dumped Villa out of the League Cup at the second-round stage 6–1 at the Hawthorns on their way to reaching the final that season. If there was any consolation for Villa, it came in the final itself when Third Division Queens Park Rangers came from behind to win 3–2 at Wembley. On the same day former Villa favourite Frank Moss senior died at his home in Worcester.

1977 Aston Villa had qualified for the UEFA Cup for a second time, again through victory in the previous season's League Cup. This time they were drawn at home in the first leg of the first round, with the visit of Turkish side Fenerbahce attracting a crowd of 30,351 to Villa Park. This time there was a goal or two to cheer, with Andy Gray, John Deehan (two) and Brian Little giving Villa a four goal lead to take into the second leg.

1983 Sixth place in the First Division in 1982–83 was sufficient to take Villa into the UEFA Cup (Manchester United, third, qualified for the European Cup-Winners' Cup, whilst Villa's own European Cup triumph of 1981–82 ensured England had a full quota of places for the UEFA Cup) and they took on Portuguese side Vitoria Guimaraes in the first round first leg. A second-half penalty conversion from Gregorio enabled the Portuguese to win 1–0.

1986 Aston Villa manager Graham Turner was sacked by the club. Villa were second from bottom of the First Division and the previous day had lost 6–0 at Nottingham Forest whilst the reserves were being humbled 7–0 by Manchester United in the Central League.

1888 Villa gained their very first League win with a 5–1 victory over Stoke at Perry Barr in front of a crowd of 2,000. The League had opened the previous week with a 1–1 draw with local rivals Wolves.

1920 Both Frank Barson and Clem Stephenson were suspended by the club for failing to turn up for the match at Bolton, which the Trotters won 5–0. Clem Stephenson had joined the club in March 1910 but struggled to command a regular place in the side during his early days at Villa, being loaned out to Stourbridge for a year. Upon his return he slotted in at inside left and helped the club to the FA Cup final in 1913. After guesting for Leeds during the First World War he returned to Villa and helped them to the FA Cup final again in 1920, but his refusal to move to the Midlands from his home base in the North East, travelling down on match days, had brought him into dispute with the club. Shortly after his suspension he was sold to Huddersfield Town in March 1921 for £3,000, and here he helped the club to the FA Cup final in 1922 and three consecutive League titles, the first time such a feat had been achieved. He later managed the same club.

1944 Graham Taylor born in Worksop. After spending his playing career with Grimsby and Lincoln City, he began his managerial career with Lincoln and took them to the Fourth Division title in 1976. In June 1977 Elton John persuaded him to return to the Fourth Division in order to revive the fortunes of Watford, and over the next ten years he guided them to the First Division for the first time in their history and the FA Cup final in 1984 and qualified for Europe. After ten years he announced he needed a fresh challenge and accepted an offer to take over at Villa Park in July 1987, restoring the club to the First Division at the end of his first season in charge. After a barren time back in the top flight he led them to challenge for the League title, with his undoubted abilities in great demand. He replaced Bobby Robson as England manager after the 1990 World Cup, taking them to the 1992 European Championships, but a poor showing here followed by failing to qualify for the 1994 World Cup finals left him little option but to resign. In April 1994 he joined Wolves with a brief to get them into the Premier League, but after 20 months and with the top flight still some way off he had resigned from this position, subsequently returning to Watford.

1979 Having won the first leg against Colchester United 2–0 away from home, the return leg should have been a formality, but somehow Villa contrived to almost gift the game to their opponents. A goal in each half from Lee and Gough brought United level on aggregate, but still Villa failed to raise their game to dispose of the Third Division side. Extra time brought no further goals although plenty of scares for Villa and then it went to a penalty shoot out. Villa finally recovered their composure enough to win 9–8!

1982 Technically, the gate figure for the European Cup tie with Besiktas at Villa Park was nil, for the game was ordered to be played behind closed doors by UEFA as a result of crowd trouble in the competition involving Villa the previous season. It was not an easy way to start the defence of the European Cup won in such magnificent fashion the previous May, but a professional performance and goals from Peter Withe, Tony Morley and Dennis Mortimer gave Villa a 3–1 win to take to Turkey in two weeks' time.

1993 Aston Villa battled their way to a goalless draw in Czechoslovakia against Slovan Bratislava in the UEFA Cup first round first leg.

1994 Villa were faced with an extremely difficult assignment in the UEFA Cup first round: Internazionale of Milan, who had beaten them in the competition in 1990. There was only one goal scored in the first leg in Milan, where 22,639 were gathered (a far cry from the 90,000 who had seen the meeting four years previously) and it was Dennis Bergkamp who got it, from the penalty spot in the second half.

SEPTEMBER 16TH

1911 Villa's best away performance of the season; a 6–2 win over Manchester City.

1917 Frank Moss junior born in Birmingham. The son of former Villa and England player Frank Moss senior, he joined Villa from Wolves for £2,000 in 1938 and made his debut for the club at the beginning of the 1938–39 season. Just as Frank senior's career was interrupted by the First World War, so Frank junior suffered with the second altercation with the Germans, although he guested for Birmingham and Northampton during the hostilities before returning to Villa Park at the end of the war. He was a regular in the side for eight seasons until his career was effectively ended following a tackle by Duncan Edwards in 1954, although he did make one final appearance for the club before retiring.

1923 Colin H. Gibson born in Normanby. He began his career with Cardiff City before switching to Newcastle United for £15,000, but after only 23 games he was sold on to Villa for an additional £2,000 more than United had paid for him. He spent seven years at Villa Park before joining Lincoln City for £6,000 in 1956 where he finished his career.

1939 Villa played their first match since the outbreak of the Second World War, a friendly fixture with Leicester at Filbert Street that the home side won 3–0. Villa would not play another first-team game until the following April.

1942 Barry Hole born in Swansea. A member of a football dynasty, with his father and both brothers having played League football, he began his career with Cardiff City and joined Villa from Blackburn Rovers in September 1968, the last signing made by Tommy Cummings. He remained with the club for nearly two years, although at one point he walked out following a bust-up with caretaker manager Arthur Cox, making 47 League appearances before heading off to Swansea where he finished his career.

1981 Aston Villa began their European Cup trail with an easy 5–0 win over Icelandic champions Valur at Villa Park, the goals coming from Tony Morley, Peter Withe (two) and Terry Donovan (two) in front of a crowd of 20,481.

1997 An excellent defensive performance in Bordeaux in front of a crowd of 16,000 saw Villa return home with a 0–0 draw in the UEFA Cup first round first leg.

SEPTEMBER 17TH

1892 Sunderland were on their way to retaining their League title, with Villa finishing in fourth place. Despite this a then record crowd of 16,000 were at Perry Barr to see Sunderland put on a display worthy of champions, winning 6–1.

1966 Three days after conceding six goals at West Bromwich Albion, Villa were hit for six again, this time at Chelsea where Bobby Tambling scored five of the Londoners' goals at Villa Park.

1969 Jimmy Brown made his debut for Villa to become the youngest ever player to have represented Villa in a senior first-team match, being 15 years and 349 days old in the 2–1 defeat at Bolton.

1975 Aston Villa made their debut in European competition, their victory in the League Cup the previous season earning them qualification for the UEFA Cup. It was not to be an auspicious start either, for despite scoring a potentially vital away goal through Ray Graydon, Antwerp scored four in Belgium and effectively ended Villa's interest in the competition.

SEPTEMBER 18TH

1948 Villa's 3–3 draw at home to Huddersfield Town helped to create a piece of League history; there were eight other draws in the division on the same day, a record for any division of the League in a single day.

1965 Craven Cottage was the setting for a remarkable match between Fulham and Villa. Tony Hateley gave Villa the lead after only two minutes, with Phil Woosnam extending Villa's advantage to 2–0 after 20 minutes. Fulham pulled one back shortly before half-time, equalised five minutes into the second half and then took the lead shortly before the hour was up, all their goals being scored by Graham Leggatt. That spurred Villa into action, with Mike Tindall levelling the game five minutes later. Both teams now looked to gain the upper hand, and it was Villa who struck first, Hateley putting them back in the lead on the 65th minute mark. Three minutes later Johnny MacLeod took the score to 5–3 in Villa's favour, and Willie Hamilton completed the scoring 15 minutes from time for a 6–3 Villa victory. It was the 11th time Villa had visited Craven Cottage and, fittingly enough, the 11th time they had scored six or more goals away from home!

1974 Villa were in magnificent form at Goodison Park, seeing off their First Division rivals Everton in the League Cup second-round replay. A goalless first half had made the Everton supporters in the 24,595 crowd restless, and this seemed to convey itself to the Everton team. As their attacks became more frantic, so the composure of Villa took over. Goals from Sammy Morgan, Frank Carrodus and Ray Graydon won the game 3–0 in Villa's favour, with Everton trooping off the field to a chorus of whistles.

SEPTEMBER 19TH

1957 Les Sealey born in London. He began his professional career with

Coventry City in 1976 and moved on to Luton in 1983. A member of the side that finished runners-up in the League Cup in 1989, he joined Manchester United on loan in December 1989 and again in March 1990, the loan due to expire at the end of the season. United had won through to the FA Cup final and Sealey was expected to provide cover for first choice Jim Leighton, but Leighton's nervous performance in the first match prompted Alex Ferguson to drop him for the replay and bring Sealey in. Sealey's performance not only helped United lift the cup but was also responsible for gaining the goalkeeper a one-year contract. At the end of that term he helped United win the European Cup-Winners' Cup. He then joined Aston Villa but was unable to claim a regular place and had loan spells with Coventry and Birmingham City before returning to United for a second spell. Although he made only two appearances this time round, they came in the FA Cup quarter-final and League Cup final, the latter against Aston Villa which Villa won 3–1. He was released on a free transfer in 1993 and has since played for Blackpool, West Ham, Leyton Orient and West Ham for a second time.

1990 A crowd of 27,317 was at Villa Park as Aston Villa, along with Manchester United in the European Cup-Winners' Cup, spearheaded England's re-entry into European competition. Villa were drawn with Banik Ostrava and goals from David Platt, Derek Mountfield and Ian Olney enabled them to win 3–1 in the UEFA Cup first round first leg.

1992 Having scored only ten goals since the start of the season it was obvious where Villa's problems lay if they were to challenge for the top honours, and the sudden swoop for Dean Saunders nine days earlier had come as a surprise – not because of any shortcomings in his play, for he was a proven goalscorer, but simply because no one believed Liverpool would part with him. But part they did and Saunders came back to haunt them almost immediately, scoring twice on his home debut against his old club, of all teams. Dalian Atkinson and Garry Parker added the others in a sparkling 4–2 win that kick-started Villa's season.

SEPTEMBER 20TH

1896 The defence of the League title began with a 2–1 win over Stoke at Perry Barr thanks to goals from John Cowan (James' brother) and John Devey in front of a crowd of 6,000.

1914 Joe Rutherford born in Chester-le-Street. After 88 appearances in goal for Southport he was signed by Villa in 1939 for £2,500 and made his debut in March of that year. Unfortunately the outbreak of the Second World War brought his career to a temporary halt but he returned in 1946 to become first choice for the goalkeeper's jersey. He made 156 appearances for the first team before his retirement in 1951, although he retained his connection with Villa, helping run the club's Pools

Development Department and later working at Bodymoor Heath, the training ground.

1969 Villa's worst ever start to a season finally came to an end, for having failed to win any of their nine League and one League Cup matches, they recorded a 3–2 home win over Hull City thanks to goals from Brian Godfrey, Lew Chatterley and David Rudge. Although this match heralded an upturn in Villa's fortunes, going on to lose only one of their next seven matches, they were still relegated to the Third Division for the first time in their history at the end of the season.

1974 Julian Joachim born in Peterborough. Signed by Leicester City as a trainee, he graduated through the ranks to become an important part of the side, although he was sidelined for two months after breaking a foot. In February 1996 Brian Little swooped on his former club and paid £1.5 million to take him to Villa Park.

1986 Manager-less Villa dropped to the bottom of the First Division after a 4–1 home defeat by Norwich. Graham Turner had been sacked the week previously and numerous names were being linked to the vacant seat at Villa Park, but whoever took over the position faced an uphill struggle to get Villa out of trouble.

1995 Three goals in each half saw off Peterborough United in the Coca-Cola Cup second round first leg at Villa Park; Mark Draper, Dwight Yorke (two, both from the penalty spot), Tommy Johnson, Gareth Southgate and an own goal from Heald supplying the goals in a 6–0 win.

SEPTEMBER 21ST

1889 Aston Villa became the first side to beat Preston North End in the Football League; Preston had gone through the entire first season of the League unbeaten (the only side ever to have accomplished this since the creation of the League) and made a 10–0 winning start to this season the previous week against Stoke. Today they lost in the League for the first time, going down 5–3 at Aston Villa (although they still finished the season as champions).

1912 The visit of local rivals West Bromwich Albion drew a then record crowd of 55,064 to Villa Park, with the visitors recording a 4–2 win.

1924 William Baxter born in Methill. He began his career with Wolves, joining the club as a junior and joining the professional ranks during the Second World War. After 43 appearances for the League side he was transferred to Villa in November 1953, making a further 100 or so appearances for the Villans before his retirement.

SEPTEMBER 22ND

1986 Manchester City manager Billy McNeill accepted an offer to take over at Villa Park, signing a four-year contract believed to be worth £70,000 a year. As a player with Celtic he won virtually every honour in the game, collecting 23 winners' medals from various competitions, including the European Cup in 1967. He began his managerial career at Clyde, returning to Celtic in May 1978 in place of Jock Stein, and remaining in charge at Parkhead for five years. He then took over at Maine Road, returning City to the First Division in 1985 before accepting the call from Villa. By the end of the season, however, it became apparent that McNeill was stepping out of the frying pan into the fire, for both Manchester City and Aston Villa were relegated!

SEPTEMBER 23RD

1938 Dave Gibson born in Winchburgh. He first made his name in the English game with Leicester after joining the Filbert Street club from Hibernian in January 1963, featuring in their FA Cup final side at the end of the season against Manchester United. He joined Villa in September 1970 but made only 19 League appearances before being released, subsequently going on to Exeter City. He won seven caps with Scotland during his career.

1980 Villa slipped out of the League Cup, beaten 2–1 at the Abbey Stadium against Second Division Cambridge United. It was a match that Villa should have won but had only Tony Morley's goal to show for their efforts.

1992 Better League Cup luck (albeit in the Coca-Cola Cup) as Villa recorded a 2–1 win at the Manor Ground against Oxford United in the second round first leg. Goals from Paul McGrath and Shaun Teale put Villa in the driving seat.

SEPTEMBER 24TH

1966 An unwanted record for Villa – they conceded their 17th goal in just ten days; beaten 6–1 at West Bromwich in the League Cup and 6–2 against Chelsea in the League, they now travelled to Filbert Street and were beaten 5–0. Former Villa player Derek Dougan rubbed salt in the wounds by netting a hat-trick.

1984 Two goals from Paul Kerr, his only strikes of the season, put Villa in a commanding position in the Milk Cup second-round first-leg tie at Scunthorpe United. A further goal from Colin Gibson enabled Villa to run out 3–2 winners.

1996 Villa huffed and puffed but proved unable to blow Helsingborg's house down, going out of the UEFA Cup at the first-round stage on away goals after drawing the first leg 1–1.

SEPTEMBER 25TH

1909 Nottingham Forest became the first team to visit Villa Park in the season and return home with even a point, drawing 0–0 after a lacklustre Villa performance. The season, however, would end in triumph for Villa, with their invincibility at Villa Park the cornerstone of their success. After Forest, only fellow citizens Notts County would earn a point, drawing 1–1 in December. By the end of the season Villa had registered 17 victories in front of their own supporters, form that saw off nearest challengers Liverpool by five points.

1946   Mick Wright born in Ellesmere Port. An England youth international, he joined Villa as an apprentice and spent his entire career at Villa Park, signing professional forms in 1963 and going on to make 315 appearances for the first team. He missed out on the club's appearance at Wembley in 1971 in the League Cup final but won a Third Division championship medal the following year before having to retire owing to injury.

1985   Simon Stainrod scored all four of Villa's goals in the 4–1 win at Exeter City in the Milk Cup second round second leg.

SEPTEMBER 26TH

1903   Villa became the first side to have scored 1,000 goals in the Football League, a total achieved with the third goal in a 3–1 win at home to Everton. Villa had achieved the total in just 445 games since the League was formed in 1888.

1939   The Football League had been abandoned at the beginning of the month following the outbreak of the Second World War and there was already talk that regional football might be organised to replace it, given that there were restrictions on the distances that could be travelled. Aston Villa held a meeting at which the situation and its implications for Villa were discussed; with 16 players already enlisted into the Police and War reserves, it was unlikely that the club would be in a position to carry on and they later declined a Football League invitation to take part in regional football.

1949   Leighton Phillips born in Briton Ferry. He began his career with Cardiff City and made 180 appearances before a £100,000 move brought him to Villa Park in September 1974. He remained with the club for four years, helping them win the League Cup in 1977, and moved on to Swansea City in 1978. After three years at Vetch Field he finished his career with short spells with Charlton and Exeter. He was capped 58 times by Wales during his career.

SEPTEMBER 27TH

1890   West Bromwich Albion were the visitors to Perry Barr for a League match which attracted a then record crowd of 12,100. Sadly, the visitors ran off with the points, beating Villa 4–0.

1919   Villa were making only their second visit to Bradford's Park Avenue ground for League points and had yet to record a win, drawing 2–2 in 1914 and crashing to a 6–1 defeat this time around. They had no further success the following year either; losing 4–0 in their last appearance on the ground in the First Division.

1988   Birmingham City had overcome local rivals Wolves over two legs in the first round of the League Cup and were rewarded with being drawn against Aston Villa, again over two legs. The first leg at St Andrew's saw Villa take command right from the start, scoring through Kevin Gage and Andy Gray in an action-packed first half to virtually guarantee their progress into the next round.

SEPTEMBER 28TH

1889   James Cowan made his debut for the club in the 3–0 defeat against West Bromwich Albion at the Hawthorns. Born in Dumbarton in October 1868, he began his career in Scotland with Vale of Leven and was destined for Warwick County until Villa nipped in and signed him first. He went on to spend 13 seasons with Villa, including four seasons in which he was an ever-present, and won two FA Cup winners' medals and five League championships. He was first capped by Scotland in 1896, winning a total of three caps for his country. He retired from playing in 1902 and later became Queens Park Rangers' manager. In 1896 Cowan was challenged by his team-mates to take part in the famous Powderhall Sprint in Edinburgh, even though it was mid-season. Cowan informed the Villa trainer that he had a spot of back trouble and needed to return home in order to recuperate. Villa were suspicious enough to request a local doctor to examine him, although he could probably have surmised that there was little wrong with Cowan when he nearly knocked him off the pavement whilst in training! Cowan duly took part in the race, under an assumed name and won, watched by a number of the Villa players who had placed bets with a local bookmaker. As fast as Cowan was, even he couldn't catch up with the bookmaker who did a runner with their winnings, and he was further punished when the Villa committee suspended him after learning of what he had been up to! He died in Scotland in 1918.

1971   Alan Wright born in Ashton under Lyne. He began his career with Blackpool and became their youngest-ever player when called from the substitutes' bench in May 1988 at the age of 16 years and 217 days. In October 1991 he was sold to Blackburn for £400,000, the first signing for Rovers by manager Kenny Dalglish and played an integral part in helping them gain promotion to the First Division. In March 1995 he joined Villa in a deal worth £1 million and helped the club win the League Cup in 1996 and later received a call-up to the England squad, having previously represented the country at Schoolboy, Youth and Under-21 levels.

1977 Villa were in Turkey to play Fenerbahce in the first round second leg of the UEFA Cup, 4–0 ahead from the first leg and in control of their own destiny. Goals from John Deehan and Brian Little ensured an easy passage into the next round 6–0 on aggregate.

1983 Peter Withe scored a hat-trick as Villa swept aside Portuguese side Vitoria Guimaraes in the UEFA Cup first round second leg, finally winning 5–0 on the night thanks to goals from Brendan Ormsby and Colin Gibson, 5–1 on aggregate.

SEPTEMBER 29TH

1888 Albert Allen became the first Villa player to score a hat-trick of goals in a League match, with three in the 9–1 victory over Notts County. The result is still County's record defeat in any competition.

1982 A sterling defensive display enabled Villa to draw 0–0 with Besiktas in the European Cup first round second leg and win 3–1 on aggregate.

1993 Villa made heavy work of it before finally despatching Slovan Bratislava from the UEFA Cup first round. After a goalless first meeting in Czechoslovakia, goals from Dalian Atkinson and Andy Townsend appeared to have put Villa home and dry by half-time, but a second-half goal from Tittel meant a second Bratislava goal would take them through on away goals. Villa's defence managed to hold them out for a 2–1 aggregate win.

1994 A night of high drama at Villa Park where 30,533 were there to see if Villa could overcome a 1–0 first leg defeat against Internazionale in the UEFA Cup. Ray Houghton eased the nerves with a goal in the 41st minute, but despite another 80 minutes' or so labours, neither side could break the stalemate. That meant a penalty shoot-out to decide who would go into the next round, and here Villa's nerve held, winning 4–3.

SEPTEMBER 30TH

1981 Aston Villa completed a 7–0 aggregate win over Valur with a 2–0 win in Iceland thanks to two goals from Gary Shaw.

1995 Villa moved up to second position in the table with an emphatic 3–0 win at Highfield Road against Coventry City. Savo Milosevic scored his second and third goals of the season, with Dwight Yorke having opened the scoring in the first half. Second place was to be the highest position attained by Villa during the season, two successive defeats sending them down five places, but they recovered in time to finish fourth and earn a place in the UEFA Cup the following season.

1997 The UEFA Cup clash between Aston Villa and French club Bordeaux was settled by a single goal over two legs, the vital strike coming from Savo Milosevic at Villa Park in front of a crowd of 33,072.

1898 Villa battled their way to a well deserved draw at Newcastle United, taking home a point after the game finished 1–1.

1923 Trevor Ford born in Swansea. Signed by his hometown club during the Second World War, he made just 16 League appearances at the end of hostilities before switching to Villa Park, signing in January 1947 for £12,000. He remained with the club for nearly four years, making 121 appearances and scoring 59 times in the League. A fee of £30,000 took him to Sunderland in October 1950, where he stayed for three years and then on to Cardiff City, finally finishing his League career with Newport County. He won a total of 38 caps for Wales.

1975 Villa Park staged its first European home match with the visit of Antwerp from Belgium in the UEFA Cup first round second leg. With Antwerp 4–1 ahead from the first leg Villa were looking for a miracle, but the 31,513 crowd were to be disappointed as the Belgians scored again to register a 5–1 aggregate win.

1939 The Football League announced plans for a regional competition to replace the abandoned Football League competition, although Villa had already declined to take part (along with Sunderland, Derby County, Exeter City, Ipswich Town and Gateshead) as their ground had been requisitioned. Birmingham City would also not be able to play their matches on their own ground, but accepted the invitation anyway.

1971 A third successive win took Villa to the top of the Third Division, this time a 1–0 win over Bristol Rovers at Eastville. Willie Anderson scored the only goal of the game, one of ten he would score during the season.

1974 A 3–0 win over Nottingham Forest halted a stuttering Villa run and began a surge up the table. Ray Graydon and Chico Hamilton gave Villa a 2–0 half-time lead, and Keith Leonard completed the scoring in the second half. That win moved Villa into fourth place.

1959 Villa made their only ever visit to Sincil Bank, the home of Lincoln City in the League, drawing 0–0. The return match at Villa Park in March was also drawn, this time 1–1.

1990 Having already won the first leg of the UEFA Cup first round Villa were in no mood to surrender their advantage and goals from Derek Mountfield and an own goal took them to a 2–1 win on the night, 5–2 on aggregate against Banik Ostrava.

1992 Wimbledon away had seldom been a fruitful journey for Villa, irrespective of whether Wimbledon were playing at Plough Lane or

Selhurst Park. Successive wins had taken Villa up to sixth in the table and hot in pursuit of the early leaders, so a win at Selhurst Park was vital. Two goals from Dean Saunders and a single strike from Dalian Atkinson finally saw Villa home, 3–2 winners on the night.

1995 Villa might have won the first leg 6–0 at Villa Park against Peterborough United, but the Second Division side were still playing for their pride in the return leg at London Road. A goal from Martindale shook Villa in the first half and only a late equaliser from Steve Staunton spared their blushes.

OCTOBER 4TH

1930 Villa hit six for the second time in the season, this time swamping Huddersfield Town 6–1 at Villa Park.

1978 Crystal Palace were the visitors for the League Cup third round and after Brian Little gave Villa a first-half lead, the 30,690 started thinking they were already home and dry. Palace had other ideas, knocking Villa out of their stride with a strong display that resulted in Gary Shelton being carried off with a nasty leg injury. If Palace were the side showing the more physical approach, then it was Villa who were the punished, conceding a penalty in the second half which Chatterton converted to earn a replay. After the game, manager Ron Saunders was furious with the Palace display, declaring 'I keep reading about these sides that want to come and play football, but all that happens is that they want to try and kick you off the pitch.'

1989 Already 2–1 ahead from the first leg of the second-round League Cup clash with Wolves, Villa got off to the perfect start when Derek Mountfield gave them the lead at Molineux. But Wolves stormed back in the second half, scoring through Steve Bull and looking as though they might draw level on aggregate to send the game into extra time. A series of saves by Nigel Spink kept them at bay and earned Villa a third-round tie with West Ham.

OCTOBER 5TH

1889 In only the second season of the Football League, Villa hit six goals away from home for the first time, beating Burnley 6–2.

1912 Harry Hampton scored five of Villa's goals in the League match at home to Sheffield Wednesday, won 10–0 by Villa, the first player to have scored as many goals in one match. The feat was later equalled by Harold Halse, Len Capewell, George Brown and Gerry Hitchens. The 10–0 defeat remains Wednesday's worst in their history.

1947 Graham Turner born in Ellesmere Port. As a player he served Wrexham, Chester and Shrewsbury and then switched to management, being appointed player-manager at Gay Meadow. In July 1984 he accepted an offer to take over at Villa Park but after two seasons and a disastrous start to the 1986–87 season he was dismissed. He later served Wolves but was replaced by Graham Taylor and then joined Hereford United.

1971 Villa produced a remarkable performance at Selhurst Park in the League Cup third round, recovering from a 2–0 deficit to force a replay. After Craven and Tambling had given the First Division side a seemingly unassailable lead, Chico Hamilton and Andy Lochhead fired home the goals that meant a replay at Villa Park.

OCTOBER 6TH

1929 Doug Winton born in Perth. He was spotted by Burnley whilst playing for Jeanfield Swifts and signed in September 1947. He left for Villa in January 1959 and made 37 appearances at full-back for the club, later finishing his career with Rochdale.

1970 Villa's charge to Wembley survived a stern test at the County Ground, Northampton, Frank Large scoring for Town and Chico Hamilton for Villa in front of 15,072.

1973 The opening seven games of the season had taken Villa to the top of the table, but consecutive defeats had pushed them down to eighth place. The slide was halted in emphatic fashion; a 5–0 win over Cardiff City at Villa Park. Villa were gifted an own goal by Woodruff and then made their superiority pay, adding goals from Ray Graydon, Willie Morgan and two from Bruce Rioch.

1982 Villa were humbled at home by Notts County in the first leg of the Milk Cup second round. Peter Withe gave Villa a dream start, firing them into the lead, but County refused to be beaten and struck twice in the second half to leave Villa facing an uphill struggle in the second leg at Meadow Lane.

1993 Birmingham City arrived at Villa Park looking to overturn a 1–0 deficit from the first leg of the Coca-Cola Cup second round, but Villa were just as determined to keep them out. Dean Saunders struck a second-half goal to confirm a 2–0 aggregate win.

OCTOBER 7TH

1959 Garry Thompson born in Birmingham. He began his career as an apprentice with Coventry, breaking into the first team shortly after signing as a professional in 1977. He moved to West Bromwich Albion in 1985 for £225,000 and two years later to Sheffield Wednesday for £450,000 where he made his name as an old fashioned striker. Villa paid £450,000 to take him to Villa Park in June 1986 and he spent two and a half years at the club, scoring 17 League goals. He was sold to Watford for £325,000 in 1988 and subsequently played for Crystal Palace, Queens Park Rangers, Cardiff and Northampton.

OCTOBER 8TH

1934 Gerry Hitchens born in Rawnsley. He began his career with non-League Kidderminster Harriers and was signed by Cardiff City in 1953. Over the next four years he developed into one of the great talents in the game and was snapped up by Villa in December 1957 for £22,500. He spent four years with Villa, his goals helping them to the Second Division title and then to reach the final of the League Cup in 1960–61, although by the time the final was played at the beginning of the following season he had gone, sold to Inter Milan for £85,000. He went on to become one of the few early British successes in Italian football, along with John Charles, and after giving Inter Milan great service went on to play for Torino, Atalanta and Cagliari during the course of eight years in the country. Capped seven times by England he returned to these shores in 1969 and played non-League football for Worcester City and Merthyr Tydfil before retiring.

1971 Neil Cox born in Scunthorpe. He began his career with the local League side and was transferred to Aston Villa for £400,000 in 1991, although he had to wait over a year before making his debut in the club's colours. He made 57 first-team appearances before a £1 million move to Middlesbrough in 1994 and later moved to Bolton for £1.2 million following their promotion to the Premier League.

1977 Play was held up for ten minutes due to pitch invasions during the match between Leicester City and Aston Villa at Filbert Street as Villa became the third side to win, goals from Gordon Cowans and Andy Gray helping them to a 2–0 victory.

OCTOBER 9TH

1897 Billy George made his debut in goal for Villa in the 1–1 draw with West Bromwich Albion. He had signed with the club after impressing in a trial friendly against the same opposition, a move which infringed an FA rule and earned Villa a £50 fine and Billy, along with Fred Rinder (the club's financial secretary) and George Ramsay, a one-month ban. Billy George recovered to become a regular for some 13 seasons, earning three caps for England and two League title medals. He finished his career with Villa in 1911 and left to become trainer at Birmingham City.

1976 A crowd of 25,000 was at Villa Park for the friendly between Aston Villa and Glasgow Rangers, but after 51 minutes the match was abandoned after supporters threw bottles on to the pitch and had fought running battles with the police.

1985 With Villa having already won the away leg with Exeter City 4–1 their progress into the third round of the Milk Cup was never going to be in any doubt, but the visit of the Grecians attracted a crowd of just 7,678 to

Villa Park for the second leg. Those who stayed away missed a goal feast; Andy Gray, Brendan Ormsby and Gary Williams all scored twice, whilst there were single strikes for Simon Stainrod and Paul Birch in an 8–1 win, Villa recording a 12–2 aggregate victory.

OCTOBER 10TH

1896 Villa's defence of their League title had not begun in an auspicious manner, with only six points gained in the opening six matches and both West Bromwich Albion and Everton having recorded victories over them. The previous week they had been held to a goalless draw at Bramall Lane by Sheffield United and really needed to move into top gear if they were to make ground on the early challengers, who by this stage comprised United themselves and Derby County. Thankfully, they gained their revenge on Albion with a 2–0 win at Perry Barr before embarking on a run of four successive victories that took them up the table and into a challenging position.

1936 Plymouth Argyle's biggest ever attendance at Home Park, 43,596, was established with the visit of Villa in a Second Division match. The game finished all square at 2–2.

1978 After a bruising first clash in the League Cup third round against Crystal Palace, Villa were at Selhurst Park for the replay. It was another stormy match which saw Villa defender Allan Evans sent off, but despite being down to ten men Villa defended admirably to hold out for a 0–0 draw.

OCTOBER 11TH

1909 Ronnie Starling born in Pelaw. He was working down the pits when he first came to the attention of Hull City in 1924, being given an office job, and played as an amateur by a Hull side desperate to get his signature. Two years later he turned professional and later joined Newcastle United for £3,750, although this move did not work out and he joined Sheffield Wednesday in 1932. Made captain he helped the club to the FA Cup in 1935 and collected two caps for England. He joined Villa in January 1937 for £7,500 and helped them in their return to the First Division. During the Second World War he was a member of the team that won the League Cup North in 1944, and at the end of the hostilities made a single appearance for the League side before retiring.

1919 An auction was held at the Hotel Metropole in Leeds – all the players from the Leeds City side that was thrown out of the League for refusing to allow the books to be inspected by the authorities were up for sale. By the time the sale was finished, little more than £10,000 had been raised, a figure considerably lower than would have been realised on an open marketplace. In particular, Aston Villa might have been expected to pay at least four or five times the £250 they forked out to take Billy Kirton to Villa Park, but at the end of an already traumatic season for him, he won an FA Cup-winners' medal and scored the winning goal! Villa also signed George Stephenson, brother of Clem who was also a Villa player. George remained with Villa until 1927 when he was sold to Derby for £2,000, later turning out for Sheffield Wednesday, Preston North End and Charlton Athletic before hanging up his boots. Just like his elder brother he had a spell in charge of Huddersfield Town, taking over in 1947 and resigning five years later.

1972   Leeds United ended Villa's interest in the League Cup, winning a third-round replay at Elland Road 2–0 in front of a crowd of 28,894. Chris Nicholl turned past Jim Cumbes to gift Leeds the first goal, with Mick Jones adding a second shortly after. Despite Villa's efforts to get back into the game, Leeds held firm.

OCTOBER 12TH

1889   Villa registered their biggest win of the season with a 7–1 win over Derby County at Perry Barr.

1939   Dave Pountney born in Baschurch. He started his League career with Shrewsbury, making 176 appearances for the Gay Meadow club before being sold to Villa in October 1963. He remained at Villa Park for nearly four and a half years, making 115 appearances in the League and then returned to Shrewsbury, finishing his career with Chester for whom he made another 135 appearances.

1946   Chris Nicholl born in Wilmslow. After failing to make the grade with Burnley he began his League career with Halifax and then had a spell with Luton before joining Villa for £75,000 in March 1972. He helped the club win the League Cup in 1975 and 1977, scoring one of the goals in the second replay against Everton, and at the end of the latter season joined Southampton, helping them to the League Cup final in 1979. He finished his playing career with Grimsby before turning to management, taking over at Southampton in 1985, and was later in charge at Walsall.

1956   Allan Evans born in Dunfermline. He began his career with Dunfermline Athletic and cost Villa £30,000 when transferred in 1977. After a spell of reserve-team football he broke into the side in time to help them win the League title and European Cup in successive seasons as well as earning four caps for Scotland. He made 469 appearances for the Villa before being released in 1990, spending a brief time in Australia before becoming assistant to Brian Little and joining him at Villa Park when he took over during the 1994–95 season.

1960   Aston Villa played their very first match in the newly inaugurated League Cup and registered a 4–1 home win over Huddersfield Town in the second round. Villa went on to win the competition at the beginning of the season, the final having been held over.

1988   Birmingham City were swept aside 5–0 on the night and 7–0 on aggregate after a stunning Villa performance. Derek Mountfield, Kevin Gage, Ian Olney and Tony Daley scored the goals that left one half of the city of Birmingham in raptures.

OCTOBER 13TH

1886 Villa's record number of goals scored in one match came in a cup-tie against Wednesbury Old Athletic at Perry Barr. Villa's goals in a 13–0 win were scored by Dennis Hodgetts, Archie Hunter and Albert Brown, all of whom scored hat-tricks, Loach (two), Davis and Burton. Hodgetts had joined Villa from Birmingham St George in February and would win two FA Cups and a League title whilst with the club, as well as representing England. He left for Small Heath in 1896.

1894 Howard Spencer made his debut for Villa in the 3–1 home win over West Bromwich Albion, thus beginning an association with the club that would stretch for 42 years. He made 294 games for the club and won four League titles and three FA Cups and represented England on six occasions. When his playing career ended he became a director of the club, serving on the board from 1909 until 1936.

1971 Andy Lochhead and Ray Graydon scored the goals that put First Division Crystal Palace out of the League Cup in a third-round replay at Villa Park in front of a crowd of 24,978. This was Villa's sixth game in the competition, having taken three games to get past Wrexham in the first round, a single match against Chesterfield in the second and two against Palace in the third.

OCTOBER 14TH

1899 The title charge gathered momentum with a 4–1 win at Notts County, meaning Villa had still only dropped four points all season.

1964 Villa produced a stunning performance to win 3–2 at Elland Road in the League Cup third round against a resurgent Leeds United to earn a home tie against Reading in the fourth round.

1978 At half-time Villa were seemingly on their way to a convincing victory over Manchester United, two goals ahead thanks to strikes from John Gregory. In the second half Villa took their foot off the pedal, allowing United back into the game and after Sammy McIlroy pulled a goal back it was backs to the wall to try and prevent an equaliser. Somehow Lou Macari found a way and the game ended 2–2, but Villa should have won.

OCTOBER 15TH

1955 Future champions Manchester United and Villa played out a highly entertaining 4–4 draw at Villa Park in a game that ebbed and flowed throughout.

1983 A first-half goal from Peter Withe settled the derby game with

Birmingham City at Villa Park in front of a crowd of 39,318. At the end of the season, City were relegated to the Second Division, leaving Villa and West Bromwich Albion as the city's representatives in the top flight.

1997 West Ham bundled Villa out of the Coca-Cola Cup with a 3–0 win at Upton Park, thus ending Villa's reign as cup holders.

OCTOBER 16TH

1974 Crewe Alexandra put up a spirited display at Villa Park in the League Cup third-round replay, but a goal from Chico Hamilton finally separated the two teams and put Villa into the fourth round, where they would face a tricky visit to Hartlepool.

1978 After two close encounters with Crystal Palace in the third round of the League Cup, Villa finally settled matters with a convincing 3–0 win at Coventry's Highfield Road in the second replay. Two goals for Andy Gray and one from John Gregory in front of a crowd of 25,445, the bulk of them having made the short trip over from Birmingham, saw Villa into the fourth round and a home draw with Luton.

OCTOBER 17TH

1910 Bob Iverson born in Folkestone. Spotted by Spurs whilst playing for Folkestone Town, he was signed and sent to the club's nursery outfit but later allowed to join Lincoln City. He later served Wolves before joining Aston Villa in 1936 and went on to become a regular in the side, continuing to play for them during the Second World War. He remained on Villa's books until 1947 when he retired to become coach to the reserve side.

1925 Len Capewell scored for Villa in the 3–3 draw at home to Birmingham City, having scored in each of the previous seven League matches for the club and thus established a new record. However, the real drama came in the final ten minutes, for with Villa 3–0 ahead many of the crowd were beginning to head for home, but two goals from City set up a nail biting finish. Villa goalkeeper Cyril Spiers was attempting to clear his line when he managed to throw the ball into his own net for a dramatic equaliser!

1931 Dai Astley made his debut for the club in the 3–0 win over Portsmouth at Fratton Park. Signed from Charlton during the previous summer he went on to score 100 goals in 173 first-team appearances for Villa and collected nine caps for Wales, having already been awarded his first whilst with Charlton. In November 1936 he was transferred to Derby County, moving to Blackpool shortly before the Second World War. At the end of hostilities he went to coach in Italy.

1987 Aston Villa became the first club to score 6,000 League goals, a feat achieved with today's 1–1 draw with Bournemouth at Villa Park. The historic goal was scored by Mark Walters.

OCTOBER 18TH

1967 Tony Daley born in Birmingham. He joined Villa straight from school and signed as a professional in May 1985, even though he had already made his debut for the club the previous month. His time with Villa was a mixture of disappointment, with relegation and a series of niggling injuries, and elation, including winning England caps during his time with the club. After 290 first-team appearances he was sold to Wolves for £1.25 million in 1994.

1971 Bruce Rioch was handed a four-week suspension by the FA Disciplinary Committee under the totting up system.

1994 Having already disposed of Internazionale in the first round of the UEFA Cup, Villa had high hopes of making further advancement in the competition against Trabzonspor. In the first leg in Turkey, however, they went down to a goal in the 78th minute from Orhan.

OCTOBER 19TH

1889 Villa's record defeat was inflicted by Blackburn Rovers in a cup-tie earlier the same year, but in the League meeting between the two sides at Ewood Park Villa also fell badly, going down 7–0.

1912 Two weeks after Harry Hampton had scored five goals in the ten goal demolition of Sheffield Wednesday to become the first Villa player to have scored five goals in a League match, Harold Halse equalled the record with all five in the victory over Derby.

1935 Villa crashed to a humiliating 7–0 defeat at home to local rivals West Bromwich Albion. The whole season was already turning out to be something of a disaster for Villa, especially at home, for by the end of the campaign they had conceded 56 goals at Villa Park. And, although Middlesbrough and Arsenal also scored seven at the same venue, none hurt the club as much as those inflicted by their local rivals.

1977 Polish side Gornik Zabrze were at Villa Park for the UEFA Cup second round first leg with a crowd of 34,138 in attendance. A goal in each half from Ken McNaught settled the game 2–0 in Villa's favour.

1983 Villa performed superbly in Russia against rising stars Moscow Spartak, scoring twice in the second half through Colin Gibson and Mark Walters. Unfortunately, Gavrilov also scored twice, the second a penalty in the very last minute, to tie the game 2–2, but Villa surely had the advantage with their away goals.

1993 Another great European result for Villa, drawing 1–1 with Deportivo La Coruna in Spain thanks to a goal from Dean Saunders.

OCTOBER 20TH

1976 Villa were in devastating form against Arsenal at Villa Park, thumping the London club 5–1 with a superlative second-half display. Dennis Mortimer and Ray Graydon had scored in the first half as Villa went into the break 2–1 ahead, but two second-half efforts from Andy Gray and a goal from Brian Little continued Villa's march up the table.

1982 Gary Shaw scored two priceless goals, one in each half, as Villa recorded a 2–0 win in Romania against Dinamo Bucharest in the European Cup second round first leg. Although the 70,000 crowd made a considerable noise at the start of the game, they had little or nothing to say at the end.

OCTOBER 21ST

1910 Ernie Callaghan born in Birmingham. John Devey had spotted him whilst Ernie was playing for Atherstone Town and he made his Villa debut in January 1933, initially as full-back but later showing his versatility by switching to centre-half. Unfortunately the Second World War cut across his career and although he was still with the club when League football resumed, he made only ten appearances before retiring and becoming maintenance man at Villa Park. Known throughout his career as Mush, he died in 1972.

1981 East German champions Dynamo Berlin were the opposition for the second round first leg of the European Cup and Villa put in an exceptional performance to record a 2–1 win in Berlin thanks to two goals from Tony Morley.

1997 Just as they had done in the first round, Villa shut up shop for the away leg of the UEFA Cup, this time in Spain to face Athletic Bilbao.

OCTOBER 22ND

1957 Roy McParland had expected to receive a hostile reception at Old Trafford in the FA Charity Shield from fans who were undoubtedly upset by his challenge on Ray Wood in the FA Cup final which had effectively ended their team's chances of winning the League and Cup double. Instead, he was greeted with a cheer, a sign that there were no hard feelings from the United followers. A Tommy Taylor hat-trick and a single strike from Johnny Berry gave them further reason to be happy. At the same time, Villa should have used the result as a warning of what was to come in the future; in order to win the League, a team needs to be consistent over 42 matches, which United undoubtedly were. To win the Cup requires luck over six games, which was what Villa had enjoyed the previous season – the gap between Villa and United couldn't have been greater as the decade headed to its conclusion.

1960 Birmingham City might well have been on their way to the final of the Inter Cities Fairs Cup final, but they were no match for Villa at Villa Park, going down to a 6–2 defeat.

1928 Keith Jones born in Kidderminster. He joined Villa in 1946 from Kidderminster Harriers and soon proved himself a more than capable goalkeeper, being capped for Wales in 1949. He played 199 games for the club until losing his place to Nigel Sims and left for Port Vale in 1957, subsequently playing for Crewe Alexandra and Southport before retiring in 1960.

1991 A crowd of only 6,447 were at Highfield Road for the Zenith Data Systems Cup second-round tie between Coventry and Villa, with Ian Olney and Dwight Yorke scoring the goals that took Villa through 2–0.

1996 A re-run of the previous season's Coca-Cola Cup final saw Villa at Elland Road to face Leeds United in the third round of the competition. Leeds took the lead after 69 minutes through Lee Sharpe but Ian Taylor equalised within a minute and then Dwight Yorke heaped more agony on the home side with a penalty conversion that took Villa into the next round.

1964 Villa were at Old Trafford for a League fixture with Manchester United and the game was a contrast of fortunes between the strikers on each side; Tony Hateley had little luck, being carried off injured, whilst his opposite number Denis Law fired home four goals in a 7–0 rout by United. It was Villa's worst defeat of a season that was already shaping up to be a struggle.

1990 The visit of Internazionale in the UEFA Cup second round first leg drew a crowd of 36,461 to Villa Park, and on one of the great European nights the stadium has witnessed, goals from Kent Nielsen and David Platt gave them a 2–0 to take to Milan for the second leg.

1919 Billy Kirton made his debut for Villa in the 4–1 win at Middlesbrough. He had joined the club earlier in the month from Leeds City for £500, the fee a ridiculously low one given his pedigree, but with Leeds being disbanded there were bargains to be had! A member of the side that reached the FA Cup finals of 1920 (he scored the winner) and 1924 he remained with Villa until 1927, joining Coventry City in September after 261 appearances for Villa. After just 16 games at Coventry he went to play non-League football.

1925 Dick York scored all three goals for Villa in the 3–2 win at Bury. An all-round sportsman he ran for Birchfield Harriers and also excelled at rugby, but whilst serving in the Royal Flying Corps during the latter stages of the First World War guested for Chelsea. At the end of hostilities he signed with Villa and made his debut during the 1919–20 season, going on to make 390 appearances for the side before joining Port Vale. He then finished his career with Brierley Hill Alliance. He scored one further hat-trick for Villa during his career, also against Bury on 13th October 1928.

1962 Steve Hodge born in Nottingham. After graduating through the ranks of the local Forest club he was something of a regular in the first team for three seasons, before being allowed to join Villa for £450,000 in 1985. His performances in the claret and blue of Villa ensured a call-up for the full England side and he went to the 1986 World Cup, playing in five of England's games. He was then sold to Spurs in 1986 but after less than a year was back at Nottingham Forest, helping them win two League Cups and reach the FA Cup final, before joining Leeds United in 1991. He later played on loan for Derby and then signed for Queens Park Rangers before retiring.

OCTOBER 26TH

1971 Villa's League Cup run came to an end at Blackpool, beaten 4–1 by the Second Division side. Having been beaten finalists the previous season and disposed of First Division opposition in the previous round, Villa had hoped they might go all the way again this time around.

1993 A superb display by Villa at Roker Park in the Coca-Cola Cup third round saw Sunderland turfed out of the competition 4–1 in front of their own supporters. Goals from Dalian Atkinson (two), Kevin Richardson and Ray Houghton won the game for the visitors in front of a crowd of 23,692.

1994 Andy Townsend scored the goal that kept Villa's grip on the Coca-Cola Cup with a 1–0 win over Middlesbrough at Villa Park. The win set up a clash with Crystal Palace in the fourth round.

OCTOBER 27TH

1894 Villa completed the double over Liverpool, following up a 2–1 win at Anfield the previous month with a 5–0 win at Perry Barr. Whilst Villa were unsuccessful in defending their League title they did win the FA Cup, whilst Liverpool finished bottom of the First Division.

1958 Gordon Cowans born in Cornforth. After graduating through the ranks at Villa he was handed a debut in 1976 and went on to help the club win the League Cup in 1977, the League in 1981 and the European Cup the following season, as well as collecting the first of his ten caps for England. A broken leg in 1983 kept him out of the side throughout 1983–84 and in 1985 he was sold to Bari in Italy for £500,000. Three years later he returned to Villa for £250,000 and re-established himself in the side before being sold to Blackburn for £200,000 in 1991. He returned to Villa Park for a third time in 1993 and took his number of first-team appearances to 527 before going to Derby for £80,000 in 1994. He has since played for Wolves, Sheffield United, Bradford City and Stockport County.

1976 Villa marched into the quarter-finals of the League Cup with a 5–1 win over Wrexham at Villa Park. Goals from Brian Little (two), Chris Nicholl, Frank Carrodus and Andy Gray overcame plucky opposition from the Third Division side.

OCTOBER 28TH

1893 Steve Smith made his debut for Villa, scoring one of their goals in the 4–0 home win over Burnley. In eight years with the club he would win two FA Cup and five League championship medals, as well as a single cap for England, scoring in the 3–0 win over Scotland in 1895. He joined Portsmouth in 1901 and later had a spell as player-manager of New Brompton, forerunners of the current Gillingham side.

1970 A single goal from Brian Tiler took Villa into the League Cup quarter-finals, 1–0 victors over Carlisle United in the fourth round at Villa Park.

1987 Villa took a notable scalp, dumping First Division Spurs out of the Littlewoods Cup 2–1 at Villa Park. Alan McInally gave them the lead in the first half and Warren Aspinall increased it in the second, and although Spurs fought back, Villa held on to make their way into the fourth round of the cup.

OCTOBER 29TH

1932 Aston Villa lost their first match of the season having been unbeaten in the opening 11 games. The run included eight wins and three draws and was brought to an end with a 3–1 defeat at West Bromwich Albion. Aston Villa went on to finish the season as League runners-up behind Arsenal.

1983 Tony Woodcock of Arsenal scored five of his side's goals in the astonishing 6–2 win over Villa at Villa Park. Given the opponents, Villa could be forgiven for paying extra special attention to the former Nottingham Forest striker as he set about single-handedly demolishing Villa's defence. It was Villa's worst home defeat for 17 years.

1986 Aston Villa were trailing 1–0 in their League Cup tie at Derby when a whistle blown in the crowd caused the Derby players to come to a standstill – Villa's Tony Daley nipped in to score the equaliser (and Villa went on to win the replay!).

OCTOBER 30TH

1884 William Suddell of Preston North End chaired another meeting of clubs in Manchester. It was proposed to form a break-away union to be known as the British Football Association – 'which shall embrace clubs and players of every nationality.' The proposal had the support of some 28 clubs (of which only Sunderland and Aston Villa were not from Lancashire) and faced with such hostility the FA finally relented and legalised professionalism.

1886 Villa established their record cup victory with a 13–0 hammering of Wednesbury Old Athletic. The goals were scored by Burton (two), R. Davis, A. Brown (three), Hunter (three), Loach (two) and Hodgetts (two).

1929 Dave Hickson born in Ellesmere Port. Signed by Everton in May 1948 from Ellesmere Port, he remained at Goodison until September 1955. He cost Villa £17,500 but remained only two months, making 12 League appearances before switching to Huddersfield for £16,000 and then returned to Everton in August 1957 for £7,500. Just over two years later he was on the move again, making the relatively short trip across Stanley Park to sign for Liverpool, and he later finished his playing career with Bury and Tranmere.

1937 A total of 68,029 people packed into Villa Park for the Second Division fixture between Aston Villa and local rivals Coventry City, the highest attendance for a Second Division match. The game ended a 1–1 draw.

1973 Michael Oakes born in Northwich. He graduated through the ranks at Villa to become a professional in 1991 and went on to win six Under-21 caps for England. As such he was a more than capable deputy whenever Mark Bosnich was not available for the side.

OCTOBER 31ST

1950 Ian Hamilton born in London. Known throughout his career as Chico, he was introduced to the League by Chelsea, making his debut in 1966. He was sold to Southend United in 1968 and cost Villa £40,000 in June 1969. He was a regular in the side for much of the next seven years, helping them to two League Cup finals, one of which was won (in 1975) and the Third Division championship. He joined Sheffield United in July 1976 before finishing off his playing career in America.

1970 Villa very nearly threw away a point against Reading in a Third Division clash at Elm Park. By half-time Villa were three goals ahead thanks to Andy Lochhead, Brian Tiler, and an own goal. Villa eased off in the second period and were nearly caught, goals from Pat McMahon and a Willie Anderson penalty finally enabling Villa to take both points in a 5–3 win.

1990 Second-half goals from Tony Cascarino and David Platt from the penalty spot saw off the challenge from Millwall in the Rumbelows League Cup clash at Villa Park.

NOVEMBER 1ST

1890 Villa won only one game away from home during the season, but as the opponents were West Bromwich Albion it tasted all the sweeter as they won 3–0 at Stoney Lane.

1902 Over 35,000 were at Villa Park for another local clash with West Bromwich Albion, with the visitors winning 3–0.

1925 Larry Canning born in Cowdenbeath. He joined Villa in October 1947 and made 39 League appearances for the club, scoring three goals from the right-half position before moving on to Northampton in June 1956. He later made a bigger name for himself as a broadcaster with the BBC.

1994 Villa's interest in the UEFA Cup ended despite a 2–1 home win over Trabzonspor, for the goal the visitors scored proved to be crucial. With the first leg having finished 1–0 against Villa, it was vital that they got an early goal to level the tie, but it took until the 77th minute before Dalian Atkinson finally made the breakthrough. That might still have been enough to force extra time and possibly a penalty shoot out, but two goals in the final minute sealed Villa's fate. Villa's second goal was scored by Ugo Ehiogu.

NOVEMBER 2ND

1962 Derek Mountfield born in Liverpool. An Everton fan as a schoolboy, he began his career with Tranmere Rovers before moving to Goodison Park for £30,000 in June 1982. Injuries to Mark Higgins finally enabled him to claim a regular place in the side and he helped Everton win the League, FA Cup and European Cup-Winners' Cup. The arrival of Dave Watson restricted his first-team opportunities with Everton and in 1988 he joined Aston Villa for £450,000. He made 120 appearances for the club until he lost his place through injury and joined Wolves, later playing for Carlisle, Northampton and Walsall.

1977 Aston Villa were in Poland for the second leg of the second round of the UEFA Cup facing Gornik Zabrze, with Villa 2–0 ahead from the first leg. A goal from Marcinkowski in the first half gave the 15,000 Polish crowd hope that their side might score again to level the tie, but a goal from Andy Gray in the second half ensured a 3–1 aggregate win for the Villa.

1983 A sad night for Villa as they became the only one of nine British sides to be eliminated from European competition, going down 2–1 at home to Moscow Spartak. Peter Withe had given Villa the lead in the first half and an overall aggregate lead, but with the Russians committed to attack in the second half, Villa found their defence breached twice by Cherenkov. With English clubs later banned from Europe as a result of the Heysel disaster, it would be another seven years before Villa Park again welcomed European competition.

NOVEMBER 3RD

1971 Dwight Yorke born in Canaan in Tobago. His performances for Trinidad and Tobago against Villa in 1989 prompted Graham Taylor to pay £120,000 to his club Signal Hill to bring him to England before word of his talent got out. After taking a while to settle in England, he became an almost permanent fixture in the side following Ron Atkinson's appointment as manager, and was top scorer for the club, scoring when they won the League Cup in 1996. After much speculation he was sold to Manchester United for £12.5 million in August 1998.

1972 Ugo Ehiogu born in Hackney. After beginning his career with West Bromwich Albion, he had made just two substitute appearances when Villa paid £40,000 to take him to Villa Park in 1991. Here he has developed into one of the best defenders in the game, helping the club win the League Cup in 1996 and earning a cap for England. He seems assured of a bright future for both club and country.

1982 Having scored twice in the first leg of the European Cup second round in Bucharest, Gary Shaw went one better with a hat-trick at Villa Park, with Mark Walters grabbing the other goal in a 4–2 win on the night, 6–2 on aggregate.

1993 Aston Villa were shocked in front of their own supporters, going down 1–0 to Deportivo La Coruna in the UEFA Cup second round second leg and 2–1 on aggregate.

NOVEMBER 4TH

1981 Villa were made to sweat before finally overcoming Dynamo Berlin in the second round of the European Cup. A superb performance in Berlin had left Villa 2–1 ahead from the first leg and seemingly all but guaranteed a place in the quarter-finals, but anyone in the 28,175 crowd expecting an easy and clear cut victory was to be disappointed. The Germans scored the only goal of the night through Terletzki and continued pressing throughout in the search for a vital second, but Villa held firm and managed to squeeze into the next round courtesy of away goals.

1986 A 2–1 win at home to Derby in the Littlewoods Cup third-round replay set up a trip to Southampton in the next round. Villa's goals were scored by Paul Birch and Garry Thompson.

1997 Once again only a single goal separated Villa and their overseas opposition in the UEFA Cup, and again it was in Villa's favour. Goals from Ian Taylor and Dwight Yorke enabled Villa to win 2–1 on the night against Athletic Bilbao in the second round second leg and progress 2–1 on aggregate.

NOVEMBER 5TH

1881 Perry Barr played host to the FA Cup first-round clash with Nottingham Forest, the appeal of the visitors attracting a then record crowd of 6,000. The home fans went home happy after a 4–1 win, even more so when it was learned that Villa had received a bye in the next round and would not therefore have to play again in the competition until the fourth round.

Quite by chance, that brought them face to face with the other side from Nottingham, Notts County!

1898 Derby County were brushed aside 7–1 in a League match at Villa Park in Villa's fifth consecutive win on their way to winning the League title.

1971 Fernando Nelson born in Portugal. Signed by Villa from Sporting Lisbon in 1996, he made his debut in the third game of the 1996–97 campaign and soon settled into a regular position as a right wing back. A full Portuguese international player he was a member of their side for the World Cup qualifiers.

1989 Everton were thumped 6–2 at Villa Park thanks to goals from Gordon Cowans, Ian Olney (two), David Platt (two) and Kent Neilsen. It was Villa's fifth consecutive win and lifted them to sixth place in the First Division.

NOVEMBER 6TH

1920 The outbreak of the First World War had forced committee member and surveyor Frederick Rinder to abandon plans to turn Villa Park into a stadium capable of accommodating 130,000 spectators, although work had begun in 1911 on transforming the ground from one in which 40,000 where cramped and had a restricted view of the proceedings into one worthy of a club of such stature. In the summer of 1914 the cycle track had been removed, the Witton Lane Stand extended and the banking behind both goals made higher. The shortage of materials during the war plus the fact the club could not be seen to be spending extravagant sums had brought the grand dreams to an end, but Villa Park could still find room for those who wished to attend. A crowd of 66,094, the first over even 60,000 for a League match, was present for the visit of local rivals West Bromwich Albion. There was little for such a vast crowd to cheer however; the game finished 0–0.

1932 Ron Saunders born in Birkenhead. As a player he began his career with Everton but made only three appearances before going off to join Gillingham in 1957. A subsequent switch to Portsmouth in 1958 revived his career and he later played for Watford and Charlton before turning to management with non-League Yeovil Town. He returned to the League with Oxford United in 1969, later moving to Norwich City and Manchester City before joining Villa in June 1974. Having previously taken both Norwich and Manchester City to the League Cup finals, it was third time lucky as he guided Villa past Norwich in the same competition in 1975. He repeated the League Cup success in 1977 and then in 1981 made them League champions for the first time in 71 years. The following season saw Villa make steady progress in the European Cup but Saunders suddenly resigned after a disagreement with the board. He became manager of Birmingham City and later had a spell in charge at West Bromwich Albion.

1965 Although Villa have been paired with Northampton Town twice in cup competition, this was the only time they visited the County Ground in the League, with Town recording a 2–1 win. Northampton also won the corresponding game at Villa Park the following April by the same score.

NOVEMBER 7TH

1931 Danny Blair made his debut for Villa in the match against Blackpool won 5–1 at Villa Park. He had been born in Glasgow and played in Canada and Ireland whilst studying agriculture and farming and only took up professional football when he returned to Scotland. He joined Villa from Clyde for a fee of £7,500 after having won six caps for Scotland prior to his arrival. He went on to make 138 first-team appearances for Villa before joining Blackpool in 1936, and later became coach.

1959 Liverpool against Aston Villa in the Second Division had an unfamiliar ring to it, but at Anfield 49,981 saw Villa go down 2–1 for their first defeat in 15 matches. They had climbed to the top of the League by that time, intent on making their season in the Second Division as brief as possible, and despite the hiccup against Liverpool stormed their way to the title at the end of the season.

1990 Villa stepped out into a cauldron of noise, generated by a sell-out crowd of 80,000 at the San Siro Stadium in Milan for the UEFA Cup second round second leg. Villa were 2–0 ahead from the first leg, but it was to be a night where little went right, especially in the second half. Jurgen Klinsmann had scored for the Italian side in the first half to reduce the aggregate lead to a single goal, and in the second half Internazionale stepped up the pace and the pressure, equalised through Nicola Berti and then won the tie with a final goal from Bianchi. Although Internazionale went on to win the cup that year, there was little compensation for Villa, inexperience after English clubs' enforced absence from European competition accounting for them as much as anything the Italians had thrown at them.

NOVEMBER 8TH

1890 Villa were held to a 4–4 draw at Perry Barr by fellow strugglers Burnley.

1930 The early pace setters, Villa and Arsenal, clashed at Highbury in the First Division's match of the day. David Jack and Cliff Bastin both scored twice for Arsenal as they put some distance between themselves and the rest of the chasing pack with a 5–2 win.

1978 Luton Town tipped Villa out of the League Cup at the fourth-round stage, winning 2–0 at Kenilworth Road.

NOVEMBER 9TH

1904 Harry Hampton made his debut for the club in the 2–1 defeat by

Manchester City at Hyde Road. Born in Wellington in 1885 he began his career with the local side and became known as the Wellington Whirlwind, scoring 54 goals in two seasons before signing for Villa. Over the next 16 years he helped the club win the FA Cup twice and the League title, as well as scoring more goals for Villa than anyone before or since. He enlisted during the First World War and saw considerable action, being gassed during one German attack on his platoon's position, but recovered sufficiently to take his place in the side when League football resumed in 1919–20. By the time he joined Birmingham City in February 1920 he had scored 242 goals in the League and cup, the 215 in the League remaining Villa's record tally. He joined Birmingham City in an effort to help them gain promotion, but his absence in the last six games cost them dearly. The following season they made no mistake, winning the Second Division title, and he then left for Newport County in September 1922. He died in Wrexham in March 1963.

1968 Another disastrous start to the season had seen Villa take only 11 points from their opening 19 matches of the season, and a 1–0 defeat at home to Preston hardly helped matters. After the game there was a mass protest outside the ground by fans fed up with the way the club was being run, with calls for the management and board to either resign or be sacked. Eventually, mounted police had to be called to clear the area, although the message delivered by the fans did get through; manager Tommy Cummings and assistant Malcolm Musgrove were sacked and coach Arthur Cox took over as caretaker manager. The board survived, for now, but by December 1968 they resigned en masse, allowing Doug Ellis to take over a club that was heavily in debt, with attendances falling week by week and little sign that matters could be turned around. The new board took immediate action to try and rectify the situation, appointing charismatic manager Tommy Docherty in charge in order to try and prevent the club from being relegated into the Third Division.

1994 Andy Townsend became the first Villa player to be dismissed in a Premier League match when sent off in the match against Wimbledon at Selhurst Park which Villa lost 4–3.

NOVEMBER 10TH

1923 In the evening after the game against Notts County (which Villa had won 1–0), Villa centre-half Thomas Ball was shot to death following an altercation with his landlord and neighbour, policeman George Stagg at Brick Kiln Lane in Perry Barr. After making his debut in 1920–21, Ball became a regular in the Villa side the following season, and played in the match against Notts County. Stagg was subsequently sentenced to death for the murder of Thomas Ball in February 1924.

1928 Tommy Thompson born in Fencehouses. He began his career with

Newcastle United but switched to Villa after only a handful of appearances for a fee of £12,500 in September 1950. He made 165 appearances in the club's colours before being surprisingly sold to Preston for £25,000 in June 1955. He later played for Stoke and Barrow and played twice for England, once whilst he was with Villa. At the end of his playing career he went back to Preston to serve under Bobby Charlton, running the club's junior teams.

1948 Villa Park staged the international match between England and Wales which England won 1–0 in front of the biggest crowd to have witnessed an international match at Villa Park, 67,770.

1950 Keith Leonard born in Birmingham. After failing to make the grade with West Bromwich Albion, he slipped into the non-League game and came to Villa's notice whilst playing for Highgate United. Signed in April 1972 he went on to make a handful of appearances before sustaining a double fracture of his right leg in a car crash. When he recovered he spent a brief spell on loan to Port Vale, returning to Villa to help them win promotion and the League Cup in 1975. Injury again hit him and he was forced to retire in 1976.

1964 Guy Whittingham born in Evesham. He bought himself out of the army in order to pursue a football career, signing with Portsmouth from non-League Yeovil in 1989. Four years later Villa paid £1.2 million to take him to Villa Park but he made only a handful of appearances before being loaned out to Wolves, subsequently being sold to Sheffield Wednesday for £700,000 in 1994.

1994 Aston Villa parted company with manager Ron Atkinson with the club languishing in 19th position in the Premier League. Despite guiding the club to the League Cup in 1994 and runners-up spot in the League in 1993, the club's woeful start to the season and dismissal from European competition in the second round counted against the flamboyant manager.

NOVEMBER 11TH

1893 By the time Villa reached the half-way stage of the season they and Sunderland, their visitors to Perry Barr, had emerged with Derby as likeliest challengers for the League title. Sunderland, the reigning champions, were going for an unprecedented three titles in a row (a feat that would not be achieved until Huddersfield in the 1920s), whilst Derby were competing in the top half of the table for the first time. Villa were able to put a little bit of daylight between themselves and their challengers with a hard fought 2–1 win over Sunderland.

1895 Villa dropped their only point at home during the season with a 2–2 draw with Sheffield United at Perry Barr. They were to finish the season champions for the second time in their history, with the 15 home matches delivering 29 points, one of the best performances in the League's history (only Sunderland, who won all 13 of their home matches in 1891–92 did better, but Villa did play two games more).

1970 Mark Draper born in Long Eaton. He first broke through with Notts County, joining the club as a trainee and rising through the ranks to full professional level. He cost Leicester City a fee of £1.25 million when signed in July 1994 and a year later switched to Villa for £3.25 million.

1987 The visit of Bradford City in the Simod Cup attracted a crowd of just 4,217 to Villa Park, one of the lowest to have witnessed a first-class fixture. Those who stayed away turned out to have been the wiser; Villa slumped to a 5–0 defeat!

1994 UEFA fined Villa £9,000 for the pitch invasion following their recent UEFA Cup exit at the hands of Turkish side Trabzonpor, with Trabzonpor also fined £6,000.

NOVEMBER 12TH

1892 Nottingham Forest and Villa were involved in a nine goal thriller at the Town Ground in Nottingham, with Villa finally winning 5–4.

1921 One week after going down 3–2 at Valley Parade against Bradford City, Villa gained ample revenge with a 7–1 win at Villa Park against the same opponents. Billy Walker scored a hat-trick for Villa, all of them from the penalty spot. Not surprisingly, this is a record achievement.

1966 After two successive victories Villa were brought back down to earth with a 5–1 defeat at Craven Cottage against fellow strugglers Fulham.

1974 Villa survived a scare at the Victoria Ground, taking the lead against Hartlepool through Charlie Aitken but then being pegged back as the Fourth Division side played above their status. They fully deserved their equaliser and could look forward to a bumper pay-day in the replay at Villa Park.

NOVEMBER 13TH

1897 Villa spiked Everton's championship aspirations with a 3–0 win at Perry Barr.

1937 Alan O'Neill born in Leadgate. He began his career with Sunderland, signing as a junior and then becoming a professional in February 1955. Villa bought him in October 1960 and he went on to make 23 League appearances before moving on to Plymouth. He finished his career with Bournemouth.

1961 Villa played a floodlight friendly against Russian side Dynamo Kiev at Villa Park, winning 2–1.

NOVEMBER 14TH

1951 Villa Park staged the international match between England and Northern

Ireland, with Nat Lofthouse of Bolton scoring both of England's goals in the 2–0 win.

1959 Five of Villa's goals in the 11–1 win over Charlton were scored by Gerry Hitchens, thus equalling the individual record for most goals in a game previously held by Harry Hampton, Harold Halse, Len Capewell and George Brown. Charlton's cause was not helped with the loss of goalkeeper Duff through an arm injury midway through the game, but by this stage Villa were 6–1 to the good and in fine form; it would not have mattered who had been in goal for the visitors on the day. Not surprisingly, this remains Charlton's worst ever defeat.

NOVEMBER 15TH

1930 There were ten goals at the Baseball Ground during the clash between Derby and Villa, but Derby got six of them to Villa's four to win the game.

1958 One less goal at Filbert Street, but still the home side scored six, with Villa going down 6–3 against Leicester City.

1960 After putting Huddersfield out of the League Cup in the second round Villa were faced with a trip to Deepdale for the third-round clash with Preston. At the time a First Division club (although they were to be relegated at the end of the season), they were a difficult proposition on their own ground, and Villa were fortunate to come away with a 3–3 draw and the chance of a replay.

1971 Bryan Small born in Birmingham. He joined Villa as a trainee and was upgraded to the professional ranks in 1990, making his debut in October 1991. Initially he was used as cover for Steve Staunton but later proved more than capable in midfield, earning a call-up for the England Under-21 squad. He went on loan to Birmingham in 1994, later joining Bolton Wanderers on a free transfer in 1996.

NOVEMBER 16TH

1963 Manchester United were already among the early leaders of the First Division and arrived at Villa Park second in the table behind Sheffield United. Villa meanwhile were fourth from bottom, but put in an excellent performance on the day to severely dent United's challenge. Villa's 4–0 win, their best of the season in front of their own fans, kept Villa in touch with the clubs immediately above them in a season in which they missed relegation by six points.

1974 This time United were making a brief appearance in the Second Division following their relegation at the end of the previous season. They had started the season in blistering form, heading the table at the end of August and never being topped by the time May came around. But Villa were part of the chasing pack and were ultimately to accompany United on their return to the First Division. A crowd of 55,615 were at Old Trafford for the top of the table clash, with Chico Hamilton giving Villa a well deserved half-time lead. United raised their game in the second period, scoring twice through Gerry Daly and took both points to maintain their position at the top. Villa took a while to recover from the defeat, slipping down as low as 7th in the League in the next few weeks, but then began a charge up the table that saw them come to rest in second place.

NOVEMBER 17TH

1888 Villa were beaten 5–1 by Blackburn Rovers, whose homes at Leamington Road and then Ewood Park were something of bogey grounds for Villa. It took until 1894 before Villa finally got a win at Ewood Park.

1970 Villa survived a League Cup quarter-final clash at Eastville against Bristol Rovers, drawing 1–1 thanks to Pat McMahon's goal to ensure a replay at Villa Park.

1994 Leicester City chairman Martin George announced that it would cost Villa £1.5 million in compensation should they wish to take Brian Little and his two assistants as the new managerial team at Villa Park.

NOVEMBER 18TH

1987 Sheffield Wednesday bundled Villa out of the Littlewoods Cup in a hard fought fourth-round tie at Villa Park. Garry Thompson scored for Villa, but Lee Chapman and West ended the Wembley dream in front of a crowd of 25,302.

1989 Villa moved up to second in the First Division table with a 4–1 win over Coventry City. With neither West Bromwich Albion or Birmingham City in the top flight, this was as close as Villa could get to a derby, and goals from Ian Ormandroyd (two), a David Platt penalty and an own goal from the unfortunate Trevor Peake wrapped up the points for Villa.

NOVEMBER 19TH

1923 The funeral of Tommy Ball took place at St John's Church in Perry Barr. Ball had been murdered nine days previously by his landlord and neighbour George Stagg and thousands of Villa fans lined the route as the coffin was taken to the church and then the graveyard following the burial service. A tribute to the player can still be seen in the churchyard in the form of a granite football.

1932 Just as they had been two years earlier, Villa and Arsenal were the season's early title challengers, and the clash at Villa Park saw Villa looking to extend a good run against the Gunners, for Arsenal had won only one of their 13 League visits. They went home empty handed again, beaten 5–3 in an exhilarating game.

1991 Villa made their last appearance in the Zenith Data Systems Cup, going out in the quarter-final 2–0 to Nottingham Forest at Villa Park in front of a crowd of 7,858.

NOVEMBER 20TH

1920 Alan Wakeman born in Walsall. Initially taken on at Villa as an office boy, he signed professional forms in December 1938 and made his debut in goal the same month. During the war he combined guesting for a number of clubs and working as a Bevin Boy and returned to Villa at the end of hostilities. Unfortunately he was third in line for the number one jersey and in 1950 he moved on to Doncaster Rovers, later finishing his career with Shrewsbury.

1942 Richard Edwards born in Kirksey. He began his career with Notts County, making over 220 appearances at centre-half for the club before joining Mansfield in March 1967. Villa signed him a year later and he remained with the club for over two years before switching to Torquay, later playing for Mansfield before winding down his career.

1962 Paul Birch born in Birmingham. Signed by the club as an apprentice he was a member of the FA Youth Cup winning side in 1980 and broke into the first team three years later. He made over 200 appearances for the first team before a £400,000 move to Wolves in February 1991. He later played for Preston, Doncaster and Exeter.

1965 Jimmy MacEwan became the first ever Villa substitute when he came on for Tony Scott during the 3–1 defeat at Turf Moor against Burnley.

1971 Villa's interest in cup competition for the season came to an end, beaten 1–0 at Southend in the FA Cup first round, leaving them to concentrate on winning the Third Division championship.

NOVEMBER 21ST

1888 Villa collected 15 points without having need to kick a ball; although the Football League had kicked off in September the points system had not been finalised, and it was only today that the familiar two points for a win and one for a draw was agreed.

1961 Villa's reign as League Cup holders came to an end with a 3–2 home defeat by Ipswich Town. Villa were as bemused as the First Division had been by the tactics deployed by Ipswich, with a withdrawn left winger in Jimmy Leadbetter drawing the right-back towards him and creating space for Ray Crawford and Ted Phillips to exploit. Whilst Ipswich were knocked out of the cup in the next round, they did go on to win the League title.

1970 Just as relegation to the Third Division had required Villa to enter the League Cup in the first round, so they were expected to join the FA Cup at the same stage. The draw gave them a long trip to Torquay's Plainmoor ground, where a 3–1 defeat sent Villa tumbling out of the cup. Thankfully, the League Cup was proving a better alternative as a way to Wembley.

NOVEMBER 22ND

1890 Villa won only seven of their games during the course of the season, finishing fourth from bottom of the First Division. They did, however, register a 5–0 win over Bolton with one of their best displays of the campaign.

1969 At half-time in the clash at Bramall Lane Villa were one goal behind but giving a good account of themselves and hoped to get back on level terms. A second-half collapse, however, saw them concede four goals and put paid to a mini revival they had been staging at the bottom of the Second Division.

1997 Villa and Everton were not usually cast in the roles of strugglers, but neither had started the season with much conviction, Villa taking five games to register their first win of the season and Everton stuttering towards another last gasp escape. The clash at Villa Park drew a crowd of 39,389, a truer reflection of the stature of the clubs, where goals from Ugo Ehiogu and Savo Milosevic ensured a 2–1 win for Villa. The result lifted them to 11th place in the table.

NOVEMBER 23RD

1938 Johnny MacLeod born in Edinburgh. He began his career in Scotland with Hibernian, earning a move to Arsenal in June 1961 soon after winning four caps for Scotland. He cost Villa £29,500 in September 1964, a then record fee, and proved an immediate hit with the fans who delighted in his play on the right wing. After 123 League appearances he left to join Belgian side KV Mechelen, finishing his career back in Scotland with Raith Rovers.

1960 Villa eased past Preston in the League Cup third-round replay 3–1 at Villa Park to set up a clash with Plymouth in the next round.

1964 A 7–1 win over Bradford City in the League Cup fifth round took Villa through to meet Chelsea over two legs in the semi-final.

1977 Athletic Bilbao were the visitors for the UEFA Cup third round first leg, a game that drew 32,973 to Villa Park. An own goal in the first half, courtesy of Iribar, settled Villa and a second-half strike from John Deehan gave them a convincing 2–0 lead to take to Spain for the second leg.

NOVEMBER 24TH

1928 Pongo Waring scored his first hat-trick in Villa's League colours in the 5–2 win at Highbury against Arsenal. He went on to score a further nine hat-tricks and a total of 167 goals for Villa during his career.

1970 Pat McMahon scored the only goal of the game as Villa beat Bristol Rovers 1–0 in the replay of the League Cup fifth round. A crowd of 36,483 were at Villa Park and Villa's reward was a money-spinning clash with Manchester United over two legs in the semi-final.

NOVEMBER 25TH

1933 Joe Tate made his last appearance in a Villa shirt in the 3–2 home defeat by Newcastle United. He had joined the club in April 1925 and proved a more than adequate replacement for Frank Moss senior when he moved on to Cardiff. He remained a regular in the side until midway through the 1932–33 season and left Villa in May 1935. He won three caps for England whilst a Villa player.

1953 Brian Little born in Durham. Signed by Villa as an apprentice, he turned professional in 1971 and made his debut the same year against Blackburn. He went on to make 301 first-team appearances, helping the club win the League Cup in 1975 and 1977, as well as promotion to the First Division. A reliable performer for Villa he won his only cap for England in 1975, coming on for the final ten minutes of the match against Wales. In 1979 a proposed move to Birmingham for £160,000 fell through on medical grounds and he was forced to give up the game at the end of the 1980–81 season. He then switched to management, with Wolves, Darlington (who went out of the Football League but returned a year later as GM Vauxhall Conference champions) and Leicester City before accepting an offer to take over at Villa Park in November 1994. Midway through the 1997–98 season he announced his decision to resign, despite having guided the club to the League Cup in 1996. He then took over at Stoke City.

1971 Jim Cumbes joined Villa from West Bromwich Albion for £36,000 and went on to make 157 League appearances for the club.

1997 The UEFA Cup third-round draw had paired Villa with Steaua Bucharest with the first leg to be played in Romania. Despite a 2–1 defeat, the goal scored by Dwight Yorke would undoubtedly prove vital if they were to progress into the next round.

NOVEMBER 26TH

1898 Villa were playing a League match against Wednesday at Sheffield and were 3–1 down when bad light forced the referee to abandon the game. Rather than play the entire game again, the Football League ordered the remaining ten minutes be played when the two sides met again on 13th March 1899! The date of this game is usually recorded as 13th March in history books. Frank Bedingfield was making his debut for Villa in the first match and this was his only appearance for Villa in the League!

1947 Ian Ross born in Glasgow. Discovered by Bill Shankly, he signed with

Liverpool in August 1965 but found it difficult to force his way into the side on a regular basis, subsequently joining Villa in February 1972 for £70,000. He was captain when Villa won the League Cup in 1975 and made 204 appearances in Villa's colours before moving on to Peterborough in 1976.

1958 Villa Park was the venue for the England and Wales match which was drawn 2–2. It was the seventh and last time Villa Park has played host to the national side, although the venue was later used for three group matches in the 1966 World Cup and three group and a quarter-final match in the 1996 European Championships.

NOVEMBER 27TH

1941 Alan Deakin born in Birmingham. Signed by the club in December 1958, he finally became a regular in the side in 1960–61, helping the club to the final of the League Cup (which was played at the start of the following season). He broke his leg midway through the 1964–65 season but returned to the side, going on to make 270 appearances during his time. In October 1969 he was transferred to Walsall and later played non-League football.

1971 Andy Lochhead hit a hat-trick for Villa as they beat Oldham Athletic 6–0. What made the result all the more impressive was the fact that Villa were the away side, thus registering their biggest away win of the season.

NOVEMBER 28TH

1931 In the pre-match kick-about before the game against Manchester City goalkeeper Fred Biddlestone, who had joined the club a year earlier, was injured and could not take part. Luckily for Villa Harry Morton had journeyed over to Maine Road in order to watch the team and an immediate call went out for him to come down to the dressing-room and get changed! Despite the rather bizarre nature of his debut for the club, Harry Morton went on to make over 200 appearances for the club before joining Everton in 1937 and finishing his career with Burnley. The match against Manchester City finished a 3–3 draw.

1989 Just 2,888 were at Hull City's Boothferry Park to see Villa, a side battling for the League title, take on the home side in the Zenith Data Systems Cup. Villa won the game 2–1 thanks to goals from Derek Mountfield and David Platt.

1990 A close match with Middlesbrough finally saw Villa triumph 3–2 in the Rumbelows Cup fourth round at Villa Park. Ian Ormondroyd and Tony Daley had earlier scored for Villa before David Platt converted a crucial penalty.

1995 The march to Wembley in the Coca-Cola Cup continued with a home win over Queens Park Rangers, Andy Townsend scoring the only goal of the game.

NOVEMBER 29TH

1890 Villa crashed to a 7–1 defeat at Notts County, their heaviest defeat of the season. Villa were to win only two of their away games during the campaign.

1902 It was Villa's turn to fire seven goals, with Newcastle the luckless victims. After a poor start to the season Villa had rediscovered their form and were marching relentlessly up the table, finally battling it out with Sheffield United for the League title.

1977 League Cup holders Villa were at the City Ground for a fourth-round tie against Nottingham Forest, newly promoted to the First Division and already top of the table on their way to the title. The cup clash between the two sides was one-way traffic in the first half, with Larry Lloyd, Viv Anderson and Peter Withe firing Forest into a 3–0 lead. Villa staged a second-half revival, getting on the scoresheet through Brian Little and Frank Carrodus, but a final Forest goal from Tony Woodcock ended Villa's interest. Forest were to make it a double that season, lifting the League Cup as well as the League.

NOVEMBER 30TH

1944 George Graham born in Bargeddie. If ever a player deserved the tag of 'the one that got away' then it is surely him, for having graduated through the ranks at Villa he made just eight League appearances before being sold to Chelsea for just £5,000 in July 1964. He helped them win the League Cup before joining Arsenal, where he won medals in the League, FA Cup and Inter-Cities Fairs Cup, including the double in 1971 before moving on to play for Manchester United. He later played for Portsmouth and Crystal Palace before turning to coaching and management, with his most successful spell coming back at Arsenal, taking them to two League titles, the FA Cup, the European Cup-Winners' Cup and two League Cups. Dismissed and banned from football for a year after it was revealed he accepted a payment for a transfer, he resurfaced at Leeds United once the suspension was over.

1955 Andy Gray born in Glasgow. A powerfully built striker, he began his career with Dundee United and cost Villa £110,000 when he joined in 1975, helping the club win the League Cup in 1977. A then record fee of £1.5 million took him to Wolves in September 1979 but his time at Molineux was hit by injury. He moved on to Everton in 1983 for £250,000, a move that revitalised his career and inspired the club to considerable success over the next two years. He won an FA Cup winners' medal in 1984 and the following season helped them to a double of League title and European Cup-Winners' Cup, only missing out in the FA Cup final to Manchester United. He returned to Villa Park in 1985 for

£150,000, spent a spell on loan to Notts County and then joined West Bromwich Albion in 1987. He returned a third time to Villa Park in 1991 as assistant to manager Ron Atkinson but resigned in 1992 in order to concentrate on his career as a broadcaster with Sky Television. A full Scottish international, he won 20 caps during his career.

1970   Villa were reported to be considering a £70,000 bid for Rotherham striker turned centre-half Dave Watson, although the player later joined Sunderland for £100,000.

1993   Coca-Cola Cup holders Arsenal had gone 26 cup-ties without defeat prior to the meeting with Villa at Highbury, having also won the FA Cup the previous season and making progress towards the European Cup-Winners' Cup final. That run came to an end thanks to Dalian Atkinson's goal which put Villa into the fifth round of the competition.

DECEMBER 1ST

1900   Villa registered their biggest win in the season with a 7–1 hammering of Manchester City at Villa Park.

1976   Victories over Manchester City, Norwich City and Wrexham had made the prospect of a return to Wembley for the League Cup final a distinct possibility, and when the fifth-round draw paired them with Millwall at Villa Park, the twin towers came closer into view. Whilst Millwall were particularly difficult to beat at their own ground, they were not so invincible on their travels, and goals in either half from Chris Nicholl and Brian Little in front of a crowd of 37,147 took Villa into the semi-finals to face Queens Park Rangers.

1981   Villa were made to come from behind before finally seeing off Wigan Athletic in the fourth round of the League Cup at Springfield Park. Peter Houghton gave the Third Division side a half-time lead, but goals from Gordon Cowans from the penalty spot and Peter Withe took Villa into their second quarter-final of the season, having already qualified in the European Cup.

DECEMBER 2ND

1893   Villa slipped to their only home defeat of the season, a 1–0 reverse against Bolton Wanderers at Perry Barr. At the end of the season they finished as League champions, whilst Bolton were fourth from bottom, making this defeat all the more surprising.

1899   Preston North End were the first side to dominate the Football League, winning it for the first two years and finishing runners-up the following year. The players who took them to such success, however, were never adequately replaced, and within 11 years they would be relegated. Villa had taken over their mantle, winning the League four times in the 1890s, emulating Preston's double achievement, and were on their way to retaining the title; new players were regularly introduced to keep Villa at the top of the tree. The passing fortunes of the two clubs were probably best summed up in the match played at Deepdale; Villa won 5–0 in a canter and could have had more.

1945　Villa Park had been due to host a friendly fixture between the touring Russian side Moscow Dynamo and an FA XI, with the representative side announced as Swift, Scott, Hardwick, Soo, Franklin, Mercer, Matthews, Carter or Pye, Lawton, Shackleton and Leslie Smith (in effect the full England national side). Arrangements were already well advanced, for Villa had printed up 70,000 tickets for the match (the Russians had just attracted 90,000 for their friendly at Ibrox against Rangers) and anticipated a bumper gate on the day. Sadly it never happened, for news was picked up that Moscow had recalled the team home, though quite why no one was sure. Certainly, the touring Russians expected to play the game, although they had to content themselves with a friendly in Sweden against Norrkoping on their way home, a game they won 5–0.

DECEMBER 3RD

1919　Dickie Dorsett born in Brownhills. He signed with Wolves before the Second World War and helped them reach the FA Cup final in 1939 where they were beaten by Portsmouth. At the end of hostilities he joined Aston Villa, making 256 League appearances before retiring in 1953 when he switched to coaching, remaining at Villa Park with the A team. He later had a spell at Anfield.

1938　Villa's first goal in the 2–0 win over Charlton was scored by Bob Iverson after just 9.6 seconds of the game, the quickest goal ever scored by a Villa player.

1967　Although Villa were destined for relegation and Manchester United the League championship, Villa could still upset the form book, winning a close match 2–1 at Villa Park. Unfortunately, there were too few occasions during the season when Villa were capable of raising their game to such levels, but the United result was a well deserved victory.

DECEMBER 4TH

1926　Len Capewell scored a hat-trick for Villa in the 5–3 home win over Everton, despite suffering from a dislocated shoulder during the match! Villa at one point had been 3–2 behind before mounting a recovery. He had joined Villa from Wellington Town in 1920 and soon established himself as a prolific goalscorer, once netting five goals in a game against Burnley and four against Port Vale, going on to net 100 for the club in 156 League and cup matches. He finished his League career with Walsall and then returned to non-League circles with Wellington Town in 1931.

1959　Paul McGrath born in Ealing. Despite his English birthplace he was discovered by Manchester United playing for St Patrick's Athletic in Eire! Signed in April 1982 for £30,000 he developed into one of the best defenders in the game, helping the club win the FA Cup in 1985 and earning the first of his caps for his country. In August 1989 he was surprisingly allowed to join Aston Villa in a £400,000 deal, United believing he was too susceptible to injuries to stand the rigours of football at the top level, but with Villa he proved each and every one of his critics wrong. A member of the side that won the League Cup in both 1994 and 1996 he continued to impress not only for club but for country as well, stretching his cap tally whilst a Villa player to 51, a record for the club. He was finally allowed to leave in 1996 and remained in the Premier League with Derby County.

1962 Kevin Richardson born in Newcastle. He came through the ranks at Everton and was a member of the side that won the FA Cup in 1984, the League in 1985 and the European Cup-Winners' Cup the same year before being sold to Watford for £225,000 in 1986. He returned to the top flight with Arsenal in 1987 following a £200,000 transfer, earning a second League championship medal in 1989. He then went to Real Sociedad for £750,000 in 1990, returning a year later to Aston Villa for £450,000 and completed his set of domestic medals with the League Cup in 1994. A move to Coventry followed in 1995 for £300,000. He won one cap for England.

DECEMBER 5TH

1891 Perry Barr was not a particularly happy hunting ground for Burnley in the first few years of the Football League, with Villa registering a 6–1 win to leave Burnley still searching for their first win at the ground.

1987 Villa were made to work hard for their 2–1 victory over Swindon in the Second Division, not making the crucial breakthrough until the second half. Then two goals from Garry Thompson enabled Villa to take control and keep their push towards the top of the table in motion.

1992 A 2–1 win at Sheffield Wednesday took Villa back up to third position in the table, Dalian Atkinson scoring both of their goals. There was further good news with Blackburn being beaten, so Villa had gained valuable ground on another rival.

DECEMBER 6TH

1890 Blackburn Rovers proved too strong for Villa as they romped to an easy 5–1 victory at Ewood Park. It was Villa's first visit to Blackburn's new enclosure, the ground having opened only two months previously.

1930 Better luck for Villa on their travels as they registered a 4–3 win at Bramall Lane against Sheffield United to keep the pressure on Arsenal at the top of the table.

1997 Villa warmed up for the forthcoming vital UEFA Cup match with Steaua Bucharest with a 3–0 win over Coventry at Villa Park. A crowd of 33,250 saw goals from Stan Collymore, Julian Joachim and Lee Hendrie wrap up the points.

DECEMBER 7TH

1889 Stoke were to finish the season bottom of the table and voted out of the Football League in preference to Sunderland. Villa helped send them on their way with a 5–1 home win.

1907 Tom Lyons made his debut for Villa in the 5–0 defeat at Anfield against Liverpool. He remained with Villa until the outbreak of the First World War caused the abandonment of the League in 1915, by which time he had made 237 first-team appearances. He retired during the war.

1935 Alex Massie made his debut for Villa in the 5–0 defeat at Maine Road against Manchester City. He had begun his career with Partick Thistle and then Ayr United before trying his luck in England with Bury, joining the club for £1,000. After being released by the club he spent a spell playing in America before returning to Scotland with Hearts, winning the first of his 18 Scottish caps in 1931 and costing Villa £6,000 when they signed him in December 1935. His initial introduction to the Villa side was a baptism of fire, for Villa conceded 17 goals in three games (the 5–0 defeat being followed by the reverse against Arsenal and Blackburn, 7–1 and 5–2 respectively), and with the club relegated at the end of the season. He helped them bounce back two years later as champions and helped them throughout the Second World War, winning a Football League Cup (North) medal in 1944. In September 1945 he retired from playing in order to become manager at Villa Park, a position he held for five years before leaving for Plainmoor, taking over at Torquay United.

1977 Villa had learnt much on their European travels that would serve them in good stead in the years to come, not least the need to silence a home crowd with a goal, especially if the home side were pressing to get back into the tie. A goal, therefore, from Dennis Mortimer in the first half gave Villa a 3–0 aggregate lead over Athletic Bilbao and although Dani pulled a goal back in the second half, Villa were seldom in danger of allowing any further Spanish goals.

DECEMBER 8TH

1888 Villa registered their second away win of the season with a 4–2 win at Notts County and thus recorded their first double, having already beaten the same opposition 9–1 at home.

1923 In the 1923–24 season it was usual to play home and away against the same sides on consecutive weeks, so one week after being held to goalless draw at home to Middlesbrough, Villa travelled to Ayresome Park and returned home with a 2–0 win! The same thing happened a few weeks earlier against Liverpool; a draw at home and a win away.

1973 Defender Charlie Aitken made his 479th League appearance and therefore overtook Billy Walker's record. Charlie had made his debut for the club in the last League match of 1960–61 and had helped the club win the Third Division title in 1972 and reach the League Cup finals of 1963 and 1971. He went on to stretch the record for League appearances to 561 before retiring. Unfortunately Sunderland spoilt the celebration with a 2–0 win at Roker Park.

DECEMBER 9TH

1961 Although Ipswich were to win the First Division title in their very first season in the top flight, Villa inflicted one of their biggest defeats, winning 3–0 at Villa Park. Villa had obviously learnt a lesson or two during the League Cup defeat the previous month, nullifying the threat from Crawford and Phillips and carving plenty of chances of their own.

1989 The First Division's match of the day was the clash between two of the top three at Anfield; Liverpool versus Villa. Villa started brighter, taking the game to Liverpool and taking a deserved lead through Ian Olney. The home side fought back in the second half, roared on by the majority of the supporters in the 37,435 crowd, and Peter Beardsley finally hit an equaliser. Whilst Villa were content with the draw, it did allow Arsenal to go two points clear at the top of the table.

1997 Villa Park was packed with 35,102 fans eager to see if Villa could overturn a 2–1 first-leg defeat by Steaua Bucharest in the UEFA Cup third round. Ian Taylor and Savo Milosevic scored the goals that took Villa through 3–2 on aggregate.

DECEMBER 10TH

1923 Johnny Dixon born in Spennymoor. He began his career playing for Spennymoor United during the Second World War and was spotted by Villa, for whom he made a number of appearances in wartime football. After the war he resumed his career and went on to make over 400 appearances for the club, captaining the side to the 1957 FA Cup final and the Second Division title in 1959–60. He played his last game in 1961 and then spent six years coaching the youth side.

1966 Villa manager Dick Taylor had gone on to the transfer market and bought the veteran Wolves striker Peter Broadbent, hoping his goals would fire Villa out of trouble. He might have been better advised looking at what was already the worst defence in the First Division – 35 goals in the League and six in the League Cup, the cup tally coming in one game. And it got worse; with former Villan Harry Burrows leading the torment Stoke City hit Villa for another six in the 6–1 drubbing at the Victoria Ground. Burrows scored a hat-trick playing on the wing!

DECEMBER 11TH

1886 Aston Villa faced Wolves in the FA Cup third round at Perry Barr and drew 2–2. The two sides would battle out a further two draws (1–1 and 3–3) before Villa finally overcame their local rivals and progressed into the next round. Fortunately, after the exertions required to get into the fourth round, Villa had to use very little energy passing into the sixth round; they were given a bye.

1897 Defending champions Villa were in scintillating form at Villa Park, beating Blackburn Rovers 5–1. Although the title was relinquished, Villa were already beginning to assemble another great side ready for a fresh assault on the League.

1937 Villa were on their way to the Second Division title at the end of the season, finishing four points ahead of Manchester United and hitting 50 goals in their 21 home matches. Seven of them came in the 7–1 win over Stockport County (who ended the season bottom of the table), with Frank Shell grabbing a hat-trick in only his second match for the club.

1948 Middlesbrough inflicted Villa's biggest defeat of the season with a 6–0 win at Ayresome Park, although at the end of the season Middlesbrough missed relegation by a single point!

DECEMBER 12TH

1920 Billy Goffin born in Tamworth. He signed as a professional with Villa in December 1937 but had yet to make his debut when the Second World War broke out and normal League football was abandoned. He resumed his career at the end of hostilities and went on to make 158 appearances in the League side, scoring 36 goals. In August 1954 he made the short journey up the road to Walsall but played only eight games before drifting into the non-League game.

1968 Barely 12,747 fans, the lowest to have witnessed a Saturday League match at Villa Park, were present for the visit of Charlton Athletic. Those who did attend went home wishing they hadn't; a goalless 0–0 draw made Christmas shopping a viable alternative!

1982 After winning the European Cup the previous season Aston Villa were in Tokyo to face Penarol of Uruguay in the World Club Championship. The competition had a chequered history; first introduced in the 1960s and played over two legs, the battles (and they were often just that) had been littered with fouls, sending offs and a host of unsavoury incidents, prompting some, such as Ajax, to refuse to enter. The introduction of a sponsor and the switch to a single tie on neutral territory, with the rest of the world watching the game on television, had done much to restore the prestige of the competition. Penarol had twice before won the trophy (1961 and 1966) and were to take their tally to three, beating Villa 2–0 on the day in front of a crowd of 62,000. It would not be until 1985 that the European Cup winners, in this case Juventus, finally overcame the Copa Libertadores winners.

1986 When the six English clubs banned from European competition organised their own competition, what became the Screen Sport Super Cup, there were those at other clubs who believed they should have a competition of their own. Thus, spurred on by the likes of Ken Bates at Chelsea, the Full Member's Cup was born. Even though the Super Cup was abandoned after only one season, the Full Member's Cup limped along for considerably longer, with Villa making their debut in the competition with a 4–1 win over Derby County at Villa Park. Villa's goals were scored by Gary Shaw (two), Allan Evans and Tony Daley in front of a crowd of just 5,124.

DECEMBER 13TH

1960 First Division Villa were held to a 3–3 draw at home to Second Division Plymouth Argyle in the League Cup fourth round in one of the shock results of the competition. It would take a further two games (although one was abandoned) before Villa finally got through to the quarter-finals.

1980 Local rivals Birmingham City were the visitors for the local derby with the bulk of the crowd of 41,101 looking to see Villa maintain their title challenge. Birmingham frustrated them throughout the first half even though Villa were fully in control. The vital breakthrough came in the second half, and goals from David Geddis, who scored twice, and Gary Shaw finally saw them home.

DECEMBER 14TH

1907 Middlesbrough were the victims as Villa registered their biggest win of the season, a 6–0 win at Villa Park. Villa also hit five on three occasions during the campaign, against Liverpool, Notts County and Sheffield Wednesday on their way to finishing runners-up behind Manchester United.

1935 Villa Park witnessed a historical occasion, although it was perhaps one they could have done without. With Villa battling against relegation, a win over Arsenal would have been vital and they certainly started brightly enough. But Arsenal in general and Ted Drake in particular recovered to take the points; Drake scored all seven of his side's goals from only eight attempts on goal – the other effort hit the underside of the bar – to equal James Ross' record set in 1888 (although there is considerable doubt about Ross' tally). The Villa fans sportingly applauded Ted Drake off the pitch at the end of the game, whilst all the players who took part signed the match ball which was presented to Drake.

1974 Goals from Ray Graydon, Chris Nicholl, Brian Little and Chico Hamilton saw off York City 4–0 at Villa Park and took Villa up to sixth place in the Second Division.

DECEMBER 15TH

1906 Sheffield United were one of the teams battling at the top of the table, but their title hopes took a dive with a 5–1 defeat at Villa Park. United finally finished the season in fifth place, one ahead of Villa but six points behind the champions Newcastle.

1976 One of the most astonishing first-half displays of football Villa Park has ever witnessed saw League champions Liverpool blitzed five goals to one. Andy Gray and John Deehan both scored twice, Brian Little once as Villa tore in to a side destined to win both the First Division and European Cup and reach the final of the FA Cup in the same season. On the evidence of their first-half display, it was Villa who looked more like European champions and a crowd of 42,851 roared their approval. Villa were unable to maintain the form into the second half, primarily because the Liverpool team were given a roasting at half-time by their manager and recovered their composure, if not their pride, in the second half. Still, the 5–1 win Villa recorded sent shock waves across English football that evening!

DECEMBER 16TH

1899 Villa made their only ever visit to North Road, Glossop, in the League. Glossop had joined the League in 1898 and won promotion to the First Division at the end of their first season. They thus became the smallest town (then only 25,000 inhabitants) to have supported a First Division side, but they were destined to finish the season bottom and were relegated back again. Villa's only visit was not one they would care to recall, Glossop winning 1–0, one of only four games they won all season.

1969 Simon Grayson born in Ripon. He began his career as a trainee with Leeds United but made only four first-team appearances before being sold to Leicester City for £50,000 in March 1992. There he slotted in at either full-back or midfield and helped the club win the League Cup in 1997. When his contract ran out that summer, he joined Villa and proved a valuable acquisition, scoring the last-minute goal that kept the club in the FA Cup against Portsmouth.

1970 Villa had beaten Notts County, Burnley, Northampton, Carlisle and Bristol Rovers on their way to the League Cup semi-finals where they were paired with Manchester United. With Villa struggling to get out of the Third Division it was a tie many reckoned would be a stroll for United, but 8,000 Villa fans didn't think it a foregone conclusion and made the trek to Old Trafford for the first leg. There were 49,000 inside Old Trafford on the night to see Andy Lochhead shock the First Division side by giving Villa the lead after 40 minutes, and although Brian Kidd soon equalised, Villa more than held their own throughout the 90 minutes. A 1–1 draw left the tie evenly balanced with everything to play for in the second leg a week later.

DECEMBER 17TH

1922 Herbert Smith born in Birmingham. Signed by Villa from Moor Green in May 1947, he made 51 League appearances and scored eight goals during his seven years with the club. He left in June 1954 and joined Southend United.

1969 Ian Olney born in Luton. He won a place in the Villa side on a regular basis during the 1989–90 season but found the going somewhat tougher the following season and was subsequently sold to Oldham Athletic for £700,000 during Ron Atkinson's reign as manager.

1983 Villa and Ipswich had competed to the last hurdle for the League title two years previously, and whilst Villa were in something of a transitional period after their European Cup success, Ipswich's side of the same era had all aged together without adequate replacements. At Villa Park Villa swept to a 4–0 win, taking a first-half lead through Paul Rideout and adding three goals in the second thanks to Steve McMahon, Allan Evans from the penalty spot and Peter Withe.

DECEMBER 18TH

1968 Tommy Docherty was appointed manager of Aston Villa; his third club in six weeks. He had resigned as manager of Rotherham United in order to take over at Queens Park Rangers but after 28 days walked out following a row with the chairman, subsequently resurfacing at Villa Park.

1987 Villa's brief sojourn in the Second Division gave them an opportunity to renew battle with local rivals Birmingham City and West Bromwich Albion. A crowd of 24,437 were at Villa Park for the visit of an Albion side desperately struggling to avoid relegation to the Third Division. A goalless draw was always the most likeliest of outcomes, although Villa created the better chances.

DECEMBER 19TH

1903 Albert Hall made his debut for the club and scored one of the goals in the 7–3 win over Nottingham Forest at the City Ground, the first time Villa had scored as many as seven goals on an opponent's ground. He was an almost permanent fixture in the side for the next ten years, helping them win the FA Cup and League title during that time and also earning a single cap for England. He lost his place to Joe Bache in 1913 when Villa went on to win the FA Cup again and subsequently left the club for

Millwall Athletic where he finished his career in 1916. Also making his debut for the club in the same match was Freddie Miles, signed from Aston St Miles. He initially formed an effective full-back partnership with Howard Spencer, but it was his subsequent pairing with Tommy Lyons that reaped dividends for the club, helping them win the League title in 1910. After 269 first-team appearances Miles retired and became the club's trainer.

1964 Villa made their first appearance on the BBC's *Match of the Day* programme, with the evening's programme showing their 3–1 victory over Arsenal.

DECEMBER 20TH

1911 William McGregor, founder of the Football League, former Aston Villa chairman and later chairman and president of the Football League, died. Born in Perthshire in 1847 he moved to Birmingham and bought a drapery shop near Villa Park, although he had no interest in playing. 'I've never taken part in active football. I tried it once when I was very young and had to take to bed for a week.' Luckily, he was an organiser and administrator and got involved with Aston Villa, later penning his now famous letter to other clubs of the era and forming the Football League. McGregor himself once said 'I really believe that the game would have received a very severe check, and its popularity would have been paralysed once and for all, if the League had not been founded. I am not saying that football would have died, because football will never die. Even if the time should come when it ceases to be the highly organised sport it is today, it will still be the pastime of the juveniles, because it is not easy to conceive the introduction of a game which will prove its superior.'

DECEMBER 21ST

1946 Dave Roberts born in Birmingham. He rose through the ranks at Villa and signed professional forms in December 1963, going on to make 16 appearances and scoring one goal for the club in the League. He then joined Shrewsbury and finished his career with Swansea.

1968 Although Villa spent much of the season at the wrong end of the table and finished in 18th position, their home form was better than average, with only three games lost all season. Twenty-eight of their 38 points were secured at Villa Park, including both in a 2–1 win over Norwich. If their performances on their travels had matched those at home, then Villa might have been challenging for promotion.

DECEMBER 22ND

1894 Villa got something of a Christmas present from Wolves, winning 4–0 at Molineux.

1932 Phil Woosnam born in Carsws. He represented Wales at schoolboy, youth and amateur level before signing with Manchester City as a professional. He made only one appearance for the club, however, as he combined his football with studying at university and then national service, and joined Orient in 1954. Four years later he cost West Ham £30,000 and remained at Upton Park for a further four years before joining Villa in a £27,000 deal in November 1962. He made 111 League appearances for the club before accepting an offer to become manager and coach to the Atlanta Chiefs in America in 1966. Three years later he was appointed Commissioner of the North American Soccer League and has remained connected with the administration of football in the USA ever since, being largely responsible for the hosting of the 1994 World Cup finals in the country.

1984 Paul Rideout hit a hat-trick as Villa overwhelmed Newcastle United 4–0 at Villa Park. The other goal was scored by Allan Evans from the penalty spot, although the crowd was a disappointing one of only 14,491.

1989 Another low crowd, this time 6,530, were at Villa Park for the Zenith Data Systems Cup clash with Nottingham Forest. Villa won 2–1 thanks to goals from David Platt from the penalty spot and Derek Mountfield.

DECEMBER 23RD

1958 Joe Mercer was appointed manager of the club in place of Eric Houghton. The former Everton and Arsenal player had begun his managerial career with Sheffield United in 1955, a year after breaking his leg and finishing his playing career. He joined Villa, a club steeped in tradition, FA Cup winners as recently as 1957 but languishing at the bottom of the First Division (albeit one point behind both Portsmouth and Spurs), with a simple brief: keep the club up. Though he ultimately failed in that, he did restore them to former glories in time and also guided them to the final of the League Cup twice during his time at Villa Park.

1971 An unbelievable crowd of 62,500 (paying receipts of £28,260) were at Villa Park for the League Cup semi-final clash between Villa and Manchester United, the first leg having finished all square at 1–1. Brian Kidd gave United the lead but Andy Lochhead equalised before half-time and Pat McMahon score a late header to send Villa to Wembley at United's expense 2–1 on the night, 3–2 on aggregate. Five days later United manager Wilf McGuinness was sacked!

DECEMBER 24TH

1912 Aston Villa paid £1,950 to Bolton Wanderers for Tommy Barber. He had been a member of the side that had won the promotion to the First Division in 1911 and impressed in the top flight prior to his arrival at Villa Park and went on to be a vital member of the side that won the FA

Cup in 1913, scoring the only goal of the game. During the First World War he joined the Footballers' Battalion and at the end of hostilities resumed his playing career with Stalybridge, Merthyr Tydfil and Walsall. He died from tuberculosis in 1925 at the age of 39.

1927 Leslie J. Smith born in Halesowen. He first appeared in the League with Wolves immediately after the Second World War and joined Villa in February 1956. He went on to make 114 appearances and scored 24 goals for the club over the next three years.

1954 Another new signing at Villa Park, this time Tommy Southern who joined the club from West Ham for a fee of £12,000.

DECEMBER 25TH

1896 After a hesitant start to the season Villa had hit good form at the beginning of October and made steady progress up the table, coming to rest at the top following a draw with Bury at the beginning of November and then winning four straight matches. A crowd of 15,000 were at Anfield to see Villa maintain their unbeaten run with a close 3–3 draw.

1938 Frederick Rinder died. In his 80s at the time of his death he had been associated with Villa for decades and had been the prime force behind making Villa Park one of the greatest grounds in the country. But for the First World War, when building materials were in short supply, his dream of having a ground capable of holding 130,000 spectators might have been realised, but attention was diverted elsewhere and something slightly over half that figure had to be accepted. He devoted his life to football and was a senior vice-president of the Football Association at the time of his death.

1956 The last game Villa played on Christmas Day was a 1–0 defeat at Roker Park.

DECEMBER 26TH

1866 John Devey born in Birmingham. One of the greatest names in Villa's history was signed by the club after appearing for local sides Excelsior, Aston Unity, Mitchell St George's and Aston Manor, joining Villa in March 1891. He made his League debut in the opening game of the following season and finished the campaign as top goalscorer with 29 goals to his credit, as well as helping Villa reach the FA Cup final. He subsequently became captain and guided the club to five League championships, two FA Cups and also won two caps for England. He was something of an all-round sportsman, for he also represented Warwickshire at cricket and scored over 6,500 runs. When he retired as a player he continued to serve Villa as a director, being appointed in 1902 and continuing in that capacity until 1934. He died in Birmingham in October 1940.

1894 Whilst Villa were moving towards their first League title, Darwen were headed in the opposite direction, having to compete in the Test Matches at the end of the season and being relegated. Villa's 9–0 win at Perry Barr hardly helped the Darwen cause either. This was the last time Villa were to play Darwen in the League, with Villa having won three and drawn the other in the four meetings between the two. Villa scored 22 goals and conceded just two!

1896 Villa finished the year with a 2–1 win at Molineux, thereby confirming their place at the top of the First Division table.

1902 Top of the table Sheffield Wednesday were the visitors to Villa Park, an attraction that drew the biggest crowd of the season, over 40,000 to see whether a revived Villa could maintain their own mounting challenge for the title. A penalty in Villa's favour, calmly converted by the ice-cool Billy Garraty, ensured Villa took both points and kept the pressure on Wednesday at the top.

1921 Villa were up against the other Sheffield club, United at Bramall Lane in a League fixture. The winning goal in the 3–2 victory was scored by the legendary Frank Barson, from fully 30 yards with a header. This was a record until beaten by another Villa player, Peter Aldis in 1950.

1947 The Boxing Day clash with Wolves drew a crowd of 68,099, setting a new record for Villa Park in the League. The visitors won 2–1 and the following day beat Villa 4–1 at Molineux.

DECEMBER 27TH

1920 Even though Manchester United and Villa were occupying mid-table positions in the First Division, the clash at Old Trafford between the two sides attracted what is still a record League crowd for the stadium; 70,504 spectators, although a further 1,500 were believed to have sneaked in without paying, pushing the final figure towards 72,000. Villa won 3–1.

1930 Manchester United were at Villa Park looking to avenge an opening day defeat at Old Trafford, Villa having triumphed 4–3. They were out of luck at Villa Park as well; Villa tanked them 7–0 to inflict United's worst ever defeat!

1932 Joe Nibloe made his debut for the club in the 4–2 win at Molineux against Wolves. Signed in September from Kilmarnock he remained with Villa until 1934 when he joined Sheffield Wednesday in part exchange for George Beeson, winning an FA Cup winners' medal during his time with his new club.

1948 Trevor Ford scored four of Villa's goals as they humbled visitors Wolves 5–1 in a League match in front of a crowd of 63,572.

1949 The biggest ever League attendance at Villa Park was the 69,492 who witnessed a 4–1 defeat inflicted by local rivals Wolverhampton Wanderers.

DECEMBER 28TH

1891 Everton had been only the second side to have won the Football League, ending Preston's successes in the first two seasons with a championship in 1890–91. Their visit to Perry Barr was therefore likely to be the biggest attraction of the season, with 14,000 present to see the visitors record a 4–3 win.

1927 Villa signed Derby County's reserve goalkeeper Ben Olney. Olney had made his debut for Derby in the last game of the 1920–21 season and been a permanent fixture of the side for the next six years until he lost his place to Harry Wilkes. By chance, Villa were also in desperate need of an experienced goalkeeper and, after suffering successive defeats over the Christmas period, signed Olney. Four months later he was in the England team, collecting two caps. He remained with Villa until 1930 when he moved into the non-League game, later turning to management with Walsall and Shrewsbury.

DECEMBER 29TH

1936 Geoff Sidebottom born in Maplewell. A product of the Wolves youth scheme, he made 28 appearances for the Molineux club before a transfer to Villa in February 1961 and appeared in goal in the second leg of the League Cup final at the beginning of the 1961–62 season. He made 70 appearances in the League before joining Scunthorpe and finished his career with Brighton.

1963 Dean Glover born in Birmingham. Signed by Villa as an apprentice, he graduated through the ranks and made 38 appearances for the club before joining Middlesbrough in 1987. He later played for Port Vale.

1979 At Ashton Gate Gary Shaw scored the first hat-trick of his career in the 3–1 win for Villa over Bristol City. Interestingly enough, Gary had made his debut for the club against the same opponents the previous year in a League match.

DECEMBER 30TH

1972 A third consecutive draw for Villa as they were held 1–1 at Leeds Road by Huddersfield Town. Villa were still in touch with the leaders of the Second Division, but the point dropped meant they slipped down to fifth place in the table. Alun Evans scored the second-half goal that brought Villa level on the day.

1989 Villa's good form over the Christmas and New Year holiday period continued with a 2–1 win over Arsenal at Villa Park. David Platt gave Villa a first-half lead and Derek Mountfield ensured all three points as Villa held on to second spot in the First Division.

1881 The FA Cup fourth round pitted Villa at home to Notts County, one of the oldest sides in the country (County were formed in 1863, some 11 years before Villa). A then record crowd of 7,000 turned out to see a 2–2 draw between the two sides.

1965 Tony Dorigo born in Melbourne in Australia. He arrived in England to sign as a schoolboy with Villa in January 1982 and made his debut at the end of the 1983–84 season. After 133 first-team appearances he was sold to Chelsea for £475,000 and thereafter broke into the England side. He was sold to Leeds United for £1.3 million in 1991 and helped them win the League title. Has won 15 caps for England.